DW 2.0
The Architecture for the Next Generation of
Data Warehousing

The Morgan Kaufmann Series in Data Management Systems

Joe Celko's Thinking in Sets
Joe Celko

Business Metadata
Bill Inmon, Bonnie O'Neil and Lowell Fryman

Unleashing Web 2.0
Gottfried Vossen and Stephan Hagemann

Enterprise Knowledge Management
David Loshin

Business Process Change, Second Edition
Paul Harmon

IT Manager's Handbook, Second Edition
Bill Holtsnider and Brian Jaffe

Joe Celko's Puzzles and Answers, Second Edition
Joe Celko

Making Shoes for the Cobbler's Children
Charles Betz

Java Data Mining: Strategy, Standard, and Practice
Mark Hornik, Erik Marcade, and Sunil Venkayala

Joe Celko's Analytics and OLAP in SQL
Joe Celko

Data Preparation for Data Mining Using SAS
Mamdouh Refaat

Querying XML: XQuery, XPath, and SQL/XML in Context
Jim Melton and Stephen Buxton

Data Mining: Concepts and Techniques, Second Edition
Jiawei Han and Micheline Kamber

Database Modeling and Design: Logical Design, Fourth Edition
Toby J, Teorey, Sam S. Lightstone, and Thomas P. Nadeau

Foundations of Multidimensional and Metric Data Structures
Hanan Samet

Joe Celko's SQL for Smarties: Advanced SQL Programming, Third Edition
Joe Celko

Moving Objects Databases
Ralf Hartmut Güting and Markus Schneider

Joe Celko's SQL Programming Style
Joe Celko

Data Mining, Second Edition: Concepts and Techniques
Ian Witten and Eibe Frank

Fuzzy Modeling and Genetic Algorithms for Data Mining and Exploration
Earl Cox

Data Modeling Essentials, Third Edition
Graeme C. Simsion and Graham C. Witt

Location-Based Services
Jochen Schiller and Agnès Voisard

Database Modeling with Microsft® Visio for Enterprise Architects
Terry Halpin, Ken Evans, Patrick Hallock, and Bill Maclean

Designing Data-Intensive Web Applications
Stephano Ceri, Piero Fraternali, Aldo Bongio, Marco Brambilla, Sara Comai, and Maristella Matera

Mining the Web: Discovering Knowledge from Hypertext Data
Soumen Chakrabarti

Advanced SQL: 1999—Understanding Object-Relational and Other Advanced Features
Jim Melton

Database Tuning: Principles, Experiments, and Troubleshooting Techniques
Dennis Shasha and Philippe Bonnet

SQL:1999—Understanding Relational Language Components
Jim Melton and Alan R. Simon

Information Visualization in Data Mining and Knowledge Discovery
Edited by Usama Fayyad, Georges G. Grinstein and Andreas Wierse

Transactional Information Systems
Gerhard Weikum and Gottfried Vossen

Spatial Databases
Philippe Rigaux, Michel Scholl, and Agnes Voisard

Information Modeling and Relational Database
Terry Halpin

Component Database Systems
Edited by Klaus R. Dittrich and Andreas Geppert

Managing Reference Data in Enterprise Database
Malcolm Chisholm

Understanding SQL and Java Together
Jim Melton and Andrew Eisenberg

Database: Principles, Programming, and Performance, Second Edition
Patrick and Elizabeth O'Neil

The Object Data Standar
Edited by R. G. G. Cattell and Douglas Barry

Data on the Web: From Relations to Semistructured Data and XML
Serge Abiteboul, Peter Buneman, and Dan Suciu

Data Mining: Practical Machine Learning Tools and Techniques with Java Implementations
Ian Witten and Eibe Frank

Joe Celko's SQL for Smarties: Advanced SQL Programming, Second Edition
Joe Celko

Joe Celko's Data and Databases: Concepts in Practice
Joe Celko

Developing Time-Oriented Database Applications in SQL
Richard T. Snodgrass

Web Farming for the Data Warehouse
Richard D. Hackathorn

Management of Heterogeneous and Autonomous Database Systems
Edited by Ahmed Elmagarmid, Marek Rusinkiewicz, and Amit Sheth

Object-Relational DBMSs: Second Edition
Michael Stonebraker and Paul Brown, with Dorothy Moore

A Complete Guide to DB2 Universal Database
Don Chamberlin

Universal Database Management: A Guide to Object/Relational Technology
Cynthia Maro Saracco

Readings in Database Systems, Third Edition
Edited by Michael Stonebraker and Joseph M. Hellerstein

Understanding SQL's Stored Procedures: A Complete Guide to SQL/PSM
Jim Melton

Principles of Multimedia Database Systems
V. S. Subrahmanian

Principles of Database Query Processing for Advanced Applications
Clement T. Yu and Weiyi Meng

Advanced Database Systems
Carlo Zaniolo, Stefano Ceri, Christos Faloutsos, Richard T. Snodgrass, V. S. Subrahmanian, and Roberto Zicari

Principles of Transaction Processing
Philip A. Bernstein and Eric Newcomer

Using the New DB2: IBMs Object-Relational Database System
Don Chamberlin

Distributed Algorithms
Nancy A. Lynch

Active Database Systems: Triggers and Rules for Advanced Database Processing
Edited by Jennifer Widom and Stefano Ceri

Migrating Legacy Systems: Gateways, Interfaces, & the Incremental Approach
Michael L. Brodie and Michael Stonebraker

Atomic Transactions
Nancy Lynch, Michael Merritt, William Weihl, and Alan Fekete

Query Processing for Advanced Database Systems
Edited by Johann Christoph Freytag, David Maier, and Gottfried Vossen

Transaction Processing
Jim Gray and Andreas Reuter

Building an Object-Oriented Database System: The Story of O₂
Edited by François Bancilhon, Claude Delobel, and Paris Kanellakis

Database Transaction Models for Advanced Applications
Edited by Ahmed K. Elmagarmid

A Guide to Developing Client/Server SQL Applications
Setrag Khoshafian, Arvola Chan, Anna Wong, and Harry K. T. Wong

The Benchmark Handbook for Database and Transaction Processing Systems, Second Edition
Edited by Jim Gray

Camelot and Avalon: A Distributed Transaction Facility
Edited by Jeffrey L. Eppinger, Lily B. Mummert, and Alfred Z. Spector

Readings in Object-Oriented Database Systems
Edited by Stanley B. Zdonik and David Maier

DW 2.0: The Architecture for the Next Generation of Data Warehousing
William H. Inmon, Derek Strauss, and Genia Neushloss

DW 2.0
The Architecture for the Next Generation of Data Warehousing

W. H. Inmon
Forest Rim Technology

Derek Strauss
Gavroshe

Genia Neushloss
Gavroshe

ELSEVIER

AMSTERDAM • BOSTON • HEIDELBERG • LONDON
NEW YORK • OXFORD • PARIS • SAN DIEGO
SAN FRANCISCO • SINGAPORE • SYDNEY • TOKYO

Morgan Kaufmann Publishers is an imprint of Elsevier.

MORGAN KAUFMANN PUBLISHERS

Morgan Kaufmann Publishers is an imprint of Elsevier.
30 Corporate Drive, Suite 400, Burlington, MA 01803, USA

This book is printed on acid-free paper.

Library of Congress Cataloging-in-Publication Data

Inmon, William H.
    DW 2.0 : the architecture for the next generation of data warehousing/William H. Inmon,
Derek Strauss, Genia Neushloss.
          p. cm.
    Includes index.
    ISBN 978-0-12-374319-0 (pbk. : alk. paper) 1. Data warehousing. I. Strauss, Derek. II.
Neushloss, Genia. III. Title. IV. Title: Data warehousing 2.0.
    QA76.9.D37I4563 2008
    005.74--dc22
                                        2008011044

ISBN: 978-0-12-374319-0

For information on all Morgan Kaufmann publications,
visit our Web site at www.mkp.com or www.books.elsevier.com

Printed in the United States
08 09 10   5 4 3 2 1

Dedication for Lynn Inmon, my wife and partner

Contents

Preface...xvii

Acknowledgments.. xx

About the Authors... xxi

**CHAPTER 1   A brief history of data warehousing and first-generation
data warehouses**..1

Data base management systems..1
Online applications..2
Personal computers and 4GL technology..3
The spider web environment..4
Evolution from the business perspective 5
The data warehouse environment...6
What is a data warehouse?...7
Integrating data—a painful experience 7
Volumes of data..8
A different development approach..8
Evolution to the DW 2.0 environment 9
The business impact of the data warehouse 11
Various components of the data warehouse environment 11
    ETL—extract/transform/load 12
    ODS—operational data store 13
    Data mart 13
    Exploration warehouse...13
The evolution of data warehousing from the business perspective...........14
Other notions about a data warehouse...14
The active data warehouse 15
The federated data warehouse approach..16
The star schema approach...18
The data mart data warehouse...20
Building a "real" data warehouse 21
Summary..22

CHAPTER 2   An introduction to DW 2.0..23

DW 2.0—a new paradigm 24
DW 2.0—from the business perspective..24
The life cycle of data..27
Reasons for the different sectors...30
Metadata 31
Access of data..33
Structured data/unstructured data..34

Textual analytics 35
Blather...38
The issue of terminology...38
Specific text/general text...40
Metadata—a major component 40
Local metadata 43
A foundation of technology...45
Changing business requirements 47
The flow of data within DW 2.0...48
Volumes of data...50
Useful applications...51
DW 2.0 and referential integrity..52
Reporting in DW 2.0 53
Summary...53

CHAPTER 3   DW 2.0 components—about the different sectors...........................55

The Interactive Sector 55
The Integrated Sector...62
The Near Line Sector 71
The Archival Sector..76
Unstructured processing 86
From the business perspective 90
Summary...92

CHAPTER 4   Metadata in DW 2.0...95

Reusability of data and analysis 96
Metadata in DW 2.0 96
Active repository/passive repository.......................................99
The active repository 100
Enterprise metadata.. 101
Metadata and the system of record.. 102
Taxonomy 104
Internal taxonomies/external taxonomies............................. 104
Metadata in the Archival Sector... 105
Maintaining metadata... 106
Using metadata—an example... 106
From the end-user perspective... 109
Summary.. 110

CHAPTER 5   Fluidity of the DW 2.0 technology infrastructure............................. 111

The technology infrastructure.. 112
Rapid business changes... 114

The treadmill of change 114

Getting off the treadmill 115

Reducing the length of time for IT to respond 115

Semantically temporal, semantically static data................................. 115

Semantically temporal data 116

Semantically stable data.. 117

Mixing semantically stable and unstable data.................................... 118

Separating semantically stable and unstable data.............................. 118

Mitigating business change... 119

Creating snapshots of data 120

A historical record 120

Dividing data... 121

From the end-user perspective.. 121

Summary.. 122

CHAPTER 6   **Methodology and approach for DW 2.0** 123

Spiral methodology—a summary of key features 124

The seven streams approach—an overview 129

Enterprise reference model stream 129

Enterprise knowledge coordination stream 129

Information factory development stream 133

Data profiling and mapping stream 133

Data correction stream.. 133

Infrastructure stream 133

Total information quality management stream 134

Summary.. 137

CHAPTER 7   **Statistical processing and DW 2.0**..141

Two types of transactions.. 141

Using statistical analysis.. 143

The integrity of the comparison 144

Heuristic analysis... 145

Freezing data.. 146

Exploration processing.. 146

The frequency of analysis 147

The exploration facility 147

The sources for exploration processing... 149

Refreshing exploration data.. 149

Project-based data 150

Data marts and the exploration facility 152

A backflow of data... 152

Using exploration data internally.. 155

From the perspective of the business analyst.. 155
Summary.. 156

CHAPTER 8   Data models and DW 2.0..157

An intellectual road map 157
The data model and business 157
The scope of integration 158
Making the distinction between granular and summarized data........... 159
Levels of the data model 159
Data models and the Interactive Sector 161
The corporate data model... 162
A transformation of models 163
Data models and unstructured data.. 164
From the perspective of the business user 166
Summary.. 167

CHAPTER 9   Monitoring the DW 2.0 environment.................................169

Monitoring the DW 2.0 environment.. 169
The transaction monitor 169
Monitoring data quality..170
A data warehouse monitor...171
The transaction monitor—response time 171
Peak-period processing 172
The ETL data quality monitor.. 174
The data warehouse monitor... 176
Dormant data 177
From the perspective of the business user 178
Summary.. 179

CHAPTER 10 DW 2.0 and security.. 181

Protecting access to data 181
Encryption 181
Drawbacks.. 182
The firewall 182
Moving data offline.. 182
Limiting encryption.. 184
A direct dump... 184
The data warehouse monitor... 185
Sensing an attack... 185
Security for near line data 187
From the perspective of the business user 187
Summary.. 188

CHAPTER 11   Time-variant data.. 191

　　　All data in DW 2.0—relative to time..191
　　　Time relativity in the Interactive Sector.. 192
　　　Data relativity elsewhere in DW 2.0... 192
　　　Transactions in the Integrated Sector 193
　　　Discrete data 194
　　　Continuous time span data 194
　　　A sequence of records... 196
　　　Nonoverlapping records 197
　　　Beginning and ending a sequence of records 197
　　　Continuity of data 198
　　　Time-collapsed data 198
　　　Time variance in the Archival Sector 199
　　　From the perspective of the end user 200
　　　Summary.. 200

CHAPTER 12   The flow of data in DW 2.0 203

　　　The flow of data throughout the architecture 203
　　　Entering the Interactive Sector..203
　　　The role of ETL 205
　　　Data flow into the Integrated Sector 205
　　　Data flow into the Near Line Sector 207
　　　Data flow into the Archival Sector...209
　　　The falling probability of data access 209
　　　Exception-based flow of data... 210
　　　From the perspective of the business user 213
　　　Summary..214

CHAPTER 13   ETL processing and DW 2.0...215

　　　Changing states of data...215
　　　Where ETL fits...215
　　　From application data to corporate data 216
　　　ETL in online mode..216
　　　ETL in batch mode 217
　　　Source and target...218
　　　An ETL mapping...219
　　　Changing states—an example 219
　　　More complex transformations 221
　　　ETL and throughput 222
　　　ETL and metadata.. 223
　　　ETL and an audit trail.. 223

ETL and data quality 224

Creating ETL 224

Code creation or parametrically driven ETL 225

ETL and rejects 225

Changed data capture 226

ELT 226

From the perspective of the business user 227

Summary 228

CHAPTER 14 DW 2.0 and the granularity manager 231

The granularity manager 231

Raising the level of granularity 232

Filtering data 232

The functions of the granularity manager 234

Home-grown versus third-party granularity managers 236

Parallelizing the granularity manager 237

Metadata as a by-product 237

From the perspective of the business user 238

Summary 238

CHAPTER 15 DW 2.0 and performance 239

Good performance—a cornerstone for DW 2.0 239

Online response time 240

Analytical response time 241

The flow of data 241

Queues 242

Heuristic processing 243

Analytical productivity and response time 243

Many facets to performance 244

Indexing 245

Removing dormant data 245

End-user education 246

Monitoring the environment 246

Capacity planning 247

Metadata 249

Batch parallelization 249

Parallelization for transaction processing 250

Workload management 250

Data marts 251

Exploration facilities 253

Separation of transactions into classes 253

Service level agreements 254

Protecting the Interactive Sector 254
Partitioning data.. 255
Choosing the proper hardware... 255
Separating farmers and explorers 256
Physically group data together... 257
Check automatically generated code... 257
From the perspective of the business user 258
Summary.. 259

CHAPTER 16 Migration 261

Houses and cities.. 261
Migration in a perfect world 262
The perfect world almost never happens 262
Adding components incrementally... 262
Adding the Archival Sector.. 264
Creating enterprise metadata... 265
Building the metadata infrastructure 266
"Swallowing" source systems... 266
ETL as a shock absorber 267
Migration to the unstructured environment... 267
From the perspective of the business user 269
Summary.. 270

CHAPTER 17 Cost justification and DW 2.0.. 271

Is DW 2.0 worth it? 271
Macro-level justification.. 271
A micro-level cost justification 272
Company B has DW 2.0... 273
Creating new analysis.. 273
Executing the steps 274
So how much does all of this cost? 276
Consider company B 276
Factoring the cost of DW 2.0 277
Reality of information.. 278
The real economics of DW 2.0 279
The time value of information 279
The value of integration 280
Historical information 280
First-generation DW and DW 2.0—the economics................................ 281
From the perspective of the business user 282
Summary.. 282

CHAPTER 18   Data quality in DW 2.0 285

The DW 2.0 data quality tool set.. 287
Data profiling tools and the reverse-engineered data model................. 288
Data model types 289
Data profiling inconsistencies challenge top-down modeling.............. 294
Summary... 296

CHAPTER 19   DW 2.0 and unstructured data...299

DW 2.0 and unstructured data 299
Reading text 299
Where to do textual analytical processing 300
Integrating text..301
Simple editing 302
Stop words 302
Synonym replacement 303
Synonym concatenation 303
Homographic resolution 303
Creating themes.. 304
External glossaries/taxonomies 304
Stemming...305
Alternate spellings 305
Text across languages...305
Direct searches 306
Indirect searches 306
Terminology...307
Semistructured data/VALUE = NAME data 307
The technology needed to prepare the data... 308
The relational data base 309
Structured/unstructured linkage...309
From the perspective of the business user 310
Summary... 310

CHAPTER 20   DW 2.0 and the system of record 313

Other systems of record 319
From the perspective of the business user 319
Summary...321

CHAPTER 21   Miscellaneous topics..323

Data marts 323
The convenience of a data mart... 324
Transforming data mart data 325

Contents **xv**

Monitoring DW 2.0..326
Moving data from one data mart to another.........................327
Bad data 329
A balancing entry..330
Resetting a value 330
Making corrections..330
The speed of movement of data 331
Data warehouse utilities..332
Summary..337

CHAPTER 22 Processing in the DW 2.0 environment..339

Summary..345

CHAPTER 23 Administering the DW 2.0 environment 347
The data model...347
Architectural administration..348
  Defining the moment when an Archival Sector will be needed 348
  Determining whether the Near Line Sector is needed........................349
Metadata administration 351
Data base administration..352
Stewardship 353
Systems and technology administration...............................355
Management administration of the DW 2.0 environment.....................358
  Prioritization and prioritization conflicts 358
  Budget 358
  Scheduling and determination of milestones....................................359
  Allocation of resources...359
  Managing consultants 359
Summary..361

Index 363

Preface

Data warehousing has been around for about 2 decades now and has become an essential part of the information technology infrastructure. Data warehousing originally grew in response to the corporate need for information—not data. A data warehouse is a construct that supplies integrated, granular, and historical data to the corporation.

But there is a problem with data warehousing. The problem is that there are many different renditions of what a data warehouse is today. There is the federated data warehouse. There is the active data warehouse. There is the star schema data warehouse. There is the data mart data warehouse. In fact there are about as many renditions of the data warehouse as there are software and hardware vendors.

The problem is that there are many different renditions of what the proper structure of a data warehouse should look like. And each of these renditions is architecturally very different from the others. If you were to enter a room in which a proponent of the federated data warehouse was talking to a proponent of the active data warehouse, you would be hearing the same words, but these words would be meaning very different things. Even though the words were the same, you would not be hearing meaningful communication. When two people from very different contexts are talking, even though they are using the same words, there is no assurance that they are understanding each other.

And thus it is with first-generation data warehousing today.

Into this morass of confusion as to what a data warehouse is or is not comes DW 2.0. DW 2.0 is a definition of the next generation of data warehousing. Unlike the term "data warehouse," DW 2.0 has a crisp, well-defined meaning. That meaning is identified and defined in this book.

There are many important architectural features of DW 2.0. These architectural features represent an advance in technology and architecture beyond first-generation data warehouses. The following are some of the important features of DW 2.0 discussed in this book:

- The life cycle of data within the data warehouse is recognized. First-generation data warehouses merely placed data on disk storage and called it a warehouse. The truth of the matter is that data—once placed in a data warehouse—has its own life cycle. Once data enters the data warehouse it starts to age. As it ages, the probability of access diminishes. The lessening of the probability of access has profound implications on the technology that is appropriate to the management of the data. Another phenomenon that happens is that as data ages, the volume of data increases. In most cases this increase is dramatic. The task of handling large volumes of data with a decreasing probability of access requires special design considerations lest the cost of the data warehouse become prohibitive and the effective use of the data warehouse becomes impractical.

■ The data warehouse is most effective when containing both structured and unstructured data. Classical first-generation data warehouses consisted entirely of transaction-oriented structured data. These data warehouses provided a great deal of useful information. But a modern data warehouse should contain both structured and unstructured data. Unstructured data is textual data that appears in medical records, contracts, emails, spreadsheets, and many other documents. There is a wealth of information in unstructured data. But unlocking that information is a real challenge. A detailed description of what is required to create the data warehouse containing both structured and unstructured data is a significant part of DW 2.0.

■ For a variety of reasons metadata was not considered to be a significant part of first-generation data warehouses. In the definition of second-generation data warehouses, the importance and role of metadata are recognized. In the world of DW 2.0, the issue is not the need for metadata. There is, after all, metadata that exists in DBMS directories, in business objects universes, in ETL tools, and so forth. What is needed is enterprise metadata, where there is a cohesive enterprise view of metadata. All of the many sources of metadata need to be coordinated and placed in an environment where they work together harmoniously. In addition, there is a need for the support of both technical metadata and business metadata in the DW 2.0 environment.

■ Data warehouses are ultimately built on a foundation of technology. The data warehouse is shaped around a set of business requirements, usually reflecting a data model. Over time the business requirements of the organization change. But the technical foundation underlying the data warehouse does not easily change. And therein lies a problem—the business requirements are constantly changing but the technological foundation is not changing. The stretch between the changing business environment and the static technology environment causes great tension in the organization. In this section of the book, the discussion focuses on two solutions to the dilemma of changing business requirements and static technical foundations of the data warehouse. One solution is software such as Kalido that provides a malleable technology foundation for the data warehouse. The other solution is the design practice of separating static data and temporal data at the point of data base definition. Either of these approaches has the very beneficial effect of allowing the technical foundation of the data warehouse to change while the business requirements are also changing.

There are other important topics addressed in this book. Some of the other topics that are addressed include the following:

■ Online update in the DW 2.0 data warehouse infrastructure.
■ The ODS. Where does it fit?
■ Research processing and statistical analysis against a DW 2.0 data warehouse.
■ Archival processing in the DW 2.0 data warehouse environment.
■ Near-line processing in the DW 2.0 data warehouse environment.

- Data marts and DW 2.0.
- Granular data and the volumes of data found in the data warehouse.
- Methodology and development approaches.
- Data modeling for DW 2.0.

An important feature of the book is the diagram that describes the DW 2.0 environment in its entirety. The diagram—developed through many consulting, seminar, and speaking engagements—represents the different components of the DW 2.0 environment as they are placed together. The diagram is the basic architectural representation of the DW 2.0 environment.

This book is for the business analyst, the information architect, the systems developer, the project manager, the data warehouse technician, the data base administrator, the data modeler, the data administrator, and so forth. It is an introduction to the structure, contents, and issues of the future path of data warehousing.

March 29, 2007
WHI
DS
EN

Acknowledgments

Derek Strauss would like to thank the following family members and friends:

My wife, Denise, and my daughter, Joni, for their understanding and support;

My business partner, Genia Neushloss, and her husband, Jack, for their friendship and support;

Bill Inmon, for his mentorship and the opportunity to collaborate on DW 2.0 and other initiatives;

John Zachman, Dan Meers, Bonnie O'Neil, and Larissa Moss for great working relationships over the years.

Genia Neushloss would like to thank the following family members and friends:

My husband, Jack, for supporting me in all my endeavors;

My sister, Sima, for being my support system;

Derek Strauss, the best business partner anyone could wish for;

Bill Inmon, for his ongoing support and mentorship and the opportunity to collaborate on this book;

John Zachman, Bonnie O'Neil, and Larissa Moss for great working relationships over the years.

About the Authors

W. H. Inmon, the father of data warehousing, has written 49 books translated into nine languages. Bill founded and took public the world's first ETL software company. He has written over 1000 articles and published in most major trade journals.

Bill has conducted seminars and spoken at conferences on every continent except Antarctica. He holds nine software patents. His latest company is Forest Rim Technology, a company dedicated to the access and integration of unstructured data into the structured world. Bill's web site—inmoncif.com—attracts over 1,000,000 visitors a month. His weekly newsletter at b-eye-network.com is one of the most widely read in the industry and goes out to 75,000 subscribers each week.

Derek Strauss is founder, CEO, and a principal consultant of Gavroshe. He has 28 years of IT industry experience, 22 years of which were in the information resource management and business intelligence/data warehousing fields.

Derek has initiated and managed numerous enterprise programs and initiatives in the areas of business intelligence, data warehousing, and data quality improvement. Bill Inmon's *Corporate Information Factory* and John Zachman's *Enterprise Architecture Framework* have been the foundational cornerstones of his work. Derek is also a Specialist Workshop Facilitator. He has spoken at several local and international conferences on data warehousing issues. He is a Certified DW 2.0 Architect and Trainer.

Genia Neushloss is a co-founder and principal consultant of Gavroshe. She has a strong managerial and technical background spanning over 30 years of professional experience in the insurance, finance, manufacturing, mining, and telecommunications industries.

Genia has developed and conducted training courses in JAD/JRP facilitation and systems reengineering. She is a codeveloper of a method set for systems reengineering. She has 22 years of specialization in planning, analyzing, designing, and building data warehouses. Genia has presented before audiences in Europe, the United States, and Africa. She is a Certified DW 2.0 Architect and Trainer.

A brief history of data warehousing and first-generation data warehouses

In the beginning there were simple mechanisms for holding data. There were punched cards. There were paper tapes. There was core memory that was hand beaded. In the beginning storage was very expensive and very limited.

A new day dawned with the introduction and use of magnetic tape. With magnetic tape, it was possible to hold very large volumes of data cheaply. With magnetic tape, there were no major restrictions on the format of the record of data. With magnetic tape, data could be written and rewritten. Magnetic tape represented a great leap forward from early methods of storage.

But magnetic tape did not represent a perfect world. With magnetic tape, data could be accessed only sequentially. It was often said that to access 1% of the data, 100% of the data had to be physically accessed and read. In addition, magnetic tape was not the most stable medium on which to write data. The oxide could fall off or be scratched off of a tape, rendering the tape useless.

Disk storage represented another leap forward for data storage. With disk storage, data could be accessed directly. Data could be written and rewritten. And data could be accessed en masse. There were all sorts of virtues that came with disk storage.

DATA BASE MANAGEMENT SYSTEMS

Soon disk storage was accompanied by software called a "DBMS" or "data base management system." DBMS software existed for the purpose of managing storage on the disk itself. Disk storage managed such activities as

- identifying the proper location of data;
- resolving conflicts when two or more units of data were mapped to the same physical location;
- allowing data to be deleted;
- spanning a physical location when a record of data would not fit in a limited physical space;
- and so forth.

Among all the benefits of disk storage, by far and away the greatest benefit was the ability to locate data quickly. And it was the DBMS that accomplished this very important task.

ONLINE APPLICATIONS

Once data could be accessed directly, using disk storage and a DBMS, there soon grew what came to be known as online applications. Online applications were applications that depended on the computer to access data consistently and quickly. There were many commercial applications of online processing. These included ATMs (automated teller processing), bank teller processing, claims processing, airline reservations processing, manufacturing control processing, retail point of sale processing, and many, many more. In short, the advent of online systems allowed the organization to advance into the 20th century when it came to servicing the day-to-day needs of the customer. Online applications became so powerful and popular that they soon grew into many interwoven applications.

Figure 1.1 illustrates this early progression of information systems.

In fact, online applications were so popular and grew so rapidly that in short order there were lots of applications.

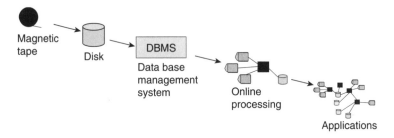

■ **FIGURE 1.1** The early progression of systems.

And with these applications came a cry from the end user—"I know the data I want is there somewhere, if I could only find it." It was true. The corporation had a whole roomful of data, but finding it was another story altogether. And even if you found it, there was no guarantee that the data you found was correct. Data was being proliferated around the corporation so that at any one point in time, people were never sure about the accuracy or completeness of the data that they had.

PERSONAL COMPUTERS AND 4GL TECHNOLOGY

To placate the end user's cry for accessing data, two technologies emerged—personal computer technology and 4GL technology.

Personal computer technology allowed anyone to bring his/her own computer into the corporation and to do his/her own processing at will. Personal computer software such as spreadsheet software appeared. In addition, the owner of the personal computer could store his/her own data on the computer. There was no longer a need for a centralized IT department. The attitude was—if the end users are so angry about us not letting them have their own data, just give them the data.

At about the same time, along came a technology called "4GL"— fourth-generation technology. The idea behind 4GL technology was to make programming and system development so straightforward that anyone could do it. As a result, the end user was freed from the shackles of having to depend on the IT department to feed him/her data from the corporation.

Between the personal computer and 4GL technology, the notion was to emancipate the end user so that the end user could take his/her own destiny into his/her own hands. The theory was that freeing the end user to access his/her own data was what was needed to satisfy the hunger of the end user for data.

And personal computers and 4GL technology soon found their way into the corporation.

But something unexpected happened along the way. While the end users were now free to access data, they discovered that there was a lot more to making good decisions than merely accessing data. The end users found that, even after data had been accessed,

- if the data was not accurate, it was worse than nothing, because incorrect data can be very misleading;
- incomplete data is not very useful;

- data that is not timely is less than desirable;
- when there are multiple versions of the same data, relying on the wrong value of data can result in bad decisions;
- data without documentation is of questionable value.

It was only after the end users got access to data that they discovered all the underlying problems with the data.

THE SPIDER WEB ENVIRONMENT

The result was a big mess. This mess is sometimes affectionately called the "spider's web" environment. It is called the spider's web environment because there are many lines going to so many places that they are reminiscent of a spider's web.

Figure 1.2 illustrates the evolution of the spider's web environment in the typical corporate IT environment.

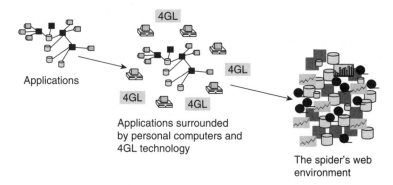

Applications

4GL

Applications surrounded by personal computers and 4GL technology

The spider's web environment

■ **FIGURE 1.2**   The early progression led to the spider's web environment.

The spider's web environment grew to be unimaginably complex in many corporate environments. As testimony to its complexity, consider the real diagram of a corporation's spider's web of systems shown in Figure 1.3.

One looks at a spider's web with awe. Consider the poor people who have to cope with such an environment and try to use it for making good corporate decisions. It is a wonder that anyone could get anything done, much less make good and timely decisions.

The truth is that the spider's web environment for corporations was a dead end insofar as architecture was concerned. There was no future in trying to make the spider's web environment work.

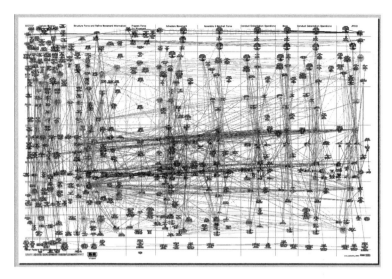

■ FIGURE 1.3   A real spider's web environment.

The frustration of the end user, the IT professional, and management resulted in a movement to a different information architecture. That information systems architecture was one that centered around a data warehouse.

EVOLUTION FROM THE BUSINESS PERSPECTIVE

The progression that has been described has been depicted from the standpoint of technology. But there is a different perspective—the perspective of the business. From the perspective of the business person, the progression of computers began with simple automation of repetitive activities. The computer could handle more data at a greater rate of speed with more accuracy than any human was capable of. Activities such as the generation of payroll, the creation of invoices, the payments being made, and so forth are all typical activities of the first entry of the computer into corporate life.

Soon it was discovered that computers could also keep track of large amounts of data. Thus were "master files" born. Master files held inventory, accounts payable, accounts receivable, shipping lists, and so forth. Soon there were online data bases, and with online data bases the computer started to make its way into the core of the business. With online data bases airline clerks were emancipated. With online processing, bank tellers could do a whole new range of functions. With online processing insurance claims processing was faster than ever.

It is in online processing that the computer was woven into the fabric of the corporation. Stated differently, once online processing began to be used by the business person, if the online system went down, the entire business suffered, and suffered immediately. Bank tellers could not do their job. ATMs went down. Airline reservations went into a manual mode of operation, and so forth.

Today, there is yet another incursion by the computer into the fabric of the business, and that incursion is into the managerial, strategic decision-making aspects of the business. Today, corporate decisions are shaped by the data flowing through the veins and arteries of the corporation.

So the progression that is being described is hardly a technocentric process. There is an accompanying set of business incursions and implications, as well.

THE DATA WAREHOUSE ENVIRONMENT

Figure 1.4 shows the transition of the corporation from the spider's web environment to the data warehouse environment.

The data warehouse represented a major change in thinking for the IT professional. Prior to the advent of the data warehouse, it was thought that a data base should be something that served all purposes for data. But with the data warehouse it became apparent that there were many different kinds of data bases.

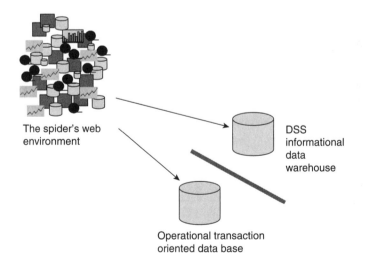

The spider's web environment

DSS informational data warehouse

Operational transaction oriented data base

■ **FIGURE 1.4**   A fundamental division of data into different types of data bases was recognized.

WHAT IS A DATA WAREHOUSE?

The data warehouse is a basis for informational processing. It is defined as being

- subject oriented;
- integrated;
- nonvolatile;
- time variant;
- a collection of data in support of management's decision.

This definition of a data warehouse has been accepted from the beginning.

A data warehouse contains integrated granular historical data. If there is any secret to a data warehouse it is that it contains data that is *both* integrated and granular. The integration of the data allows a corporation to have a true enterprise-wide view of the data. Instead of looking at data parochially, the data analyst can look at it collectively, as if it had come from a single well-defined source, which most data warehouse data assuredly does not. So the ability to use data warehouse data to look across the corporation is the first major advantage of the data warehouse. Additionally, the granularity—the fine level of detail—allows the data to be very flexible. Because the data is granular, it can be examined in one way by one group of people and in another way by another group of people. Granular data means that there is still only one set of data—one single version of the truth. Finance can look at the data one way, marketing can look at the same data in another way, and accounting can look at the same data in yet another way. If it turns out that there is a difference of opinion, there is a single version of truth that can be returned to resolve the difference.

Another major advantage of a data warehouse is that it is a historical store of data. A data warehouse is a good place to store several years' worth of data.

It is for these reasons and more that the concept of a data warehouse has gone from a theory derided by the data base theoreticians of the day to conventional wisdom in the corporation today.

But for all the advantages of a data warehouse, it does not come without some degree of pain.

INTEGRATING DATA—A PAINFUL EXPERIENCE

The first (and most pressing) pain felt by the corporation is that of the need to integrate data. If you are going to build a data warehouse, you *must* integrate data. The problem is that many corporations have legacy systems that are—for all intents and purposes—intractable. People are really reluctant to make any changes in their old legacy systems, but building a data warehouse requires exactly that.

So the first obstacle to the building of a data warehouse is that it requires that you get your hands dirty by going back to the old legacy environment, figuring out what data you have, and then figuring out how to turn that application-oriented data into corporate data.

This transition is *never* easy, and in some cases it is almost impossible. But the value of integrated data is worth the pain of dealing with unintegrated, application-oriented data.

VOLUMES OF DATA

The second pain encountered with data warehouses is dealing with the volumes of data that are generated by data warehousing. Most IT professionals have never had to cope with the volumes of data that accompany a data warehouse. In the application system environment, it is good practice to jettison older data as soon as possible. Old data is not desirable in an operational application environment because it slows the system down. Old data clogs the arteries. Therefore any good systems programmer will tell you that to make the system efficient, old data must be dumped.

But there is great value in old data. For many analyses, old data is extremely valuable and sometimes indispensible. Therefore, having a convenient place, such as a data warehouse, in which to store old data is quite useful.

A DIFFERENT DEVELOPMENT APPROACH

A third aspect of data warehousing that does not come easily is the way data warehouses are constructed. Developers around the world are used to gathering requirements and then building a system. This time-honored approach is drummed into the heads of developers as they build operational systems. But a data warehouse is built quite differently. It is built iteratively, a step at a time. First one part is built, then another part is built, and so forth. In almost every case, it is a prescription for disaster to try to build a data warehouse all at once, in a "big bang" approach.

There are several reasons data warehouses are not built in a big bang approach. The first reason is that data warehouse projects tend to be large. There is an old saying: "How do you eat an elephant? If you try to eat the elephant all at once, you choke. Instead the way to eat an elephant is a bite at a time." This logic is never more true than when it comes to building a data warehouse.

There is another good reason for building a data warehouse one bite at a time. That reason is that the requirements for a data warehouse are often not known when it is first built. And the reason for this is that the end users of the data warehouse do not know exactly what they want. The end users operate in a mode of discovery. They have the attitude—"When I see what the possibilities are, then I will be able to tell you what I really want." It is the act of building the first iteration of the data warehouse that opens up the mind of the end user to what the possibilities really are. It is only after seeing the data warehouse that the user requirements for it become clear.

The problem is that the classical systems developer has never built such a system in such a manner before. The biggest failures in the building of a data warehouse occur when developers treat it as if it were just another operational application system to be developed.

EVOLUTION TO THE DW 2.0 ENVIRONMENT

This chapter has described an evolution from very early systems to the DW 2.0 environment. From the standpoint of evolution of architecture it is interesting to look backward and to examine the forces that shaped the evolution. In fact there have been many forces that have shaped the evolution of information architecture to its highest point—DW 2.0.

Some of the forces of evolution have been:

- The demand for more and different uses of technology: When one compares the very first systems to those of DW 2.0 one can see that there has been a remarkable upgrade of systems and their ability to communicate information to the end user. It seems almost inconceivable that not so long ago output from computer systems was in the form of holes punched in cards. And end user output was buried as a speck of information in a hexadecimal dump. The truth is that the computer was not very useful to the end user as long as output was in the very crude form in which it originally appeared.

- Online processing: As long as access to data was restricted to very short amounts of time, there was only so much the business person could do with the computer. But the instant that online processing became a possibility, the business opened up to the possibilities of the interactive use of information intertwined in the day-to-day life of the business. With online processing, reservations systems, bank teller processing, ATM processing, online inventory management, and a whole host of other important uses of the computer became a reality.

■ The hunger for integrated, corporate data: As long as there were many applications, the thirst of the office community was slaked. But after a while it was recognized that something important was missing. What was missing was corporate information. Corporate information could not be obtained by adding together many tiny little applications. Instead data had to be recast into the integrated corporate understanding of information. But once corporate data became a reality, whole new vistas of processing opened up.

■ The need to include unstructured, textual data in the mix: For many years decisions were made exclusively on the basis of structured transaction data. While structured transaction data is certainly important, there are other vistas of information in the corporate environment. There is a wealth of information tied up in textual, unstructured format. Unfortunately unlocking the textual information is not easy. Fortunately, textual ETL (extract/transform/load) emerged and gave organizations the key to unlocking text as a basis for making decisions.

■ Capacity: If the world of technology had stopped making innovations, a sophisticated world such as DW 2.0 simply would not have been possible. But the capacity of technology, the speed with which technology works, and the ability to interrelate different forms of technology all conspire to create a technological atmosphere in which capacity is an infrequently encountered constraint. Imagine a world in which storage was held entirely on magnetic tape (as the world was not so long ago.) Most of the types of processing that are taken for granted today simply would not have been possible.

■ Economics: In addition to the growth of capacity, the economics of technology have been very favorable to the consumer. If the consumer had to pay the prices for technology that were used a decade ago, the data warehouses of DW 2.0 would simply be out of orbit from a financial perspective. Thanks to Moore's law, the unit cost of technology has been shrinking for many years now. The result is affordability at the consumer level.

These then are some of the evolutionary factors that have shaped the world of technology for the past several decades and have fostered the architectural evolution, the epitome of which is DW 2.0.

THE BUSINESS IMPACT OF THE DATA WAREHOUSE

The impact of the data warehouse on business has been considerable. Some of the areas of business that are directly impacted by the advent of the data warehouse are:

- The frequent flyer programs from the airline environment: The single most valuable piece of technology that frequent flyer programs have is their central data warehouse.

- Credit card fraud analysis: Spending profiles are created for each customer based on his/her past activities. These profiles are created from a data warehouse. When a customer attempts to make a purchase that is out of profile, the credit card company checks to see if a fraudulent use of the credit card is occurring.

- Inventory management: Data warehouses keep detailed track of inventory, noting trends and opportunities. By understanding— at a detailed level—the consumption patterns for the goods managed by an organization, a company can keep track of both oversupply and undersupply.

- Customer profiles: Organizations wishing to "get to know their customer better" keep track of spending and attention patterns as exhibited by their customers and prospects. This detailed information is stored in a data warehouse.

And there are many other ways in which the data warehouse has impacted business. In short the data warehouse becomes the corporate memory. Without the data warehouse there is—at best—a short corporate memory. But with a data warehouse there is a long and detailed corporate memory. And that corporate memory can be exploited in many ways.

VARIOUS COMPONENTS OF THE DATA WAREHOUSE ENVIRONMENT

There are various components of a data warehouse environment. In the beginning those components were not widely recognized.

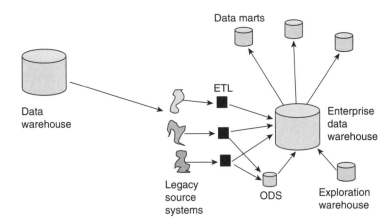

■ **FIGURE 1.5** Soon the data warehouse evolved into a full-blown architecture sometimes called the corporate information factory.

But soon the basic components of the data warehouse environment became known.

Figure 1.5 illustrates the progression from an early stand-alone data warehouse to a full-fledged data warehouse architecture.

The full-fledged architecture shown in Figure 1.5 includes some notable components, which are discussed in the following sections.

ETL—extract/transform/load

ETL technology allows data to be pulled from the legacy system environment and transformed into corporate data. The ETL component performs many functions, such as

- logical conversion of data;
- domain verification;
- conversion from one DBMS to another;
- creation of default values when needed;
- summarization of data;
- addition of time values to the data key;
- restructuring of the data key;
- merging of records;
- deletion of extraneous or redundant data.

The essence of ETL is that data enters the ETL labyrinth as application data and exits the ETL labyrinth as corporate data.

ODS—operational data store

The ODS is the place where online update of integrated data is done with online transaction processing (OLTP) response time. The ODS is a hybrid environment in which application data is transformed (usually by ETL) into an integrated format. Once placed in the ODS, the data is then available for high-performance processing, including update processing. In a way the ODS shields the classical data warehouse from application data and the overhead of transaction integrity and data integrity processing that comes with doing update processing in a real-time mode.

Data mart

The data mart is the place where the end user has direct access and control of his/her analytical data. The data mart is shaped around one set of users' general expectations for the way data should look, often a grouping of users by department. Finance has its own data mart. Marketing has a data mart. Sales has a data mart, and so forth. The source of data for each data mart is the data warehouse. The data mart is usually implemented using a different technology than the data warehouse. Each data mart usually holds considerably less data than the data warehouse. Data marts also generally contain a significant amount of summarized data and aggregated data.

Exploration warehouse

The exploration warehouse is the facility where end users who want to do discovery processing go. Much statistical analysis is done in the exploration warehouse. Much of the processing in the exploration warehouse is of the heuristic variety. Most exploration warehouses hold data on a project basis. Once the project is complete, the exploration warehouse goes away. It absorbs the heavy duty processing requirements of the statistical analyst, thus shielding the data warehouse from the performance drain that can occur when heavy statistical use is made of the exploration warehouse.

The architecture that has been described is commonly called the corporate information factory.

The simple data warehouse, then, has progressed from the notion of a place where integrated, granular, historical data is placed to a full-blown architecture.

THE EVOLUTION OF DATA WAREHOUSING FROM THE BUSINESS PERSPECTIVE

In the earliest days of computing end users got output from computers in a very crude manner. In those days end users read holes punched in cards and read hexadecimal dumps in which one tiny speck of information hid in a thousand pages of cryptic codes. Soon reports became the norm because the earliest forms of interface to the end users were indeed very crude.

Soon end users became more sophisticated. The more power the end user got, the more power the end user could imagine. After reports came, online information was available instantaneously (more or less).

And after online transaction processing, end users wanted integrated corporate data, by which large amounts of data were integrated into a cohesive whole. And then end users wanted historical data.

Throughout this progression came a simultaneous progression in architecture and technology. It is through first-generation data warehouses that the end user had the ultimate in analytical capabilities.

Stated differently, without first-generation data warehouses, the end user was left with only a fraction of the need for information being satisfied. The end user's hunger for corporate information was the single most important driving force behind the evolution to first-generation data warehousing.

OTHER NOTIONS ABOUT A DATA WAREHOUSE

But there are forces at work in the marketplace that alter the notion of what a data warehouse is. Some vendors have recognized that a data warehouse is a very attractive thing, so they have "mutated" the concept of a data warehouse to fit their corporate needs, even though the data warehouse was never intended to do what the vendors advertised.

Some of the ways that vendors and consultants have mutated the notion of a data warehouse are shown in Figure 1.6.

Figure 1.6 shows that there are now a variety of mutant data warehouses, in particular,

- the "active" data warehouse;
- the "federated" data warehouse;

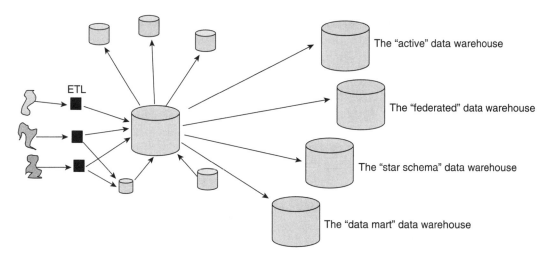

The "active" data warehouse

The "federated" data warehouse

The "star schema" data warehouse

The "data mart" data warehouse

■ FIGURE 1.6   Soon variations of the data warehouse began to emerge.

- the "star schema" data warehouse (with conformed dimensions);
- the "data mart" data warehouse.

While each of these mutant data warehouses has some similarity to what a data warehouse really is, there are some major differences between a data warehouse and these variants. And with each mutant variation come some major drawbacks.

THE ACTIVE DATA WAREHOUSE

The active data warehouse is one in which online processing and update can be done. High-performance transaction processing is a feature of the active data warehouse.

Some of the drawbacks of the active data warehouse include:

- Difficulty maintaining data and transaction integrity: When a transaction does not execute properly and needs to be backed out, there is the problem of finding the data that needs to be plucked out and either destroyed or corrected. While such activity can be done, it is usually complex and requires considerable resources.

- Capacity: To ensure good online response time, there must be enough capacity to ensure that system resources will be available during peak period processing time. While this certainly can be done, the result is usually massive amounts of capacity sitting unused for long periods of time. This results in a very high cost of operation.

- Statistical processing: There is always a problem with heavy statistical processing conflicting with systems resource utilization for standard data warehouse processing. Unfortunately, the active data warehouse vendors claim that using their technology eliminates this problem.

- Cost: The active data warehouse environment is expensive for a myriad of reasons—from unused capacity waiting for peak period processing to the notion that all detail should be stored in a data warehouse, even when the probability of access of that data has long since diminished.

Figure 1.7 outlines some of the shortcomings of the active data warehouse approach.

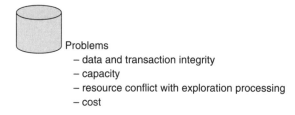

Problems
— data and transaction integrity
— capacity
— resource conflict with exploration processing
— cost

■ **FIGURE 1.7**   The active data warehouse.

THE FEDERATED DATA WAREHOUSE APPROACH

In the federated data warehouse approach, there is no data warehouse at all, usually because the corporation fears the work required to integrate data. The idea is to magically create a data warehouse by gluing together older legacy data bases in such a way that those data bases can be accessed simultaneously.

The federated approach is very appealing because it appears to give the corporation the option of avoiding the integration of data. The integration of old legacy systems is a big and complex task wherever and whenever it is done. There simply is no way around having to do integration of older data unless you use the federated approach.

But, unfortunately, the federated approach is more of an illusion than a solution. There are *many* fundamental problems with the federated approach, including but not limited to:

- Poor to pathetic performance: There are many reasons federating data can lead to poor performance. What if a data base that needs to be joined in the federation is down or is currently being reorganized? What if the data base needed for federation is participating in OLTP? Are there enough machine cycles to service both the OLTP needs and the federated needs of the data base? What if the same query is executed twice, or the same data from different queries is needed? It has to be accessed and federated each time it is needed, and this can be a wasteful approach to the usage of resources. This is just the short list of why performance is a problem in the federated environment.

- Lack of data integration: There is no integration of data with the federated approach. If the data that is being federated has already been integrated, fine; but that is seldom the case. Federation knows little to nothing about the integration of data. If one file has dollars in U.S. dollars, another file has dollars in Canadian dollars, and a third file has dollars in Australian dollars, the dollars are all added up during federation. The fundamental aspects of data integration are a real and serious issue with the federated approach.

- Complex technical mechanics: However federation is done, it requires a complex technical mechanism. For example, federation needs to be done across the DBMS technology of multiple vendors. Given that different vendors do not like to cooperate with each other, it is no surprise that the technology that sits on top of them and merges them together is questionable technology.

- Limited historical data: The only history available to the federated data base is that which already exists in the federated data warehouse data bases. In almost every case, these data bases jettison history as fast as they can, in the quest for better performance. Therefore, usually only a small amount of historical data ever finds its way into the federated data warehouse.

- Nonreplicable data queries: There is no repeatability of queries in the federated environment. Suppose a query is submitted at 10:00 AM against data base ABC and returns a value of $156.09. Then, at 10:30 AM a customer comes in and adds a payroll deposit to his account, changing the value of the account to $2971.98. At 10:45 AM the federated query is repeated. A different value is returned for the same query in less than an hour.

- Inherited data granularity: Federated data warehouse users are stuck with whatever granularity is found in the applications that support the federated query. As long as the granularity that already exists in the data base that will support federation is what users want, there is no problem. But as soon as a user wants a different level of data granularity—either higher or lower—a serious fundamental problem arises.

Figure 1.8 summarizes the fundamental problems with the federated approach to data warehousing.

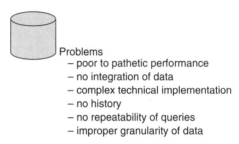

Problems
– poor to pathetic performance
– no integration of data
– complex technical implementation
– no history
– no repeatability of queries
– improper granularity of data

■ **FIGURE 1.8**   The federated data warehouse.

THE STAR SCHEMA APPROACH

The star schema approach to data warehousing requires the creation of fact tables and dimension tables. With the star schema approach, many of the benefits of a real data warehouse can be achieved. There are, nevertheless, some fundamental problems with the star schema approach to data warehousing, including:

- Brittleness: Data warehouses that consist of a collection of star schemas tend to be "brittle." As long as requirements stay exactly the same over time, there is no problem. But as soon as the requirements change, as they all do over time, either massive changes to the existing star schema must be made or the star schema must be thrown away and replaced with a new one. The truth is that star schemas are designed for a given set of requirements and only that given set of requirements.

- Limited extensibility: Similarly, star schemas are not easy to extend. They are pretty much limited by the requirements upon which they were originally based.

- One audience: Star schemas are optimized for the use of one audience. Usually one set of people find a given star schema optimal, while everyone else finds it less than optimal. The essential mission of a data warehouse is to satisfy a large and diverse audience.

A data warehouse is suboptimal if there are people who are served in a less than satisfactory manner, and creating a single star schema to serve all audiences does just that.

- Star schema proliferation: Because a single star schema does not optimally satisfy the needs of a large community of users, it is common practice to create multiple star schemas. When multiple star schemas are created, inevitably there is a different level of granularity for each one and data integrity comes into question. This proliferation of star schemas makes looking for an enterprise view of data almost impossible.

- Devolution: To solve the problem of multiple granularity across different stars, the data in each star schema must be brought to the lowest level of granularity. This (1) defeats the theory of doing star schemas in the first place and (2) produces a classical relational design, something the star schema designer finds abhorrent.

Figure 1.9 shows the challenges of using a star schema for a data warehouse.

Problems
- brittle, can't withstand change
- cannot be gracefully extended
- limited to optimization for one audience
- confused granularity
- useful only when brought to the lowest
  level of granularity

■ **FIGURE 1.9**   The star schema data warehouse.

Star schemas are not very good in the long run for a data warehouse. When there are a lot of data and a lot of users, with a lot of diversity, the only way to make the star schema approach work is to make sure the data is nonredundant and model it at the lowest level of granularity. Even then, when the requirements change, the star schema may still have to be revised or replaced.

However, in an environment in which there is little diversity in the way users perceive data, if the requirements do not change over time, and if there aren't many users, then it is possible that a star schema might serve as a basis for a data warehouse.

THE DATA MART DATA WAREHOUSE

Many vendors of online application processing (OLAP) technology are enamored of the data mart as a data warehouse approach. This gives the vendor the opportunity to sell his/her products first, without having to go through the building of a real data warehouse. The typical OLAP vendor's sales pitch goes—"Build a data mart first, and turn it into a data warehouse later."

Unfortunately there are many problems with building a bunch of data marts and calling them a data warehouse. Some of the problems are:

- No reconcilability of data: When management asks the question "What were last month's revenues?" accounting gives one answer, marketing gives another, and finance produces yet another number. Trying to reconcile why accounting, marketing, and sales do not agree is very difficult to do.

- Extract proliferation: When data marts are first built, the number of extracts against the legacy environment is acceptable, or at least reasonable. But as more data marts are added, more legacy data extracts have to be added. At some point the burden of extracting legacy data becomes unbearable.

- Change propagation: When there are multiple data marts and changes have to be made, those changes echo through all of the data marts. If a change has to be made in the finance data mart, it probably has to be made again in the sales data mart, then yet again in the marketing data mart, and so forth. When there are many data marts, changes have to be made in multiple places. Furthermore, those changes have to be made in the same way. It will not do for the finance data mart to make the change one way and the sales data mart to make the same change in another way. The chance of error quickly grows at an ever-increasing rate. The management, time, money, and discipline required to ensure that the propagating changes are accurately and thoroughly completed are beyond many organizations.

- Nonextensibility: When the time comes to build a new data mart, unfortunately most must be built from scratch. There is no realistic way for the new data mart to leverage much or even any of the work done by previously built data marts.

All of these factors add up to the fact that with the data mart as a data warehouse approach, the organization is in for a maintenance nightmare.

Problems
  – no reconcilability of data
  – the number of extracts that must be written
  – the inability to react to change
  – no foundation built for future analysis
  – the maintenance nightmare that ensues

■ **FIGURE 1.10**   The data mart data warehouse.

Figure 1.10 depicts the problems with the data mart as a data warehouse approach.

It is an interesting note that it is not possible to build a data mart and then grow it into a data warehouse. The DNA of a data mart is fundamentally different from the DNA of a data warehouse. The theory of building a data mart and having it grow up to be a data warehouse is akin to asserting that if you plant some tumbleweeds, when they grow up they will be oak trees. The DNA of a tumbleweed and the DNA of an oak tree are different. To get an oak tree, one must plant acorns. When planted, tumbleweed seeds yield tumbleweeds. The fact that in the springtime, when they first start to grow, oak trees and tumbleweeds both appear as small green shoots is merely a coincidence.

Likewise, while there are some similarities between a data mart and a data warehouse, thinking that one is the other, or that one can mutate into the other, is a mistake.

BUILDING A "REAL" DATA WAREHOUSE

The developer has some important choices to make at the architectural level and at the outset of the data warehouse process. The primary choice is, what kind of data warehouse needs to be built—a "real" data warehouse or one of the mutant varieties of a data warehouse? This choice is profound, because the financial and human resource cost of building any data warehouse is usually quite high. If the developer makes the wrong choice, it is a good bet that a lot of costly work is going to have to be redone at a later point in time. No one likes to waste a lot of resources, and few can afford to do so.

Figure 1.11 shows the dilemma facing the manager and/or architect.

One of the problems with making the choice is that the vendors who are selling data warehousing products are very persuasive. Their No. 1 goal is to convince prospective clients to build the type

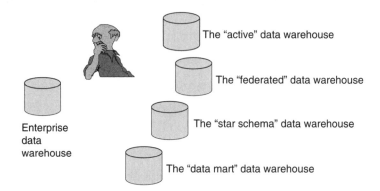

The "active" data warehouse

The "federated" data warehouse

The "star schema" data warehouse

Enterprise
data
warehouse

The "data mart" data warehouse

■ **FIGURE 1.11**   Both the long-term and the short-term ramifications are very important to the organization.

of data warehouse that requires their products and services, not necessarily the type of data warehouse that meets the business's needs. Unfortunately, falling for this type of sales pitch can cost a lot of money and waste a lot of time.

SUMMARY

Data warehousing has come a long way since the frustrating days when user data was limited to operational application data that was accessible only through an IT department intermediary. Data warehousing has evolved to meet the needs of end users who need integrated, historical, granular, flexible, accurate information.

The first-generation data warehouse evolved to include disciplined data ETL from legacy applications in a granular, historical, integrated data warehouse. With the growing popularity of data warehousing came numerous changes—volumes of data, a spiral development approach, heuristic processing, and more. As the evolution of data warehousing continued, some mutant forms emerged:

- Active data warehousing
- Federated data warehousing
- Star schema data warehouses
- Data mart data warehouses

While each of these mutant forms of data warehousing has some advantages, they also have introduced a host of new and significant disadvantages. The time for the next generation of data warehousing has come.

Chapter 2

An introduction to DW 2.0

To resolve all of the choices in data warehouse architecture and clear up all of the confusion, there is DW 2.0. DW 2.0 is the definition of data warehouse architecture for the next generation of data warehousing. To understand how DW 2.0 came about, consider the following shaping factors:

- In first-generation data warehouses, there was an emphasis on getting the data warehouse built and on adding business value. In the days of first-generation data warehouses, deriving value meant taking predominantly numeric-based, transaction data and integrating that data. Today, deriving maximum value from corporate data means taking ALL corporate data and deriving value from it. This means including textual, unstructured data as well as numeric, transaction data.

- In first-generation data warehouses, there was not a great deal of concern given to the medium on which data was stored or the volume of data. But time has shown that the medium on which data is stored and the volume of data are, indeed, very large issues.

- In first-generation data warehouses, it was recognized that integrating data was an issue. In today's world it is recognized that integrating old data is an even larger issue than what it was once thought to be.

- In first-generation data warehouses, cost was almost a nonissue. In today's world, the cost of data warehousing is a primary concern.

- In first-generation data warehousing, metadata was neglected. In today's world metadata and master data management are large burning issues.

- In the early days of first-generation data warehouses, data warehouses were thought of as a novelty. In today's world, data warehouses are thought to be the foundation on which the competitive use of information is based. Data warehouses have become essential.

- In the early days of data warehousing, the emphasis was on merely constructing the data warehouse. In today's world, it is recognized that the data warehouse needs to be malleable over time so that it can keep up with changing business requirements.

- In the early days of data warehousing, it was recognized that the data warehouse might be useful for statistical analysis. Today it is recognized that the most effective use of the data warehouse for statistical analysis is in a related data warehouse structure called the exploration warehouse.

We are indeed much smarter today about data warehousing after several decades of experience building and using these structures.

DW 2.0—A NEW PARADIGM

DW 2.0 is the new paradigm for data warehousing demanded by today's enlightened decision support community. It is the paradigm that focuses on the basic types of data, their structure, and how they relate to form a powerful store of data that meets the corporation's needs for information.

Figure 2.1 illustrates the new DW 2.0 architecture. This figure shows the different types of data, their basic structure, and how the data types relate. The remainder of the book is dedicated to explaining the many subtleties of and underlying this diagram of the DW 2.0 next-generation data warehouse architecture.

DW 2.0—FROM THE BUSINESS PERSPECTIVE

There are some powerful reasons DW 2.0 appeals to the business person. Some of those reasons are:

- The cost of data warehousing infrastructure is not constantly rising. In the first-generation data warehouse, the cost of the technical infrastructure constantly rises. As the volume of data grows, the cost of the infrastructure grows exponentially. But with DW 2.0 the cost of the data warehouse flattens.

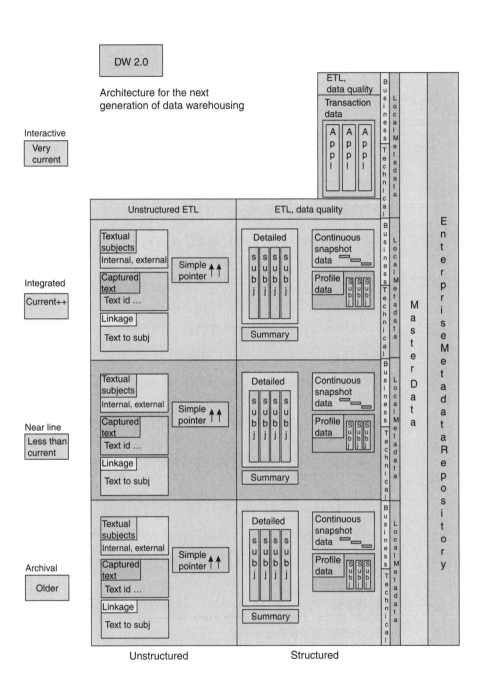

■ **FIGURE 2.1** The structure of data within DW 2.0.

- The infrastructure is held together by metadata. This means that data is not easily lost. In first-generation data warehouses, it is easy for a unit of data or a type of data to become "lost." It is like the misplacement of a book in the shelves of the New York City Library. Once the book is misfiled, it may be years before the book is replaced in a location where it can be easily located. And so it goes with data in the first-generation data warehouse environment. But the metadata that is the backbone of DW 2.0 does not allow data to become easily lost.

- Data is quickly accessible. In a first-generation data warehouse in which data is stacked upon other data, soon data becomes an impediment to access. In a first-generation data warehouse the data that is needed "hides" behind mountains of data that is not needed. The result is poor performance. In a DW 2.0 environment, data is placed according to its probability of access. The result is a much more efficient access of data than in the first-generation data warehouse environment.

- The need for archiving is recognized. In first-generation data warehouses there is little or no archiving of data. As a consequence data is stored for only a relatively short period of time. But with DW 2.0 data is stored so that it can be kept indefinitely, or as long as needed.

- Data warehouses attract volumes of data. The end user has to put up with the travails that come with managing and accessing large volumes of data with first-generation data warehousing. But with DW 2.0, because data is sectioned off, the end user has to deal with far less data.

All of these factors have an impact on the end user. There is a significantly reduced cost of the data warehouse. There is the ability to access and find data much more efficiently. There is the speed with which data can be accessed. There is the ability to store data for very long periods of time. In short these factors add up to the business person's ability to use data in a much more effective manner than is possible in a first-generation data warehouse.

So, what are some of the differences between first-generation data warehousing and DW 2.0? In fact there are very significant differences. The most stark and most important is the recognition of the life cycle of data within the data warehouse.

THE LIFE CYCLE OF DATA

In first-generation data warehousing it was thought that data need only be placed on a form of disk storage when a data warehouse was created. But that is only the beginning—data merely starts a life cycle as it enters a data warehouse. It is naïve of developers of first-generation data warehouses to think otherwise.

In recognition of the life cycle of data within the data warehouse, the DW 2.0 data warehouse includes four life-cycle "sectors" of data. The first sector is the Interactive Sector. Data enters the Interactive Sector rapidly. As data settles, it is integrated and then is passed into the Integrated Sector. It is in the Integrated Sector that—not surprisingly—integrated data is found. Data remains in the Integrated Sector until its probability of access declines. The falling off of the probability of data access usually comes with age. Typically, after 3 or 4 years the probability of data access in the Integrated Sector drops significantly.

From the Integrated Sector the data can then move on to one of two sectors. One sector that the data can go to is the Near Line Sector. In many ways, the Near Line Sector is like an extension of the Integrated Sector. The Near Line Sector is optional. Data does not have to be placed there. But where there is an extraordinarily large amount of data and where the probability of access of the data differs significantly, then the Near Line Sector can be used.

The last sector is the Archival Sector. Data residing in the Archival Sector has a very low probability of access. Data can enter the Archival Sector from either the Near Line Sector or the Integrated Sector. Data in the Archival Sector is typically 5 to 10 years old or even older.

What does the life cycle of data look like as it enters the DW 2.0 data warehouse? Figure 2.2 illustrates the DW 2.0 data life cycle.

Data enters the DW 2.0 environment either through ETL from another application or from direct applications that are housed in the Interactive Sector. The Interactive Sector is the place where online update of data occurs and where high-performance response time is found. The data that enters the Interactive Sector is very fresh, perhaps only a few seconds old. The other kind of data that is found in the Interactive Sector is data that is transacted as part of a coresident application. In this case, the data is only milliseconds old.

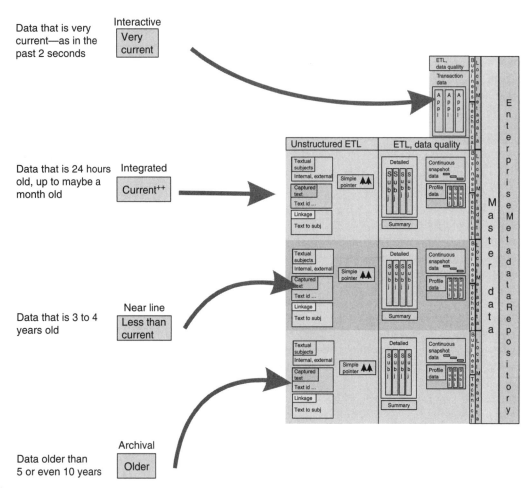

■ FIGURE 2.2 There is a life cycle of data within the DW 2.0 environment. And there is a sector of data that corresponds to the different ages of data in the data warehouse.

As an example of the data found in the interactive sector, consider an ATM transaction. In an ATM transaction, the data is captured upon the completion of an ATM activity. The data may be as fresh as less-than-a-second old when it is entered into the Interactive Sector. The data may enter the Interactive Sector in one of two ways. There may be an application outside of the DW 2.0 data warehouse by which data is captured as a by-product of a transaction. In this case, the application executes the transaction and then sends the data through ETL into the Interactive Sector of the data warehouse.

The other way the data can enter the Interactive Sector is when the application is also part of a DW 2.0 data warehouse. In this case, the application executes the transaction and enters the data immediately into the Interactive Sector.

The point is that in the Interactive Sector the application may exist outside of the sector or the application may actually exist inside the Interactive Sector.

Transaction data is inevitably application oriented, regardless of its origins. Data in the Interactive Sector arrives in an application state.

At some point in time, it is desirable to integrate transaction, application data. That point in time may be seconds after the data has arrived in the Interactive Sector or the integration may be done days or weeks later. Regardless, at some point in time, it is desirable to integrate application data. That point in time is when the data passes into the Integrated Sector.

Data enters the Integrated Sector through ETL. By passing into the Integrated Sector through ETL, the data casts off its application state and acquires the status of corporate data. The transformation code of ETL accomplishes this task.

Once in the integrated state, the data is accumulated with other similar data. A fairly large collection of data resides in the Integrated Sector, and the data remains in the integrated state as long as its probability of access is high. In many organizations, this means that the data stays in the Integrated Sector for from 3 to 5 years, depending on the business of the organization and the decision support processing that it does.

In some cases, there will be a very large amount of data in the Integrated Sector coupled with very vigorous access of the data. In this case it may be advisable to use near-line storage as a cache for the integrated data. The organization can make a very large amount of data electronically available by using the Near Line Sector. And the cost of integrated data storage with near-line storage makes the cost of the environment very acceptable. Data is placed in near-line storage when the probability of access of the data drops significantly. Data whose probability of access is high should not be placed there. It is assumed that any data placed in near-line storage has had its probability of access verified by the analyst controlling the storage location of corporate data.

The last DW 2.0 sector of data is the Archival Sector. The Archival Sector holds data that has been collected electronically and may see some usage in the future. The Archival Sector is fed by the Near Line Sector or the Integrated Sector. The probability of access of data in the Archival Sector is low. In some cases, data may be stored in the Archival Sector for legislated purposes, even where it is thought the probability of access is zero.

REASONS FOR THE DIFFERENT SECTORS

There are many reasons for the different data sectors in the DW 2.0 environment. At the heart of the different sectors is the reality that as data passes from one sector to another the basic operating characteristics of the data change. Figure 2.3 illustrates some of the fundamental operating differences between the various sectors.

Figure 2.3 shows that the probability and the pattern of access of data from sector to sector differ considerably. Data in the Interactive Sector is accessed very frequently and is accessed randomly. Data in

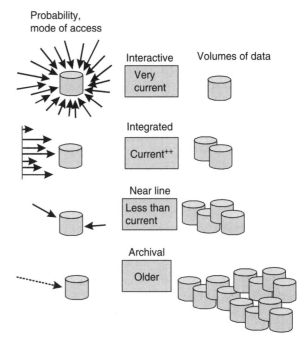

■ **FIGURE 2.3** As data goes through its life cycle within DW 2.0, its probability of access and its volume change dramatically.

the Integrated Sector is also accessed frequently, usually sequentially and in bursts. Data in the Near Line Sector is accessed relatively infrequently, but when it is accessed, it is accessed randomly. Data in the Archival Sector is accessed very infrequently, and when it is accessed, it is accessed sequentially or, occasionally, randomly.

In addition to the various patterns of access, data in different sectors are characterized by distinctly different volumes. There is relatively little data in the Interactive Sector. There is more data in the Integrated Sector. If an organization has near-line data at all, there is usually a considerable amount of data in the Near Line Sector. And Archival Sector data can mount up considerably. Even though there will be relatively little archival data in the early years of collecting it, as time passes, there is every likelihood that a large amount of data will collect in the Archival Sector.

There is a conundrum here. In the classical data warehouse, all data was just placed on disk storage, as if all data had an equal probability of access. But as time passes and the volume of data that is collected mounts, the probability of access of data drops, giving rise to a certain irony: The more data that is placed on disk storage, the less the data is used.

This is expensive, and poor performance is the result. In fact, it is *very* expensive.

Poor performance and high cost are not the only reasons first-generation data warehousing is less than optimal. There are other good reasons for dividing data up into different life-cycle sectors. One reason is that different sectors are optimally served by different technologies.

METADATA

As a case in point, consider metadata. Metadata is the auxiliary descriptive data that exists to tell the user and the analyst where data is in the DW 2.0 environment. Figure 2.4 illustrates the very different treatment of metadata in the Interactive and Archival Sectors of the DW 2.0 architecture.

Figure 2.4 shows that it is common industry practice to store metadata separately from the actual data itself. Metadata is stored in directories, indexes, repositories, and a hundred other places. In each case, the metadata is physically separate from the data that is being described by the metadata.

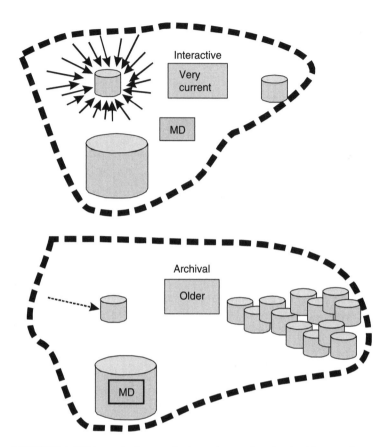

■ **FIGURE 2.4** With interactive data, metadata is stored separately; with archival data, metadata is stored directly with the data.

In contrast, metadata is stored physically with the data that is being described in the Archival Sector. The reason for including metadata in the physical embodiment in the archival environment is that archival data is like a time vault containing data that might not be used for 20 or 30 years. Who knows when in the future archival data will be used or for what purpose it will be used? Therefore, metadata needs to be stored with the actual data, so that when the archival data is examined it will be clear what it is. To understand this point better, consider the usage of archival data that is 30 years old. Someone accesses the archival data and then is horrified to find that there is no clue—no Rosetta Stone—indicating what the data means. Over the 30-year time frame, the metadata has been separated from the actual data and now no one can find the metadata. The result is a cache of archival data that no one can interpret.

However, if the metadata had been stored physically with the actual data itself, then when the archivist opened up the data 30 years later, the meaning, format, and structure of the actual data would be immediately apparent.

From the standpoint of the end user, there is a relationship between end user satisfaction and metadata. That relationship is that with metadata, the end user can determine if data and analysis already exist somewhere in the corporation. If there is no metadata, it is difficult for the business person to determine if data or analysis already is being done. For this reason, metadata becomes one of the ways in which the business person becomes enamored of the DW 2.0 environment.

ACCESS OF DATA

Access of data is another fundamental difference between the various DW 2.0 data sectors. Consider the basic issue of the access of data depicted in Figure 2.5.

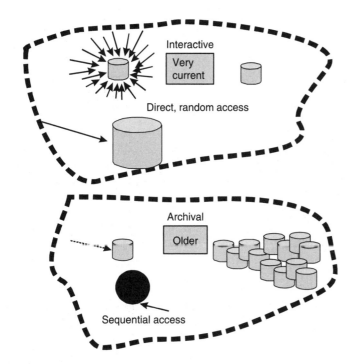

■ **FIGURE 2.5** Another major difference is in the mode of access of data.

This figure highlights the very fundamental differences in the pattern and frequency of data access in the Interactive Sector and the Archival Sector. Interactive data is accessed randomly and frequently. One second, one transaction comes in requiring a look at one unit of data. In the next second, another transaction comes in and requires access to a completely different unit of data. And the processing behind both of these accesses to data requires that the data be found quickly, almost instantaneously.

Now consider the access of archival data. In the case of archival data, there is very infrequent access of data. When archival data is accessed, it is accessed sequentially, in whole blocks of records. Furthermore, the response time for the access of archival data is relaxed.

It is seen then that the pattern of access of data is very different for each sector of data in the DW 2.0 architecture. The technology for the sectors varies as well. Therefore, it is true that no single technology—no "one size fits all" technology—is optimal for the data found in a modern data warehouse. The old notion that you just put data on disk storage and everything takes care of itself simply is not true.

While the life cycle of data is a very important aspect of DW 2.0, it is not the only departure from the first-generation data warehouse. Another major departure is the inclusion of both structured and unstructured data in the DW 2.0 environment.

STRUCTURED DATA/UNSTRUCTURED DATA

There are two basic types of data—structured and unstructured. Structured data is data that comes repetitively in the same format and layout, usually through the issuance of transactions. Typical examples of structured data include data generated by bank transactions, airline reservation transactions, insurance transactions, manufacturing transactions, retail transactions, and so forth. Structured data is conveniently stored in data base records, where there are attributes, keys, indexes, tables, and so forth. In fact the entire world of structured data is well served by standard data base technology.

The other world is that of unstructured data. Unstructured data exists in two basic forms—textual and nontextual. Textual unstructured data occurs in many places—emails, telephone conversations, PowerPoint presentations, and more. Nontextual unstructured data occurs as graphics and images, including but not limited to photographs, X-rays, MRIs, diagrams, and illustrations.

While current technology is not yet able to handle nontextual data with much elegance, textual unstructured data is another story. Textual unstructured data can be captured and manipulated. Standard data base technology has a hard time with textual data because textual data is not repetitive like structured data. However, this does not mean that there is not great value in textual data. Indeed, there is great value in it. It is just that the textual data is not easily handled and manipulated by standard data base technology.

DW 2.0 calls for unstructured textual data to be placed in a data warehouse and to be integrated along with structured data. Great opportunity for the innovative use of information arises by so doing.

Figure 2.6 shows the fundamental division between structured data and unstructured data in the DW 2.0 architecture and highlights the need to incorporate and integrate both kinds of data.

There are many challenges in the bringing together of structured and unstructured data in the DW 2.0 environment. One challenge is the integration of structured and unstructured data. Some unstructured data cannot be integrated with structured data, but other unstructured data can.

In fact unstructured data comes in two "flavors"—unstructured data and semistructured data. Unstructured data is that which is just text written in a free-form manner. A book, a manual, or a training course often has large amounts of unstructured text. Semistructured data is data that is textual, but in which there is repeatability of the format of the text. As an example, a recipe book is a single document. But within the recipe book are many recipes. Each recipe has its own ingredients and its own instructions. Each recipe is a form of semistructured data.

The integration of textual data into the DW 2.0 environment requires that both unstructured data and semistructured data be used as input.

TEXTUAL ANALYTICS

The integration of unstructured and structured data in the DW 2.0 data warehouse enables a different kind of analysis than has ever been done before—analytical processing against textual data. Analytical processing can be done against unstructured data or against a combination of structured and unstructured data, as represented in Figure 2.7.

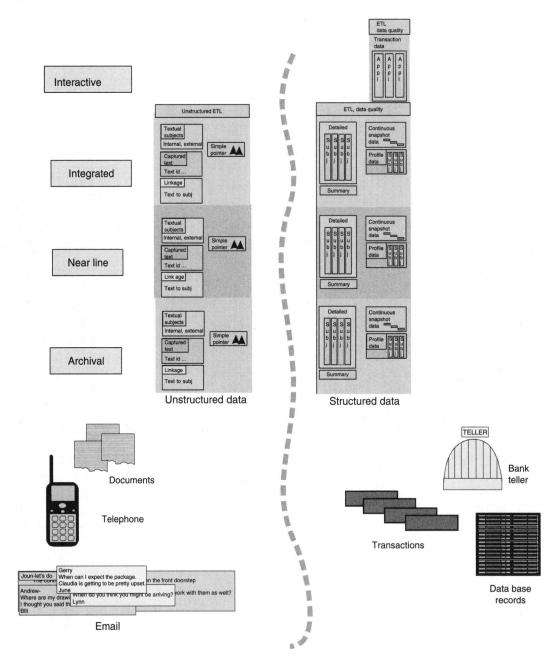

■ **FIGURE 2.6** There are two distinct worlds that are very different in many ways.

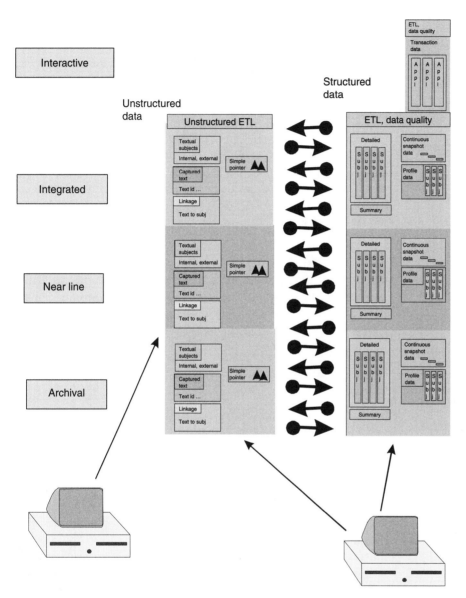

■ **FIGURE 2.7** When unstructured data is included in a data warehouse: (a) unstructured data can be accessed and analyzed by itself, (b) unstructured data and structured data can be analyzed together, and (c) some unstructured data can be closely linked with structured data.

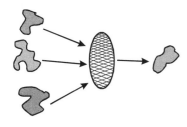

FIGURE 2.8 Unstructured data needs to be screened.

BLATHER

The challenges of incorporating unstructured data with structured data in a DW 2.0 data warehouse are many. One of the challenges is that of screening unstructured data. For a variety of reasons it is true that unstructured data contains what can be called "blather." Blather is data that has no meaning to the business of the corporation. A typical example of blather occurs in email.

Consider the email message, "Honey, what's for dinner tonight?" The world of email is full of personal content like this. Personal email has no relevance or bearing on the business of the corporation. If one is storing email, one normally does not need to see or keep blather. It just gets in the way.

Email is not the only unstructured data that needs to be screened for blather. All unstructured data needs to be screened for blather. Stated differently, if the corporation does not screen for blather, then the unstructured data that gets loaded into the DW 2.0 environment may be largely irrelevant and bloated, neither of which is conducive to good analysis. Therefore, screening is an important process in the collection and management of unstructured data.

Figure 2.8 represents the screening of unstructured data before it enters the DW 2.0 environment.

Screening unstructured data for blather is just the first of many steps that need to be done to prepare unstructured data for the DW 2.0 environment. Another major activity in the preparation of unstructured data for the DW 2.0 environment is that of creating a general (or "normalized") textual foundation of the unstructured data.

If unstructured data is going to be useful analytically, it must be transformed into data that can be analyzed both generally and specifically. To understand the need for both a general and a specific foundation for unstructured text, consider this. In almost every organizational case, unstructured text is generated by multiple sources. Whatever unstructured data is being considered, whether it be documents, emails, medical records, etc., it is a good bet that the unstructured data was not written by the same person.

THE ISSUE OF TERMINOLOGY

Because text is written by many different people, the different terminologies used by different people must be taken into consideration.

Due to differences in background, age, ethnicity, social class, education, country of origin, native language, and many other factors, people have many different ways of expressing the same thing. If these different ways of expressing the same things are not "rationalized" (or "normalized"), then it will be impossible to do a meaningful analysis on the textual data. Therefore, if textual data is to be used for textual analytics, it must first be subjected to a normalization process.

There is another reason text needs to be normalized before textual analysis can occur. That reason is that when an author writes text the author may have no idea that the text will be read and used as input into a data warehouse. Therefore there is no consideration by the author of any activity of terminology resolution. The analyst doing preparation of text for entry into a data base has the challenge of reading the text and describing to the system that will ingest the text how the text is to be interpreted. The process of describing text to a machine is not easy and must be done as part of the terminology rationalization process.

The normalization process for text requires that the text be cast in two forms—a specific form and a general form. The specific form is usually what the person has said or written. The general form is the normalized value of the data represented by what the person said or wrote.

As an example of the general and the specific forms of data, suppose that a person has written, "The tarsus has been subjected to stress and has disarticulated." This expression would be the specific original text. Now suppose someone were doing a search on broken bones. Looking up bones would not turn up tarsus, and looking up broken would not turn up disarticulated. But if the text had been preprocessed into specific and general terms, the term tarsus could have been recognized as a bone and the term disarticulated could have been recognized as an expression for broken. The creation of the general from the specific could have created two expressions—tarsus/bone and disarticulated/broken. After the connection between the specific and the general has been made, and after both the specific and the general forms have been placed in the DW 2.0 environment, an analyst looking for broken bones in the unstructured data will immediately find a disarticulated tarsus.

So a second major step in preparing unstructured data for the DW 2.0 environment is to read the specific data and to superimpose the general data over the specific to make the data fit for analysis. Anything short of that is just a waste of time and opportunity.

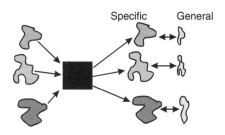

■ **FIGURE 2.9** A transformation needs to be made from raw text to specific/ general text.

SPECIFIC TEXT/GENERAL TEXT

Figure 2.9 illustrates the need for reading specific data and creating a general interpretation of the general textual data before the data is passed into a DW 2.0 environment.

The recognition of the life cycle of data in the data warehouse and the inclusion of unstructured data in the data warehouse are important advances over first-generation data warehouses. But they are not the only improvements that DW 2.0 has to offer next-generation data warehouse users.

From the business perspective it is mandatory that terminology be rationalized. If the text is not normalized, it is a futile effort to try to allow the business person to do analytical processing against textual data.

METADATA—A MAJOR COMPONENT

The DW 2.0 approach recognizes that metadata is a major and critically important part of the data warehouse infrastructure.

For a variety of reasons, metadata was never recognized or included as a major part of the first-generation data warehouse. With the advent of the next generation of data warehousing, metadata will not be forgotten again.

Metadata is the information that sits atop the data and describes what is in the actual data. Metadata is important in any environment, but is especially important in the DW 2.0 environment.

So why is metadata important to DW 2.0 when it was optional or even forgotten in first-generation data warehouses? There are some very good, very compelling reasons for the importance of metadata in the DW 2.0 architecture:

■ Size and diversity: Today's data warehouses are bigger and more diverse than previous data warehouses. While it once may have been possible to keep track of what data was in a data warehouse informally, due to the volume and diversity of data warehouse data today, it is not possible to keep track of the contents of a data warehouse.

- More diverse users: There are more, and more-diverse, users for today's data warehouses. There once were only a few users who formed a close-knit community. Today there are many users with diverse backgrounds. Keeping these users informed about what is in a data warehouse is a full-time job unto itself.

- Broad metadata scope: Metadata lies at the heart of successful DSS (Decision Support Systems) processing. To do optimal DSS processing, the end user analyst has to know many things about the data that is available for analysis. The end user analyst needs to know where the data is from, what the data means, what calculations were made, what source data was included, what source data was excluded, when the data became available, and more. All of this metadata information is important to the end user analyst.

- Administrative requirements: Administration of the data warehouse environment becomes more complex as the data warehouse ages and grows. The better the metadata, the better and easier the administration of the warehouse environment.

These, then, are just a few of the reasons for the inclusion of metadata in DW 2.0. Figure 2.10 shows the metadata layer in the DW 2.0 architecture.

In a way, the metadata component of the DW 2.0 architecture is simple—at least in concept. The metadata that resides in the DW 2.0 environment merely serves to describe the actual DW 2.0 data.

Figure 2.11 illustrates the DW 2.0 metadata perspective.

It is worth noting that DW 2.0 metadata needs to describe *both* structured and unstructured data. It is true that the classical use of metadata has been for the description of structured data. But with the inclusion of unstructured data, metadata is revealed as useful for describing the unstructured data as well.

Indeed, part of the integration of structured and unstructured data is the integration of metadata describing both of these components of the DW 2.0 data environment.

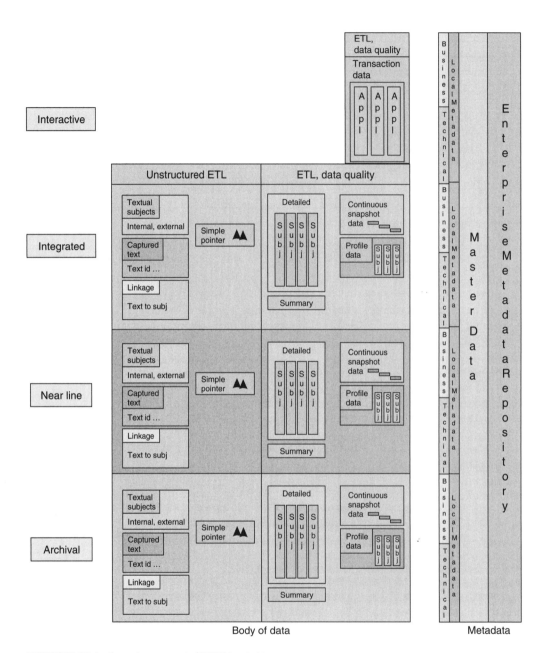

Interactive

Integrated

Near line

Archival

■ **FIGURE 2.10** Another major component of DW 2.0 is metadata.

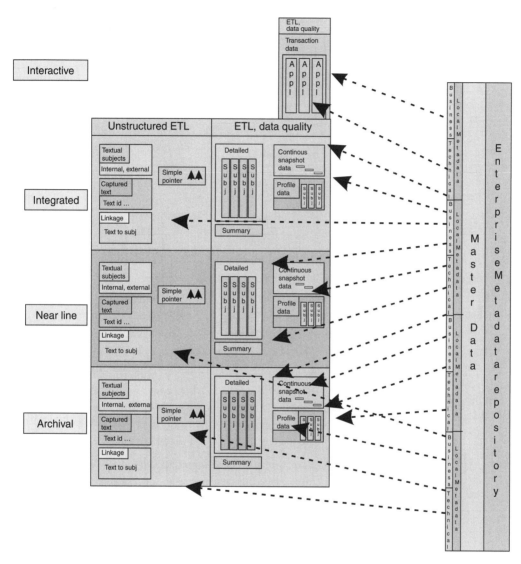

■ FIGURE 2.11 A simple way of thinking about metadata is that metadata describes one or more aspects of the body of data that lies in DW 2.0.

LOCAL METADATA

Go to any conference and listen to the speakers, and the hue and cry for metadata will be unavoidable. The fact of the matter is that there is plenty of metadata around today. There is metadata in the ETL tools, metadata in DBMS directories, metadata in BI (Business

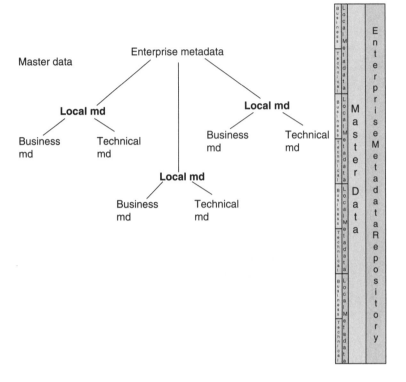

■ **FIGURE 2.12** The structure of the metadata environment.

Intelligence) tools . . . metadata everywhere! But that metadata is all specific to the tools that are being used. It can be called "local metadata." What is missing is *enterprise-wide* metadata.

DW 2.0 calls for both layers of metadata—local and enterprise-wide. Figure 2.12 illustrates the resulting DW 2.0 hierarchy, relationships, and subtypes.

Figure 2.12 shows that the DW 2.0 architecture includes several types of metadata and an overall metadata structure. There is master metadata or "reference data." There is enterprise-wide metadata. There is local metadata, such as that found in a given tool. Then, within the local metadata, there are both business and technical metadata.

Business metadata is metadata that is written in the language of the business person and is appropriate to the business of the corporation. Technical metadata (the kind most people are familiar with) is useful to and relevant to the corporation's technicians.

It is fair to say that today most metadata in the corporation is metadata relating to technology, not business.

DW 2.0 offers some major significant improvements over first-generation data warehouses. DW 2.0 offers the recognition that there is a life cycle of data once it enters the data warehouse, the notion that structured and unstructured data belong in the data warehouse, and the idea that metadata is an essential and normal part of the data warehouse.

There is yet another major change from the first-generation data warehouse environment to the DW 2.0 environment. That improvement is the notion that the technical foundation of the data warehouse should not be set in technology that cannot be easily changed.

A FOUNDATION OF TECHNOLOGY

Figure 2.13 shows the technology foundation that underlies every data warehouse.

The technology foundation is an essential part of any data warehouse. Simply stated, the data warehouse cannot exist without an underlying technology foundation. This is as true for first-generation data warehouses as it is for DW 2.0 data warehouses.

But there is a problem. The technology that houses the data warehouses roots the data warehouse to a static state. Once the data warehouse is rooted in its technology, it is very difficult to change. The technology of data warehousing tends to cast data warehouses in concrete. This is not a problem as long as there is no need to change the data warehouse. The moment it needs to be changed or updated, the extremely difficult task of uprooting and/or changing its technology foundation becomes a significant problem.

The next-generation DW 2.0 approach mandates that the data warehouse not be cast in concrete. To see how this is possible, consider that the development of a data warehouse is done by shaping it around business requirements, as suggested by Figure 2.14.

One way or another, the data warehouse is built to meet a set of business needs or requirements. The problem is that as time passes, those requirements change for many reasons, such as

- new, modified, or interpreted legislation;
- new competition;
- economic circumstances;
- new technology.

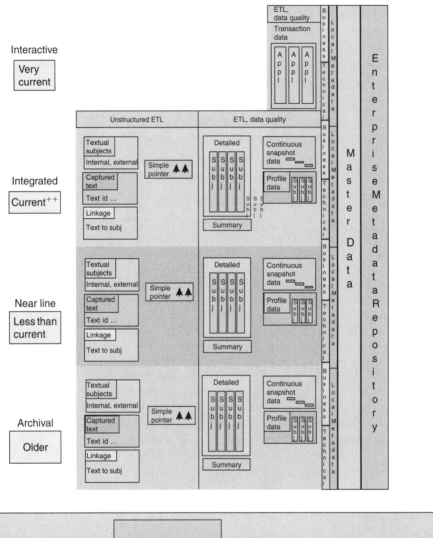

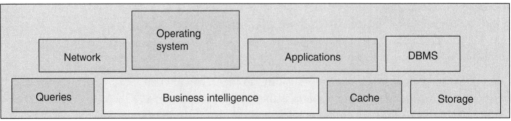

■ **FIGURE 2.13** Sitting beneath DW 2.0 is a technological foundation.

CHANGING BUSINESS REQUIREMENTS

It is said that the only two constants are death and taxes. There should be a third—business change. Business change happens to everyone, albeit at different rates and in different manners. Figure 2.15 depicts business requirements changing over time.

While business change is a predictable constant reality, changing the technological infrastructure upon which the business depends is a different matter altogether. For a variety of reasons, the technology that underpins most businesses is rooted in cement. Making changes to the technological infrastructure is very, very difficult to do.

There is a disparity, then, between business that changes all the time and a technological infrastructure that does not change. In Figure 2.16, a data warehouse has been built to meet requirements depicted as an orange box. When the business requirements and conditions change, they need to look like a blue circle. The technical infrastructure, depicted by a data can, is originally engineered to support the initial orange-box business requirements. This technical infrastructure remains static and unchanged after the changes are made in the business.

An organization's data warehouse is a significant, often mission-critical, component of its technology infrastructure. The problem is that the data warehouse cannot change easily and is designed to meet the business requirements of an earlier time. Little by little the technology

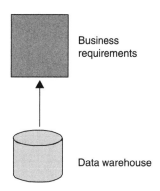

■ **FIGURE 2.14** The data warehouse is shaped by the business requirements that are known at the moment of building the data warehouse.

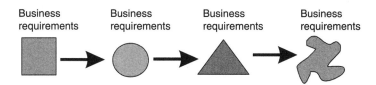

■ **FIGURE 2.15** Over time business requirements change.

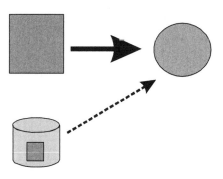

■ **FIGURE 2.16** The business requirements have changed but the data warehouse has not.

■ **FIGURE 2.17**   Unless the data warehouse can be placed on a foundation of dynamic technology, it is constantly reflecting yesterday's business requirements.

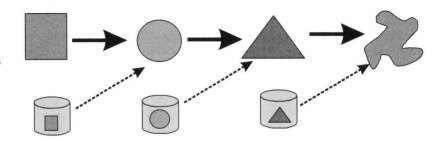

infrastructure changes, and one day the technology catches up to where it should be. But by this time the business has changed again. Figure 2.17 depicts this never-ending disparity.

This, then, is a dilemma for the data warehouse architect. DW 2.0 addresses this dilemma by mandating that the technology be placed on a foundation of dynamism, which can change over time with ease.

THE FLOW OF DATA WITHIN DW 2.0

The simple diagram that has been used to represent DW 2.0 shows the components and their approximate relationships to each other. What is not shown is the general flow of data throughout the DW 2.0 environment.

While it is possible for almost any unit of data to flow almost any-where, in general there is a predictable flow of data through the DW 2.0 for the vast majority of data.

For structured processing, data enters the system either directly through an application that is a part of the interactive environment or from an application external to the DW 2.0 environment. Data that originates in an application external to DW 2.0 is processed through an ETL interface and then flows into the Interactive Sector.

Once structured data is in the Interactive Sector, it then flows into the Integrated Sector, where the data is integrated and transformed into corporate data. Data subsequently flows from the Integrated Sector either to the Near Line Sector or to the Archival Sector. Near Line Sector data also eventually flows into the Archival Sector.

Unstructured data follows a similar path. Unstructured data begins life as a document or some other form of textual data. The textual data undergoes an ETL process for unstructured data. Then, the unstruc-tured data enters the Integrated Sector of the DW 2.0 environment.

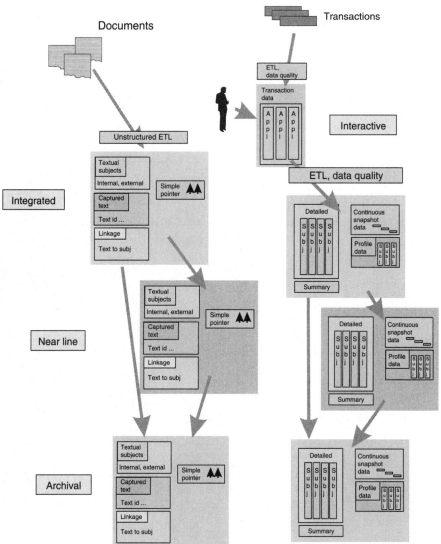

■ **FIGURE 2.18** The general flow of data throughout the DW 2.0 environment.

It is questionable if the Near Line Sector applies to unstructured data. However, if there is a need for near-line data in the unstructured environment, the unstructured data can flow into that environment.

In any case, data flows into the archival portion of unstructured data either from the Integrated Sector or from the Near Line Sector if it has been used.

The flow of both structured and unstructured data through the components of the DW 2.0 environment is depicted in Figure 2.18.

VOLUMES OF DATA

Another interesting way to view structured and unstructured data in the DW 2.0 environment is from the perspective of where the volumes of data reside, as shown in Figure 2.19.

There is typically relatively little interactive data in the structured portion of the DW 2.0 environment. The volume of structured integrated data increases substantially. When the Near Line Sector is used, the volume of structured data it must support increases yet again. And then, as the Archival Sector reaches maturity, the volume of archived structural data increases very dramatically.

In contrast, the volume of data in all of the life-cycle sectors of the unstructured environment is invariably higher and increases at a

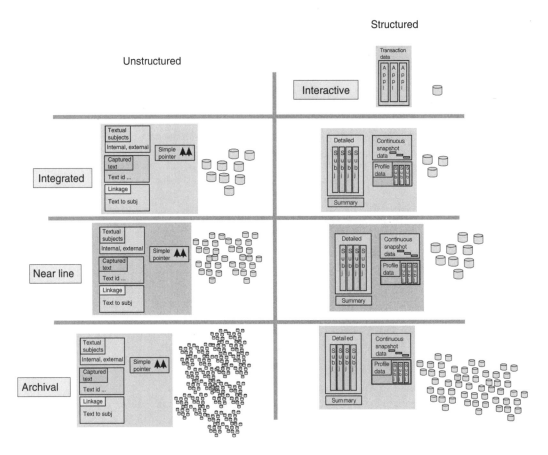

■ **FIGURE 2.19** The expected volumes of data at the different sectors in the DW 2.0 environment.

faster rate than its structured environment counterpart. It is estimated that there is four to five times as much unstructured data in the typical corporation as there is structured data. When blather and other nonuseful text are factored out, there probably remains two to three times as much data in the unstructured environment as there is in the structured environment. These proportional data volume relationships are also illustrated in Figure 2.19.

USEFUL APPLICATIONS

DW 2.0 offers the possibility of new applications that have never before been possible. DW 2.0's support for both structured and unstructured data in the data warehouse environment gives rise to some of the most interesting applications from the blending of both kinds of data.

Figure 2.20 shows that when unstructured communications, such as email, coreside in a data warehouse with demographics derived from structured data, it is possible—for the first time—to create a true 360° view of a customer.

Another useful combination of the unstructured data and structured data environment occurs when unstructured doctor's notes meet laboratory test results. A complete, composite, electronic patient record becomes possible, practical, and easy to achieve, as represented in Figure 2.21.

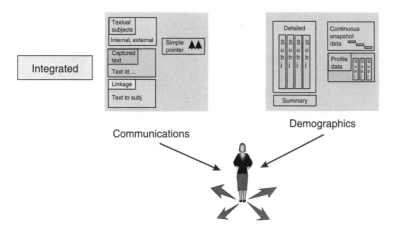

■ **FIGURE 2.20** A true 360° view of the customer.

■ **FIGURE 2.21** Creating the personal medical health record.

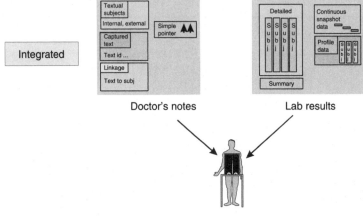

■ **FIGURE 2.22** There are two forms of referential integrity within the DW 2.0 environment—intersector and intrasector.

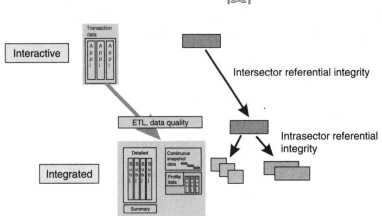

DW 2.0 AND REFERENTIAL INTEGRITY

Referential integrity has been around for a long time. Referential integrity suggests that data residing in a data base must also be governed by a set of logical rules. For example, if the medical procedure is childbirth, the patient's sex must equal female. Or, if a purchase is made, there must be a product or service that has been purchased.

The DW 2.0 approach extends the notion of referential integrity. In DW 2.0 there is intersector referential integrity and there is intrasector referential integrity. Figure 2.22 shows the two different types of referential integrity.

In Figure 2.22, intersector referential integrity refers to preservation of the integrity of data as it passes from one sector to another. Intrasector referential integrity refers to preservation of the integrity of data within a sector.

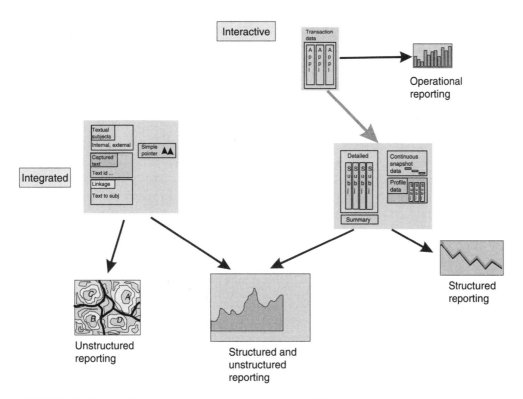

Interactive

Transaction data

Operational reporting

Integrated

Textual subjecta
Internal, external
Captured text
Text id ...
Linkage
Text to subj
Simple pointer

Detailed

Continuous snapshot data

Profile data

Summary

Structured reporting

Unstructured reporting

Structured and unstructured reporting

■ **FIGURE 2.23** There are different kinds of reporting that occur throughout the DW 2.0 environment.

REPORTING IN DW 2.0

Reporting can occur almost anywhere within the DW 2.0 environment. There is no one place where reports are run. Instead, there are different kinds of reports that are run in different places.

Figure 2.23 shows that some reports are run operationally out of the Interactive Sector. Others are run out of the Integrated Sector. Some reports are run using a combination of structured and unstructured data from the Interactive and the Integrated Sectors of the DW 2.0 environment. And yet other reports are run from the unstructured portion of the DW 2.0 environment.

SUMMARY

DW 2.0 is the next generation of architecture for the data warehouse environment. There are many differences between DW 2.0 and first-generation data warehousing. The four largest differences are

- recognition of the life cycle of data as it passes into and then resides in a data warehouse;
- inclusion of unstructured data in the data warehouse;
- inclusion of metadata in the DW 2.0 environment;
- placement of DW 2.0 on a technology foundation that can change over time.

DW 2.0 has four major data life-cycle sectors:

- Interactive Sector, where data warehousing is done in an update mode at transaction response-time rates
- Integrated Sector, where data is integrated and analytical processing can be done
- Near Line Sector, which serves as a caching area for data in the Integrated Sector
- Archival Sector, where data that may still be needed goes after a significant decline in the probability that it will be accessed

DW 2.0 includes unstructured data as well as structured data. Unstructured text that is put into a data warehouse must first go through an integration process. The integration process is necessary to prepare the unstructured text for textual analytics. If integration is not done for unstructured text, textual analytics cannot be done effectively.

One of the main tasks of preparing unstructured data for entry into the DW 2.0 environment is the removal of blather. A second necessary activity for the preparation of unstructured data is that of terminology rationalization. Text must have both specific and general references for textual analytics to be successful.

Metadata is an essential part of DW 2.0. Metadata exists at several levels:

- Enterprise level
- Local level
- Business level
- Technical level

To be successful, the DW 2.0 environment must sit on top of a technical foundation that can be changed over time.

DW 2.0 components—about the different sectors

DW 2.0 is made up of four different sectors: the Interactive Sector, the Integrated Sector, the Near Line Sector, and the Archival Sector. Depending on the size and age of the data warehouse, different sectors will either be in use or not be in use. For example, in the early days of a data warehouse, it is unlikely that any archival data will be present. For a small data warehouse, there may never be any near-line storage. The exact implementation of the DW 2.0 data warehouse varies considerably among different corporations.

Each of the different sectors has its own set of considerations and characteristics. Indeed, within the same sector, the considerations for structured data and unstructured data vary considerably.

From the business perspective, there are usually different types of users that access and analyze data from each sector. The office community makes widespread usage of the Interactive Sector. Day-to-day office activities are transacted here. The Integrated Sector indirectly supports all levels of management—from the junior level to the president of the company. The Near Line Sector is used by the analytical community, and the Archival Sector is infrequently used, or is used by an actuarial or engineering community.

There are then different communities of users who access and use the different sectors of the DW 2.0 environment.

THE INTERACTIVE SECTOR

The Interactive Sector is the place where data enters the DW 2.0 environment. Data enters either through ETL, where the application is external to DW 2.0, or as part of a transaction from an application implemented inside of the Interactive Sector. Figure 3.1 shows the various places from which data enters the Interactive Sector.

There may be multiple applications within the Interactive Sector, as depicted in Figure 3.1. The applications may or may not have integrated data. The applications in the Interactive Sector can do updates and can have high-performance transaction processing in which sub-second response time is the norm.

The workload of transactions passing through the Interactive Sector is illustrated by Figure 3.2.

In Figure 3.2 it is seen that there are many small transactions passing through the interactive workload. This is the equivalent of having a road on which only Porsches and Ferraris are allowed to run. Because

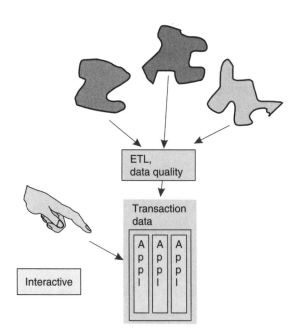

■ **FIGURE 3.1** Where input to the interactive layer comes from.

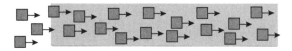

■ **FIGURE 3.2** What the workload going on inside the Interactive Sector looks like.

there are no slow-running vehicles on the road, the average speed is very fast. There is consistently good response time for the activities that are running through the system.

Another feature of the Interactive Sector is the volume of data that is managed by the technology of the sector. There is only a modest amount of data that is found in the Interactive Sector, as illustrated in Figure 3.3.

The range of data is anywhere from a few gigabytes to up to a terabyte of data running in the Interactive Sector. Relative to other parts of the DW 2.0 environment, the volumes of interactive data that are found here are small. The interactive data almost always resides on disk storage.

Because interactive data is stored on disk, and because the interactive workload is consistently made up of small, fast transactions, the response times that are achieved are very fast. Figure 3.4 represents the good response time that is the norm for the Interactive Sector.

In addition to having fast performance, the transactions that are run through the Interactive Sector are able to do updates. Data can be added, deleted, or modified, as shown in Figure 3.5 for the Interactive Sector.

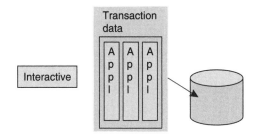

■ **FIGURE 3.3** There is a modest amount of data being managed by the interactive environment.

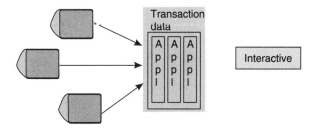

■ **FIGURE 3.4** Access to the interactive environment is measured in seconds.

One feature of the interactive environment is that because data can be updated, the value that is given to a query is relative to the moment in time the query is made. In other words, if a query is executed at one moment in time, and the same query is performed at a later point in time, the two queries will produce different answers. Figure 3.6 shows a query done at 10:31 AM yielding a value of $3000. The same query done at 10:53 AM returns a result of $4500. In between the queries, someone had added money to the account.

If data enters the Interactive Sector from an exterior application, the data flows through an ETL layer. In other words, if an application exists outside of the Interactive Sector and if it is desired to have data from that application enter the Interactive Sector, the data must be processed by an ETL tool. Figure 3.7 illustrates this circumstance.

It is possible to put data into the Interactive Sector without having to integrate the data separately using an ETL tool. In this case the data is integrated as it passes into the Integrated Sector.

Data inside the Interactive Sector may or may not have referential constraints placed on it. The choice to use or not to use referential integrity depends entirely on the application that is being run. Figure 3.8 suggests that the Interactive Sector may or may not include optional referential integrity.

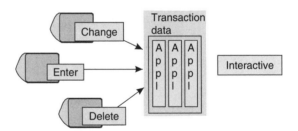

■ **FIGURE 3.5** Transactions can update data in the Interactive Sector.

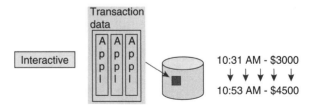

■ **FIGURE 3.6** Because data can be updated in the interactive environment, any value that has been accessed is accurate only as of the moment of access.

The pattern of access for data found in the Interactive Sector is that access is fast—in subseconds. When interactive data is accessed, there is a desire to access only a few records of data per access. And the pattern of access is random. One interactive data access will go to one location and another access will go to an entirely different and random location. Because of this pattern of access of data inside the Interactive Sector, disk storage is ideal.

Figure 3.9 depicts the general pattern of rapid, random data access in the Interactive Sector.

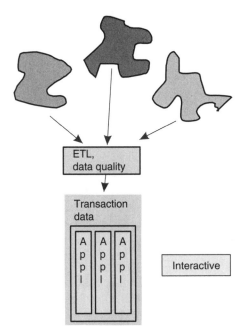

■ **FIGURE 3.7** When data enters the Interactive Sector, the data may or may not be transformed. The data normally enters via passage through an ETL layer.

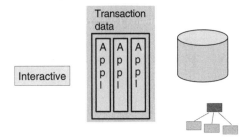

■ **FIGURE 3.8** Referential integrity can be enforced at the intrasector level in the Interactive Sector.

Only small amounts of historical data are found inside the Interactive Sector. Typical interactive historical data is a day old or even just an hour old. It is really unusual to find data as old as a month in the Interactive Sector. Data passes into the Integrated Sector before it gets to be old.

Figure 3.10 captures the notion that not much historical data is maintained in the Interactive Sector.

There is a very uneven level of granularity of data found in the Interactive Sector. Some applications will have a fine degree of granularity, while other applications will aggregate data. There just isn't any consistency of design when it comes to the granularity of application data, as shown in Figure 3.11.

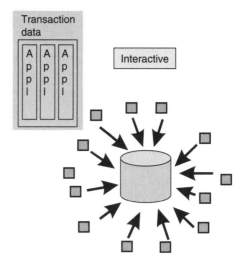

■ **FIGURE 3.9** The pattern of access: (a) fast, (b) random, and (c) for small amounts of data.

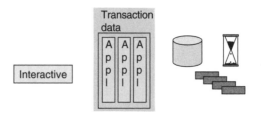

■ **FIGURE 3.10** There are only small amounts of historical data to be found in the interactive environment.

Data passes from the Interactive Sector to the Integrated Sector. If data has come from outside of the Interactive Sector, it passes to the Integrated Sector. If data comes from the execution of an application residing in the Interactive Sector, then the data is gathered as a by-product of the execution and is passed on to the Integrated Sector. Figure 3.12 shows that all data that passes into or through the Interactive Sector eventually moves into the Integrated Sector.

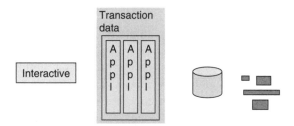

■ **FIGURE 3.11**   The granularity of the data inside the Interactive Sector varies considerably from application to application.

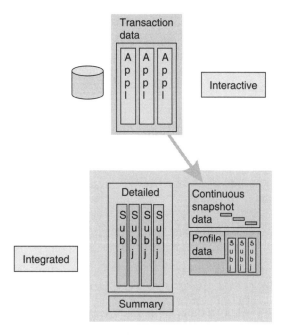

■ **FIGURE 3.12**   Where data goes after it leaves the Interactive Sector.

THE INTEGRATED SECTOR

The Integrated Sector is the place where application and transaction data eventually meet and become corporate data. As an example of the differences between application data and corporate data, consider three applications, A, B, and C, that collect revenue information. Application A collects revenue information in euros. Application B collects data in U.S. dollars. And application C collects revenue information in pesos. As this application data passes into the Integrated Sector, the data is all converted into a common currency.

And there are *many* conversions that have to be done to transform operational application and interactive transaction data into corporate data. For example, suppose application A has a month-end closing date of the 31st, application B has a closing date of the calendar end of the month, and application C has a corporate calendar closing date. It is for this reason that the closing reports from the applications will not reconcile to the corporate closing reports. They may have different actual closing dates. These inconsistencies are resolved when all three closing dates are converted to a common closing date as data is passed into the corporate Integrated Sector.

Another type of reconciliation is that of data key reconciliation. Application A has one key structure, application B has another key structure, and application C has yet another key structure. When data from these applications pass into the Integrated Sector, the keys are converted into a common key structure that serves the entire corporation.

Here is another example. Application A has a date format of YYMMDD, application B has a date format of MMDDYY, and application C has a date format of YYYYMMDD. When dates are passed into the Integrated Sector, they are all converted into a single common format.

These are just a few examples of the many types of conversion that occur as data passes from the Interactive to the Integrated Sector.

The Integrated Sector contains different kinds of structures. The following types of data structures are found in the Integrated Sector:

- Subject-oriented detailed data—This is where data is organized into major subject areas and where detail is kept. As an example of the way that detail is organized into a subject area, suppose that the particulars of a sales transaction come to the Integrated

Sector. From the sale data, the item sold will go to the products sold subject area, the person to whom the item was sold may have some purchase preference data that needs to go in the customer subject area, and the revenue amount will go to the revenue subject area.

- Small amounts of summary data—The summary data found in the Integrated Sector is summary data that is used in many places and summary data that doesn't change. For example, for a publicly traded corporation, a quarterly statement of revenue, expenses, profitability, and other information goes into a public place (i.e., the Integrated Sector) where anyone that needs this information can have access to it.

- Continuous time span data—For some data that changes slowly, it is useful to place it in a continuous time span structure. For example, a continuous time span structure can be used to track the name and address of a customer. The customer doesn't move often and the customer's name changes infrequently—only when the customer's marital status changes. Therefore, it is possible and reasonable to keep a continuous record of the information about a customer in the Integrated Sector.

- Profile data—Profile data is data collected from a wide variety of sources about a single subject. A customer record is a simple example of a profile record. A profile record for a customer is kept to track such things as the customer's demographics, the last items the customer bought, the times of day when the customer is active, the locations the customer is active in, and so forth. Looking at the profile record provides a lot of information about the customer in a thumbnail sketch.

The data in the Integrated Sector is collected after the interactive data is passed through a layer of ETL processing. It is at the moment of ETL processing that data quality processing is also done. Some simple examples of data quality processing that are done here are domain checking and range checking.

An example of domain checking is ensuring gender codes such as M (male), F (female), or U (unknown). The logic of range checking might read, if age is greater than 150, flag it as likely an error.

Once the data is collected, integrated, and passed through a data quality editor, it is then entered into the Integrated Sector, as depicted in Figure 3.13.

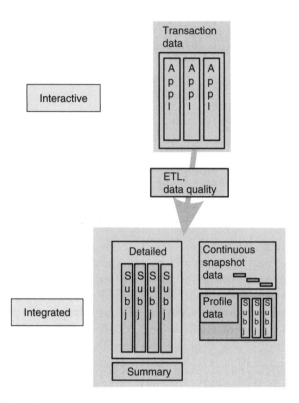

■ **FIGURE 3.13** How data enters the Integrated Sector.

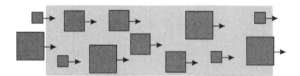

■ **FIGURE 3.14** What the workload going on inside the Integrated Sector looks like.

The workload passing through the Integrated Sector is very mixed, as illustrated by Figure 3.14.

The workload shown in Figure 3.14 is like a highway on which there are Porsches, Ferraris, and lots of semitrailers all sharing the same roadway. The speed of a vehicle on this highway depends on the vehicle in front of it. It doesn't matter that a Porsche can go 185 mph if it is stuck behind a semi going 25 mph. Contrast this workload with the workload of the Interactive Sector and it becomes clear that there is a world of difference between the two highways.

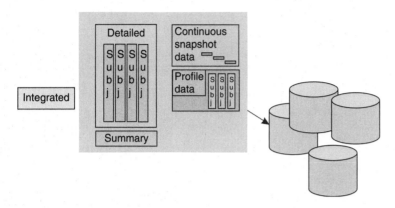

■ FIGURE 3.15 There is a fairly significant amount of data being managed by the integrated environment.

There is a good reason for the mixed workload of the Integrated Sector. Some people have to access a lot of data and other people want only a small amount of data. It is as simple as that. But all of them want it from the Integrated Sector, so there is a very mixed workload.

The Integrated Sector usually involves a significant amount of data, as depicted by Figure 3.15.

There are some good reasons for the large amount of data found in the Integrated Sector, including:

- The data is granular: There are a lot of atomic units of data to be collected and managed.
- The data is historical: There is often from 3 to 5 years' worth of data.
- The data comes from a wide variety of sources.

Combine these three factors and the result is a lot of data in the Integrated Sector.

Corresponding to the mixed workload is the response time that is expected in the Integrated Sector, where the response time varies anywhere from 10 seconds to much longer. The reason for the variance is the mixed workload. When large data retrieval jobs are being executed against the Integrated Sector, small data queries against the sector are likely to be held up and delayed. On the other hand, users who access the Integrated Sector when no one else is using it can expect good response time.

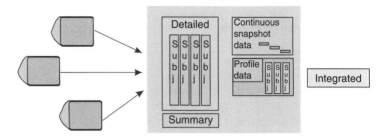

■ **FIGURE 3.16** Access to the integrated environment is measured anywhere from 10 seconds to 2 hours or more.

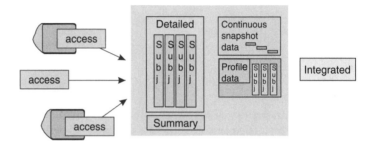

■ **FIGURE 3.17** Transactions can only access data in the Integrated Sector.

One way that people try to regulate response time is not to let the semis on the highway during rush hours—let only the Porsches and Ferraris on the road during the hours of 8:00 AM to 3:30 PM. While this works well, it penalizes the semitrailer drivers who have a legitimate need to get on the highway. In other words, the response time for small jobs that need to use Integrated Sector data can be improved during peak usage hours by confining large queries against the sector to off hours, a less than desirable situation for large query users.

So there are ways around the mixed workload found on the Integrated Sector highway. Figure 3.16 depicts the response time expectations that accompany the Integrated Sector.

The transactions that access data in the Integrated Sector can only read data. Unlike the Interactive Sector, where data can be added, deleted, or altered, the data in the Integrated Sector can only be accessed, not updated. Figure 3.17 illustrates data access from the Integrated Sector.

Because data cannot be added, deleted, or changed in the Integrated Sector does not mean that changes to data cannot be accommodated. Instead changes to data are accomplished in a different manner.

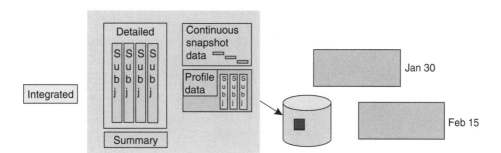

Changes to data in the Integrated Sector are done by creating a new record whenever a change is made to the data. When a bank account changes, a new record is created. When a person's address changes, a new record is created. When a person's insurance coverage changes, a new record is created, and so forth. By creating a new record every time a change is made, a historical track record of the data's evolution is maintained. In addition, once a value is correctly placed in the Integrated Sector, it is never altered. The record may be sent to near-line storage or to archival storage, but after the record is correctly created, it is never changed. This means of dealing with change is very different from that found in the Interactive Sector, where changes to the same records are made all the time.

Figure 3.18 illustrates how changes are recorded in the Integrated Sector.

There is an interesting effect of tracking historical changes to data as it is done in the Integrated Sector. Namely, once a question is asked, it will always get the same answer, even if it is asked at a later point in time. To illustrate this constancy of data, suppose that at 10:31 AM a banker wants to know what the bank's year-to-date revenues are as of 10:31 AM this morning. The answer retrieved from the Integrated Sector comes back as $3000. Now, for whatever reason, the banker asks the same question at 10:53 AM. Although the bank's revenues have changed since 10:31 in the bank's operational and interactive applications, the answer to the banker's query against the Integrated Sector of the data warehouse has not. The banker will get back the same answer—$3000.

Figure 3.19 illustrates the constancy of data that is characteristic of processing in the Integrated Sector.

Figure 3.20 emphasizes that there are no exceptions to the integration of data as it enters the Integrated Sector. Data entry to the Integrated Sector is necessarily a one-way street and a highly controlled route.

■ **FIGURE 3.18** When data values change in the Integrated Sector, a record of the change is created and entered. Thus a historical record of change is kept.

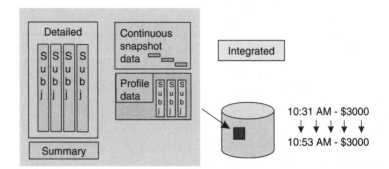

■ **FIGURE 3.19** Because data cannot be updated in the integrated environment, any value that has been accessed is accurate at any time.

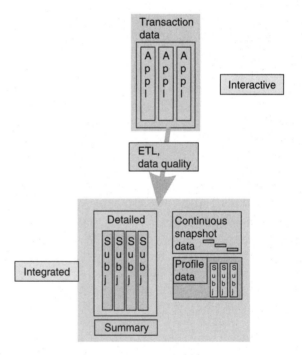

■ **FIGURE 3.20** When data enters the Integrated Sector, it is always integrated after passing through ETL processing.

There are two forms of referential integrity that are relevant to and are found in the Integrated Sector. The first type is intersector referential integrity. Intersector referential integrity refers to the integrity of data as it passes across sectors. In other words, if data passes from

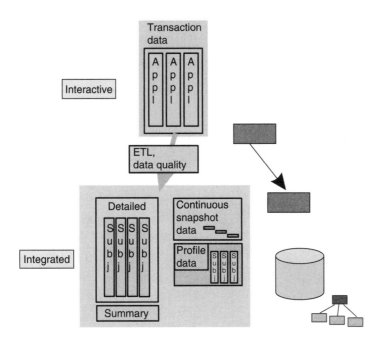

■ FIGURE 3.21 Referential integrity can be enforced at the intersector level or the intrasector level.

the Interactive Sector to the Integrated Sector, the data will recognizably have its source and its target accounted for and no data will be missing. There can be no entry of data in the Integrated Sector that does not have a corresponding entry in the Interactive Sector—and vice versa—there can be no entry of data in the Interactive Sector that does not have a corresponding entry in the Integrated Sector.

However, just because there are corresponding entries in each sector does not necessarily mean that the values of the entries are the same. One entry may be in euros and the other entry may be in U.S. dollars. Just because two data elements do not have the same value does not mean that they are not corresponding entries.

The second kind of referential integrity that can be found in the Integrated Sector is intrasector referential integrity. Intrasector referential integrity means that there may be a relationship between data elements within the same sector. Both types of referential integrity are possible in the Integrated Sector, as depicted by Figure 3.21.

In comparison to the Interactive Sector, the pattern of access for data in the Integrated Sector is one in which fewer calls for data are made, but the calls typically request more data. Figure 3.22 illustrates the

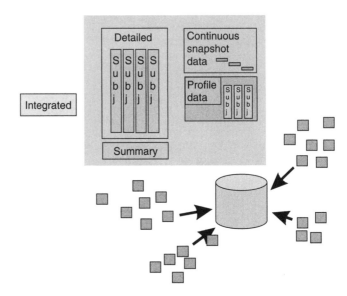

■ **FIGURE 3.22** The pattern of access: (a) relaxed speed, (b) sequentially random, (c) for large amounts of data.

general pattern of access that is expected for the Integrated Sector. This pattern of data access is expected with a mixed workload of small-to-large data retrieval requests.

Another difference between the Interactive Sector and the Integrated Sector has to do with the amount of historical data that is found in the different environments. In the integrated environment there is a significant amount of historical data. It is normal to find from 3 to 5 years' worth of data in the Integrated Sector. In contrast, it is rare to find more than 30 days' worth of data in the Interactive Sector.

Figure 3.23 illustrates the large amount of historical data that is found in the Integrated Sector.

Data granularity is another major difference between the Interactive Sector and the Integrated Sector. In the Interactive Sector, there is mixed granularity. Some data is granular and some data is not. The Integrated Sector, on the other hand, contains the lowest level of granularity of data found in the corporation. It is mandatory that the data in the Integrated Sector be at the very finest and atomic that there is. The Integrated Sector will support many forms of DSS (Decision Support Systems) processing, and each of the DSS processes will have its own requirements for data. Therefore, the lower the level of granularity at the integrated level, the more forms of DSS processing are supported. Stated differently, when the level of granularity of data is

The Near Line Sector

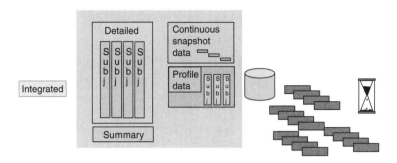

■ **FIGURE 3.23** There are fairly large amounts of historical data to be found in the integrated environment.

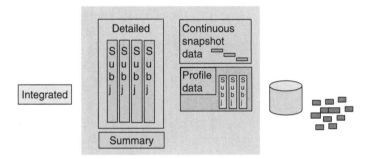

■ **FIGURE 3.24** The granularity of the data inside the Integrated Sector is as low as it gets anywhere in the information systems environment.

raised in the Integrated Sector, fewer forms of subsequent DSS processing can be supported.

Figure 3.24 depicts the need for low levels of granularity at the Integrated Sector.

Once data leaves the Integrated Sector, it can go either to the Near Line Sector or to the Archival Sector (Figure 3.25). Data goes to the Near Line Sector when there is a lot of data and there is a need for caching of data. Data goes to the archival environment when the probability of access of the data drops significantly. Usually, but not always, this means that as data ages it is sent to the archival environment.

THE NEAR LINE SECTOR

The Near Line Sector is a form of caching for the Integrated Sector. The Near Line Sector may or may not be used for caching—it

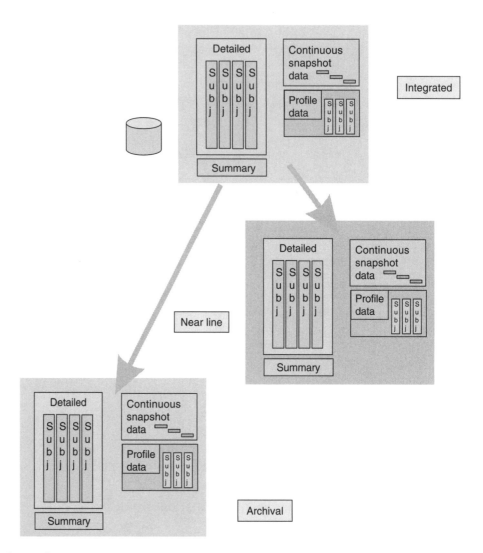

■ FIGURE 3.25 Where data goes after it leaves the Integrated Sector.

depends entirely upon the nature of the data warehouse. When a data warehouse's Integrated Sector is very large, easing the burden on the Integrated Sector by inclusion of a Near Line Sector makes sense. When there is not all that much data in the Integrated Sector, then using the Near Line Sector probably is not necessary.

There are two reasons for using the Near Line Sector—cost and performance. Near-line storage costs significantly less than disk storage. So if the hardware costs of disk storage for the Integrated Sector are

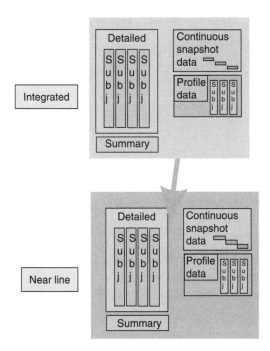

■ **FIGURE 3.26** The source of near-line data is the Integrated Sector.

prohibitive, then much of the data in the Integrated Sector can be downloaded into the Near Line Sector for tremendous cost savings.

Performance is enhanced by downloading data with a low probability of access to the Near Line Sector. Because only data with a low probability of access is sent to the Near Line Sector, the data remaining in disk storage in the Integrated Sector is freed from the overhead of "bumping into" large amounts of data that is not going to be used.

Near-line storage is sequential data storage on cartridges that are managed robotically. Near-line storage is used for storing large quantities of data very inexpensively. Data is still electronically available when it is maintained on near-line storage, but the cost of storage is significantly reduced compared to the cost of storing all data in the Integrated Sector on disk storage.

Figure 3.26 depicts Near Line Sector data arriving from the Integrated Sector.

Once data has been placed in near-line storage, it is subjected to a workload like any other environment. The typical workload for

■ **FIGURE 3.27** What the workload going on inside the Near Line Sector looks like.

near-line storage does not need much data access activity. The reason there is a diminished need for access to the near-line data is that only data with a low probability of access has been placed in near-line storage. In fact, if there is frequent access of any particular type of near-line data, then that data needs to be moved back up into the Integrated Sector.

On the relatively rare occasion when there is a need for access to near-line data, the access is either for a string of records or for a single record. Figure 3.27 depicts the typical workload associated with near-line storage.

One of the burning issues is how data moves from the Integrated Sector to the Near Line Sector. There are basically two ways that data can be managed when it comes to its placement—manually or in an automated manner.

When data is managed manually, there is an administrator who monitors the usage of the data in the Integrated Sector or receives a request for movement of data. The administrator then moves the data either to or from the Integrated Sector to the Near Line Sector.

The other alternative for the management of the movement of the data is through a CMSM—a cross-media storage manager. The CMSM sits between the Integrated Sector and the Near Line Sector. The CMSM automatically manages the placement of the data from one environment to the next.

The CMSM can operate in a mode of transparency. A transparent CMSM examines requests coming into the system and sees if any of the requests are looking for data that is managed in near-line storage. When a request for data that is being managed in near-line storage arrives, the CMSM queues the transaction, goes and finds the data in near-line storage that has been requested, and loads the data onto disk storage. Then the transaction is de-queued and executed. Upon going into execution, the transaction finds all the data it needs residing in disk storage where the CMSM put it.

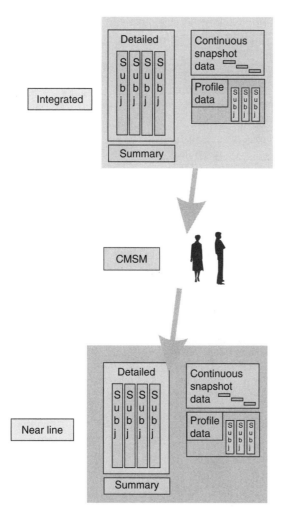

■ **FIGURE 3.28** There are essentially two ways to manage the flow of data between the Integrated Sector and the Near Line Sector.

There are other ways that the CMSM can operate. What has just been described is only one of several modes of CMSM operation.

Figure 3.28 shows the interface between the Integrated Sector and the Near Line Sector.

As a rule, the data that resides in the Near Line Sector is a mirror image of the structure and format of the data that resides in the Integrated Sector. The design of the data, the DBMS, and the release of the DBMS are all identical to their Integrated Sector counterparts.

There is a good reason for this extreme similarity of data from the integrated and near-line environments. That reason is that data needs to be effectively interchangeable between the two environments. It is certainly obvious that data moves from the integrated environment to the near-line environment. What may not be so obvious is that data also moves from the near-line environment back to the integrated environment. Data moves from the near-line environment to the integrated environment whenever the probability of the data being accessed arises. Therefore, it becomes easy to move data from the near-line environment to the integrated environment when the data is identical in format, structure, and technology. Let any one of these factors slip and it becomes much harder to move near-line data back into the integrated environment.

Figure 3.29 shows that the data is identical in structure, format, and technology in the integrated and near-line environments.

One of the main benefits of the near-line environment is that it can manage *huge* amounts of data, far more than can be managed gracefully in the interactive or integrated environments. It is possible to manage hundreds of terabytes of data in the near-line environment.

Figure 3.30 depicts the ability of the near-line environment to manage huge amounts of data.

Upon leaving the Near Line Sector, data normally moves into the Archival Sector. Note that the Archival Sector may be fed data directly from the Integrated Sector without passing through the Near Line Sector. However, if the data has been moved into the Near Line Sector, then it is normally moved from there to the Archival Sector.

The movement of data to the Archival Sector is made when the probability of accessing the data drops significantly.

Figure 3.31 illustrates the movement of data from the Near Line Sector to the Archival Sector.

THE ARCHIVAL SECTOR

The Archival Sector is the place where data goes when the probability of it being accessed becomes very small. In some cases, data is placed in the Archival Sector not due to any probability of access, but because of legislative reasons. In some cases the government mandates the storage of data for long periods of time.

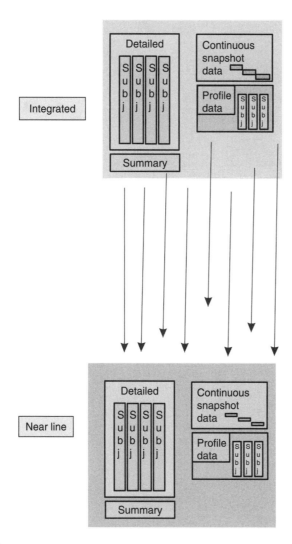

■ **FIGURE 3.29**   Structurally, the near-line environment is a carbon copy of the integrated environment.

Putting data in archives used to be a one-way street. Data that went into archives became inaccessible. Often when a person went to open a magnetic tape that had been assigned to archival processing, oxide dust fell out of the plastic container the moment it was opened. This of course meant that the magnetic tape had decomposed, which in turn meant that the tape was now useless because it could not be read.

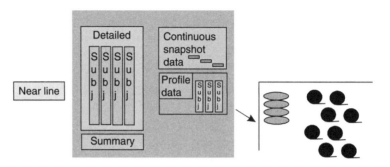

■ **FIGURE 3.30** There can be a very large amount of data being managed by the near-line environment.

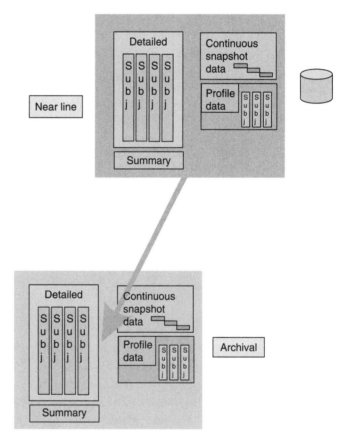

■ **FIGURE 3.31** Where data goes after it leaves the Near Line Sector.

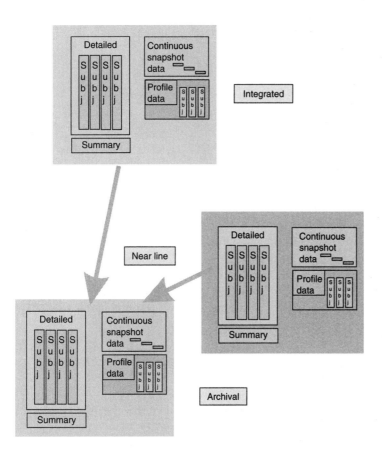

■ **FIGURE 3.32** Archival data can come from either the Integrated Sector or the Near Line Sector.

Today when data is placed in archival storage, the data must be readable at a later point in time, otherwise the archival environment is a waste of time and money.

In many ways building an archival environment is like building a time capsule. People put all sorts of things in a time capsule, not knowing when the capsule will be opened or by whom. The same analogy is true for the data stored in the archival environment. When an archival environment is populated with data, the future needs of the data's users are unknown and the moment in time when the data will be needed is also unknown.

Therefore, the archival environment needs to organize data so that it is in "time capsules" that are completely self-contained.

Figure 3.32 recaps how data enters the archival environment from either the integrated environment or the near-line environment.

■ FIGURE 3.33 What the workload going inside the Archival Sector looks like.

The workload associated with the archival environment is very unusual. For long periods of time—months or even years—there is often no access of archival data whatsoever. Then one day there is a need for the data—either a few records or a whole long sequential string of data.

The biggest problem with archival data is usually finding the required data. Whereas in other environments the emphasis is on subsecond response time, in the case of archival data the issue is that of even being able to find whatever data you are looking for. Usually there is so much archival data, and the basis for searching the data is so obscure, that finding data in the archival environment is like looking for the proverbial needle in a haystack.

Figure 3.33 depicts the workload associated with the archival environment.

The volumes of data found in the Archival Sector can be tremendous. Over time, it is expected that there will be more data in the Archival Sector than anywhere else. In the early days of a data warehouse's life cycle there usually is very little data in its archives. But over time, as the data warehouse matures, its archives can accumulate and grow to contain utterly huge amounts of data.

Figure 3.34 shows the large amount of data that can be found in the Archival Sector.

Access to the archival environment in terms of response time is measured in units of time not found elsewhere in the DW 2.0 architecture. It is normal to expect for it to take days or even weeks to find data in the archival environment. This of course depends on the volume of data in the archival environment, how well the data is indexed, the data search criteria, and the technology used to store the archival data. In some cases a search may be completed rather quickly, but general expectations for retrieving data from the archival environment had better not be set too high.

Figure 3.35 illustrates the search time expectations for an archival environment.

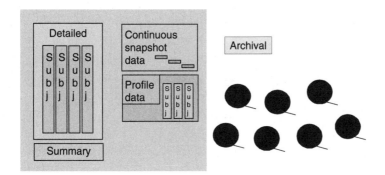

■ FIGURE 3.34 There can be a huge amount of data being managed by the archival environment.

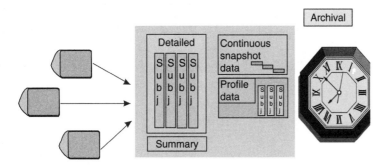

■ FIGURE 3.35 Access to the archival environment is measured in hours or even days.

On occasion, upon completing a search, data can be moved from the archival environment to the Integrated Sector. This kind of archival data restoration is indicated when there is reason to suspect that the data will be needed for lots of analysis and access. Going to the archival environment is a rather painful experience in most environments. By moving archival data that is likely to be used frequently back to the Integrated Sector, the often-painful experience of having to go back to the archival environment to retrieve it again can be mitigated.

Figure 3.36 shows that data can be restored to the Integrated Sector from the Archival Sector.

One of the most useful things that can be done with archival data is the creation of passive indexes. Usually the archival environment just sits there. Occasionally someone loads more data into the archival environment. But for the most part, the archival environment is essentially void of activity.

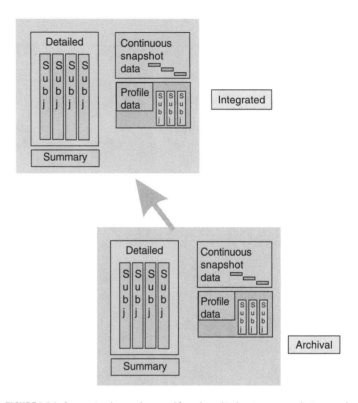

■ **FIGURE 3.36** On occasion data can be moved from the archival environment to the integrated environment.

Then along comes a day when someone wants something from the archival environment. Suddenly there is a big rush to push a lot of data through the system. In the archival environment, there are typically long periods of inactivity followed by a few short periods of frantic voluminous activity. And when it comes to finding data in the archival environment, the search is always questionable.

These are the conditions that commend the creation and use of passive indexes.

Under normal circumstances, indexes are created for the purpose of rapid access into a data base using known requirements. But in the case of archival data, there are few predictable paths of access. Therefore, while the data in the Archival Sector is just sitting there, creating indexes based on probable paths of access is a good use of time. Once several passive indexes are created, when it comes time to search the Archival Sector, with any luck the data that is being sought

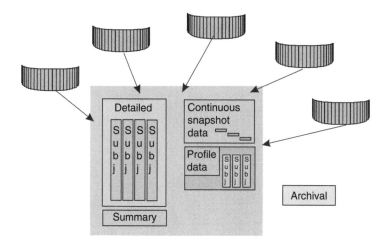

■ **FIGURE 3.37**   Archival data sits there and is not often used. It is a good idea to use this idle time to create what is termed a "passive index."

can be easily and quickly found. Only in the case in which data is being sought where a passive index has not been built will it be necessary to do a full sequential search of the data.

Figure 3.37 shows the creation of passive indexes on likely paths to and through the Archival Sector.

When data is sent to the Archival Sector, it may or may not be appropriate to preserve the structure that the data had in the integrated or near-line environments. There are advantages and disadvantages to both preserving the structure of the data and not preserving the structure of the data. One advantage of preserving the structure of the data as it passes into the Archival Sector is that it is an easy thing to do. The data is simply read in one format and written out in the same format. That is about as simple as it gets. But there are some reasons this approach may not be optimal. One reason is that once the data becomes archived, it may not be used the same way it was in the integrated environment. The format and structure of data in the Integrated Sector may not be appropriate at all for data in the Archival Sector.

In addition, data in the Integrated Sector is usually compatible with a particular release of the software that uses it. By the time archival data is retrieved from the archival environment, it is likely that the release of the software that will use it is long gone. Therefore, it may not make sense to structure the data in the Archival Sector the same way the data was structured in the Integrated Sector.

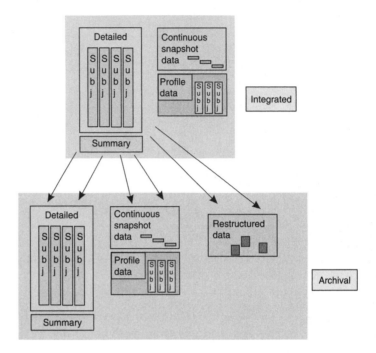

■ **FIGURE 3.38** When data is sent to the archive environment, the structure of the data may be preserved, the data may be restructured, or both.

The data can and often should be broken into finer pieces as it is placed in the Archival Sector. Then, when it is searched or when it is accessed it is simpler to query.

Additionally, there is no reason the data cannot be placed in the archival environment in two formats—in its original structure from the Integrated Sector and in a simpler, more universal format.

Figure 3.38 illustrates the dual structuring of data in the Archival Sector.

Data placed in the Archival Sector needs to be as free as possible from software release constraints and conventions.

There is a predictable pattern of access for data found in the Archival Sector, as depicted by Figure 3.39.

Archival Sector data is accessed very infrequently, and when it is accessed, it is usually the case that entire sets of archival data must be accessed. Only rarely will a single record in the archival environment need to be retrieved.

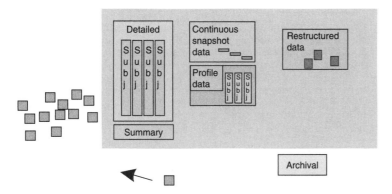

■ **FIGURE 3.39**   The pattern of access for the archival environment is: (a) very infrequent access; (b) when access occurs, most of it is for lots of sequential data; (c) a few accesses are made for specific records.

One of the interesting aspects of accessing data in the archival environment is that oftentimes the data will need to be located based on obscure fields or data values. Occasionally there is a need to access archival data by one "standard" key and identifier values. But, often there needs to be an access and qualification of data based on very nonnormal types of data.

Due to the volume of archival data and the fact that archival data is retained for long periods of time, referential integrity constraints are not a part of the Archival Sector, as illustrated in Figure 3.40.

The Archival Sector is often searched when the goal is to find *any* relevant data and move it to the Integrated Sector or an exploration facility. But there are occasions when it makes sense to search the Archival Sector by itself. In other words, the Archival Sector can be used as a basis for decision making. There are, however, some major drawbacks to this approach, including but not limited to the following:

- There is really a lot of data in the Archival Sector.
- The data in the Archival Sector needs to be searched sequentially.
- There are no indexes that are useful for the searches that need to be done.

Further, the data query and analysis technology that is available for the Archival Sector is limited, compared to what is available in other arenas.

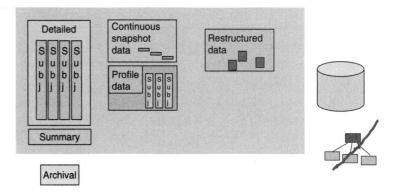

■ **FIGURE 3.40** Normally referential integrity is not enforced at the Archival Sector.

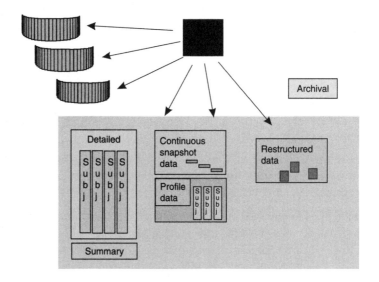

■ **FIGURE 3.41** It is always possible to search sequentially and process the archival environment by itself.

However, on occasion the Archival Sector can be accessed and analyzed in a stand-alone fashion. Figure 3.41 shows this capability.

UNSTRUCTURED PROCESSING

There are two major sides or domains to the DW 2.0 environment. Half of the DW 2.0 data architecture is designated for the structured data, which has been the main subject of this chapter so far. The other half of the DW 2.0 environment is the realm of unstructured data.

While the same four DW 2.0 sectors apply to the unstructured data side of the DW 2.0 environment, each sector has very different characteristics in the unstructured domain compared to those found in the structured side of DW 2.0. It is even questionable whether all four sectors are useful in the unstructured DW 2.0 data domain.

The input to the unstructured Integrated Sector of DW 2.0 comes from documents and other forms of text. Unstructured data input can come from practically anywhere. It can come from medical records, safety reports, contracts, spreadsheets, inspection reports, and more. The text can be in any language. The text may or may not be related.

To load unstructured data into the DW 2.0 data warehouse, the text is first gathered in an electronic format. Then the text is run through an ETL process designed for unstructured data. The unstructured text is converted into text that is suitable for analytical processing. A few of the activities that the text must undergo for it to be fit for textual analytics include

- stop word removal;
- stemming;
- specific/general analysis;
- alternate spelling analysis;
- taxonomy grouping of data.

After the text has passed through this rigorous process, the text is ready for analytical processing.

There are several kinds of data in the unstructured integrated environment. Some of the kinds of data that appear here are:

- Internal and external taxonomies: A taxonomy is a list of words in which there is some relationship between the words. The unstructured textual environment includes both taxonomies that have been created internally (sometimes called "themes") and external taxonomies that can come from practically anywhere.

- Captured, edited text: Captured, edited text is text that has passed through the unstructured ETL process and has been placed in a data base—a standard relational data base.

- Linkage: Linkages are the data that ties the unstructured data to the structured data.

- Simple pointers: Occasionally the unstructured data text will remain in another environment and only index references to it will be brought into the unstructured interactive data warehouse.

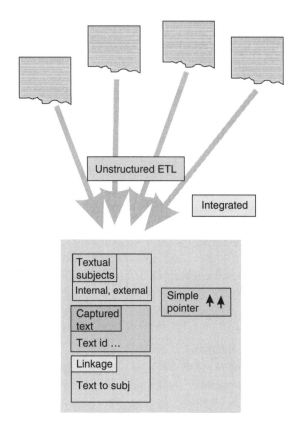

■ **FIGURE 3.42** Where input to the unstructured integrated layer comes from.

Figure 3.42 shows text passing through textual ETL and into the unstructured integrated environment.

The unstructured integrated environment has a workload just like every other DW 2.0 sector. Figure 3.43 characterizes the workload of the unstructured Integrated Sector.

Figure 3.44 highlights how the unstructured integrated workload is full of large activities, which is not surprising given the nature of the textual environment. However, because the size of textual data bases can vary so widely, there will also be some activities that are small in size in this environment.

Because the workload in the unstructured integrated environment is mixed, the response time expectations are also mixed. Figure 3.45 shows the response time expectations in the unstructured integrated environment.

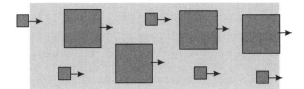

■ **FIGURE 3.43** What the workload going on inside the unstructured Integrated Sector looks like.

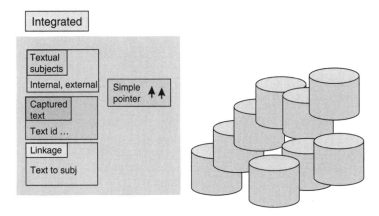

■ **FIGURE 3.44** There can be a very large amount of data being managed by the unstructured integrated environment.

There are basically two kinds of activities in the unstructured integrated environment—loading of data and accessing of data. It is almost impossible for unstructured textual data to be updated. After a textual description or work is written, if changes need to be made it is rewritten. Accordingly, incrementally or partially updating textual data is simply not a reflection of reality.

The two basic activities of the unstructured integrated environment are illustrated in Figure 3.46.

The unstructured environment is quite unlike the structured environment in DW 2.0. Usually there is only an unstructured Integrated Sector. It is questionable whether there is a need for an unstructured Near Line Sector.

There is, however, occasion to use the archival environment for unstructured data. Data is placed in the unstructured Archival Sector when the probability of access of the data diminishes. Figure 3.47

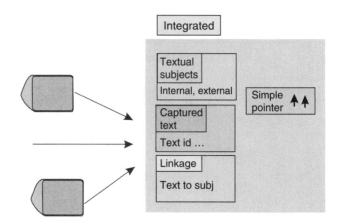

■ **FIGURE 3.45** Access to the unstructured integrated environment is measured in seconds to hours depending on the workload that is processing at the time the transaction is submitted.

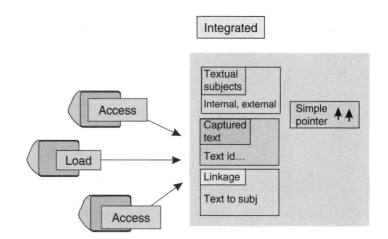

■ **FIGURE 3.46** Transactions can access data or load data in the unstructured Integrated Sector.

shows the movement of unstructured textual data into the unstructured archival environment.

FROM THE BUSINESS PERSPECTIVE

The breakup of data into different components is normal and natural to the business person. It is not good policy to present the architecture to the end user as if there were just one single store of data. The end user knows that data is placed in different places based on the age of the data.

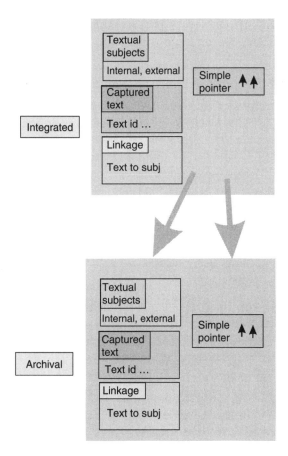

■ FIGURE 3.47 Occasionally unstructured integrated data needs to be placed in the unstructured archival environment.

In addition the end user knows that textual, unstructured data can be found in DW 2.0 and can be intermingled with queries. And the end user knows that there is a facility—metadata—that exists that allows the end user to find his/her way around the environment.

Finally, the end user knows that different kinds of processes are generally found in different places. If the end user wants to do online update and analysis, there is the Interactive Sector. If the end user wants to do integrated analytical analysis there is the Integrated Sector. If the end user wants to look at really old data there is the Archival Sector.

The only sector that is transparent to the end user is the Near Line or data warehouse utility sector. Even then, there may be occasions on which the end user may wish to access and analyze data found in the Near Line Sector.

SUMMARY

The place where data enters the DW 2.0 environment under normal circumstances is the Interactive Sector. Data can enter through ETL or directly. The Interactive Sector is application oriented, the sector in which update to data can be done, and the environment that supports 2- to 3-second response time. The workload passing through the Interactive Sector is small and fast. No large transactions are allowed to pass through the Interactive Sector.

The pattern of data access in the Interactive Sector is random, fast, and small, in terms of the amount of data accessed. There is limited historical data in the Interactive Sector.

Integrated Sector data is integrated before the data is allowed to enter the environment. The integration is normally done by an ETL tool. The integration represents a change in the state of the data. While data from the Interactive Sector is application-oriented data, that in the Integrated Sector is corporate data.

The workload of data passing into and out of the integrated environment is mixed, including both small and large transactions. The response time in the Integrated Sector is also mixed, varying from seconds to hours. There is usually a large volume of data in the Integrated Sector. The Integrated Sector usually contains 3 to 5 years' worth of data.

No data updating occurs in the Integrated Sector. Snapshots of data are taken and are inserted into the data base when a change of data is needed. A historical track record of the data is created.

The pattern of access is infrequent, and large volumes of data are accessed, often en masse.

When data leaves the Integrated Sector, the data goes either to the Near Line Sector or to the Archival Sector.

The Near Line Sector acts like a cache for the Integrated Sector. The Near Line Sector operates on non-disk-storage-based technology. The Near Line Sector contains data that is a mirror image of the data found in the Integrated Sector.

The Near Line Sector is linked to the Integrated Sector either manually or by means of a CMSM—a cross-media storage manager. The workload on the Near Line Sector is infrequent loading of data. But when data is loaded, it is loaded en masse. Data is placed in the Near Line Sector when the probability of access drops.

The Archival Sector is where data goes when the probability of access diminishes significantly. The Archival Sector contains packages of data that are self-contained. These self-contained packages are like time capsules, to be opened up at a later and unspecified moment in time. The creation of passive indexes is a good idea for archival data.

There normally is a lot of data in the archival environment. It is conceivable that there could be hundreds of years of data in the archival environment. To be useful, archival data must be free from software release and product considerations, because it is unlikely that the same releases and products will be available when the data needs to be used.

Unstructured data must first be integrated before it can be useful for textual analytics. Unstructured data passes through an ETL layer before entering the unstructured DW 2.0 environment.

There are usually large volumes of data found in the unstructured environment. There may not be an Archival Sector for unstructured data. There probably is no Near Line Sector for unstructured data.

4

Metadata in DW 2.0

One of the essential ingredients of the DW 2.0 architecture is metadata. Unlike first-generation data warehouses where metadata either was not present or was an afterthought, metadata is one of the cornerstones of the DW 2.0 data warehouse.

There are many reasons metadata is so important. Metadata is important to the developer, who must align his/her efforts with work that has been done previously. It is important to the maintenance technician, who must deal with day-to-day issues of keeping the data warehouse in order. It is perhaps most important to the end user, who needs to find out what the possibilities are for new analysis.

The best way to understand the value of metadata in DW 2.0 is to see it as acting like a card catalog in a large public library. How is information found in the public library? Do people walk in and look for a book by passing from one row of books to the next? Of course people can do that. But it is a colossal waste of time. A much more rational way to locate what you are looking for in a library is to go directly to the card catalog. Compared to manually searching through every book in the library, searching a card catalog is immensely faster.

Once the book that is desired is located in the catalog, the reader can walk directly to where the book is stored. In doing so, vast amounts of time are saved in the location of information.

Metadata in DW 2.0 plays essentially the same role as the card catalog in the library. Metadata allows the analyst to look across the organization and to see what analysis has already been done.

REUSABILITY OF DATA AND ANALYSIS

Consider the end user. End users sit on the sidelines and feel the need for information. This need for information may come from a management directive, from a corporate mandate, or simply from the end user's own curiosity. However it comes, the end user ponders how to approach the analysis. Metadata is the logical place to which to turn. Metadata enables the analyst to determine what data is available. Once the analyst has identified the most likely place to start, the analyst can then proceed to access the data.

Without metadata, the analyst has a really hard time identifying the possible sources of data. The analyst may be familiar with some sources of data, but it is questionable whether he/she is aware of all of the possibilities. In this case, the existence of metadata may save huge amounts of unnecessary work.

Similarly, the end user can use metadata to determine if an analysis has already been done. Answering a question may be as simple as looking at what someone else has done. Without metadata, the end-user analyst will never know what has already been done.

For these reasons, then (and plenty more!), metadata is a very important component of the DW 2.0 architecture.

METADATA IN DW 2.0

Metadata has a special role and implementation in DW 2.0. Separate metadata is required for each sector of DW 2.0. There is metadata for the Interactive Sector, metadata for the Integrated Sector, metadata for the Near Line Sector, and metadata for the Archival Sector.

The metadata for the Archival Sector is different from the other metadata, because Archival Sector metadata is placed directly in the archival data. The reason for this is to ensure that over time the metadata is not separated or lost from the base data that it describes.

Figure 4.1 depicts the general location of metadata in the DW 2.0 architecture.

There is a general architecture for metadata in DW 2.0. There are actually two parallel metadata structures—one for the unstructured environment and one for the structured environment. Figure 4.2 shows the high level of structure of DW 2.0 metadata.

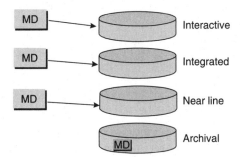

■ **FIGURE 4.1** Metadata and the DW 2.0 environment.

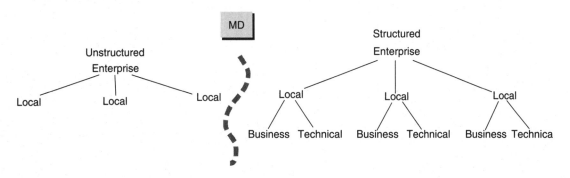

■ **FIGURE 4.2** The general structure of metadata.

For unstructured data, there are really two types of metadata—enterprise and local. The enterprise metadata is also referred to as general metadata, and the local metadata is referred to as specific metadata.

For structured metadata, there are three levels—enterprise, local, and business or technical. There is an important relationship between these different kinds of metadata. The best place to start to explain these relationships is the local level.

Local metadata is a good place to start, because most people have the most familiarity with that type of metadata. Local metadata exists in many places and in many forms. It exists inside ETL processes. It exists inside a DBMS directory. It exists inside a business intelligence universe.

Local metadata is metadata that exists inside a tool that is useful for describing the metadata immediate to the tool. For example, ETL metadata is about data sources and targets and the transformations that take place as data is passed from source to target. DBMS directory metadata is typically about tables, attributes, and indexes. Business intelligence (BI) universe metadata is about data used in analytical processing. There are many more forms of local metadata other than these common sources.

Figure 4.3 depicts examples of local metadata.

Local metadata is stored in a tool or technology that is central to the usage of the local metadata. Enterprise metadata, on the other hand, is stored in a locale that is central to all of the tools and all of the processes that exist within the DW 2.0 environment.

Figure 4.4 shows that enterprise metadata is stored for each sector of the DW 2.0 environment in a repository.

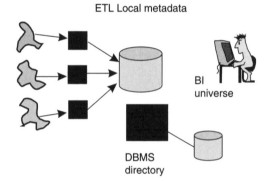

■ **FIGURE 4.3** Local metadata already exists in a lot of places.

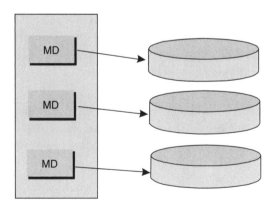

■ **FIGURE 4.4** A repository is a place where metadata is stored.

In this figure it is seen that sitting above each sector of DW 2.0 is a collection of enterprise metadata, and that all of the enterprise metadata taken together forms a repository. Actually, all of the sectors except the Archival Sector have their metadata stored in a repository.

ACTIVE REPOSITORY/PASSIVE REPOSITORY

There are two basic types of metadata repositories—active and passive. An active repository is one in which the metadata interacts in an ongoing manner with the development and query activities of the system. A passive repository is one in which the metadata does not interact in any direct manner with the development and/or the query activities of the end user.

Figure 4.5 depicts a passive metadata repository.

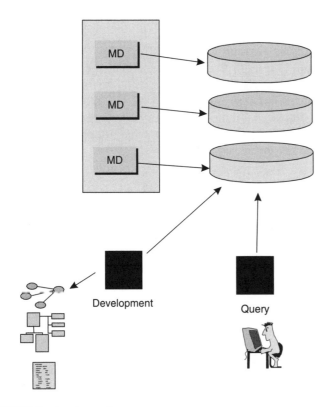

■ **FIGURE 4.5**   A passive repository.

The passive repository is the least desirable option, because end-user and developer activity is independent of the metadata repository. Any work that becomes optional quickly becomes work that is not done at all, because most organizations are compelled to minimize the amount of work, reduce costs, and meet deadlines. The passive metadata repository quickly assumes the same position as documentation. In the time-honored fashion of developers, documentation simply does not get done.

If by some miracle the passive metadata repository does get built, it is soon out of date as changes to the system are not reflected in the passive repository.

THE ACTIVE REPOSITORY

The other style of metadata repository is the active repository. The active repository is the place where enterprise metadata is kept when the metadata is actively used during the development process and for data-querying activities. Figure 4.6 shows an active metadata repository.

This figure illustrates that the development process and the query process are intimately intertwined with the metadata repository. When a change needs to be made to the data model, when the most current description of the data is needed, or when the source of data is needed, these activities and more rely on the active repository as their foundation.

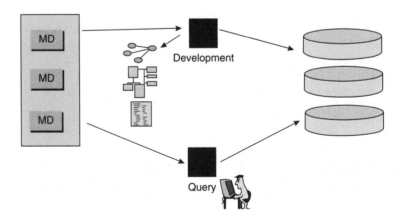

■ **FIGURE 4.6** An active repository.

ENTERPRISE METADATA

The enterprise active metadata repository is used when a query needs to be made against a table, when the relationship between the local and the global needs to be examined, or when the analyst just wishes to see what the data possibilities are.

Enterprise metadata has many different relationships with local metadata. One such relationship is semantics. In a semantics relationship, the enterprise describes a global term for the corporation. Then the local usage of that term is described, along with a pointer to the local system where the term is found. For example, suppose there is an enterprise term "revenue" and three local systems that refer to that term. In one local system the term is the same—"revenue." In another local system, the term is "money," and in another the term is "funds." These three different words mean the same thing in the example enterprise. Enterprise metadata is an excellent way to ensure that the terms are consistently recognized and interpreted as the synonyms they are in the enterprise's dialect.

Metadata provides a way to unite vocabularies at the enterprise level and the local level. This capability is illustrated in Figure 4.7.

But semantic relationships are hardly the only type of enterprise/local relationship that can be found in the metadata of the DW 2.0 environment.

Another key type of data relationship commonly found in organizations is that of enterprise subject area definitions. Figure 4.8 shows one such definition.

This figure shows a major subject area, Customer, defined at the enterprise level. The different places at the local level where information about Customer is found are shown. One local system has name and address information about a Customer. Another local system has age

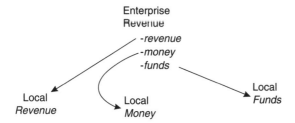

■ **FIGURE 4.7**   An example of the relationship between enterprise metadata and local metadata.

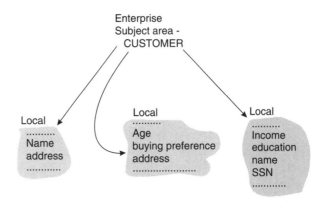

■ **FIGURE 4.8**   An example of the specification of a major subject area at the enterprise level.

and buying preference information about a Customer. Yet another local system maintains Customer income, education, and Social Security number.

The enterprise metadata level can be used to identify where the local systems have supporting data for major business subjects.

METADATA AND THE SYSTEM OF RECORD

Metadata can also be used to define the system of record for the enterprise's data subjects and their data attributes. In the system of record, the definitive source for a unit of data is declared. Figure 4.9 shows that the system of record for each element of data may be identified. It is not unusual for there to be more than one system of record for various data attributes of a major subject of the enterprise.

It is noteworthy that in the three preceding examples, there is some overlap between the definitions of data and relations defined between the local level of metadata and the enterprise level of metadata. However, there are some dissimilarities as well. The differences between the relationships that have been described are subtle. This level of subtlety can be represented by enterprise metadata and its relationship with local metadata in the DW 2.0 environment.

But there are other metadata relationships that are also important in the DW 2.0 environment. For example, there are two distinct types of metadata in the local level of metadata—business and technical.

Business metadata is information about the data that is useful to and found in the jargon of the business person. Technical metadata

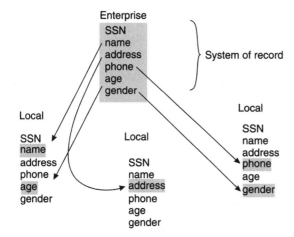

■ **FIGURE 4.9**   The system of record is identified in the enterprise level of metadata.

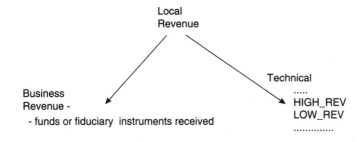

■ **FIGURE 4.10**   An example of local business metadata and local technical metadata.

is information about the data that is useful to and found in the jargon of the technician. An example of business metadata might be the definition of "revenue" as "money or instruments paid for services or products." An example of technical metadata might be the attribute definition "REV-DESIGNATED PIC 9999.99" contained in a table named "ABC."

Figure 4.10 shows that the local level of metadata has its own subdivisions for business and technical metadata.

Unstructured data in DW 2.0 has its own metadata. The metadata for the unstructured environment is very different from the metadata for the structured environment. Taxonomies are an example of metadata for the unstructured environment.

TAXONOMY

Simply stated, a taxonomy is a detailed subdivision of a larger subject. A taxonomy has a detailed breakdown of the components of a given subject. Glossaries and ontologies are related to taxonomies.

Two basic types of taxonomies are found in the unstructured DW 2.0 environment—internal and external. Internal taxonomies are constructed using only the words and phrases found in the text itself. For example, suppose the text in question is a series of contracts. The taxonomies for a group of contracts might well contain major themes, such as contract, terms, length of agreement, and payments. The internal taxonomy is a declaration of the major subject areas found within the text of unstructured data itself. Sometimes internal taxonomies are called "themes" of a text.

The other type of taxonomy found in the unstructured DW 2.0 environment is external. An external taxonomy can come from anywhere. An external taxonomy is something that is developed entirely from the "real world." Examples of some external taxonomies include

- Sarbanes Oxley;
- Basel II;
- import/export regulations;
- major league baseball;
- Dewey decimal numbering scheme;
- recipes from Emeril.

There may or may not be a relationship between an external taxonomy and a body of unstructured data. For example, suppose the external taxonomy major league baseball is compared to some unstructured contract text. Unless the contracts are for baseball players, there most likely is little or no overlap between the contracts and major league baseball. In contrast, suppose the body of text is a collection of emails authorizing corporate expenditures and the external taxonomy is Sarbanes Oxley. In this case there would indeed be major overlap between the taxonomy and the body of unstructured data.

INTERNAL TAXONOMIES/EXTERNAL TAXONOMIES

Figure 4.11 shows that there are two different kinds of taxonomies.

There are many different forms of unstructured metadata. Figure 4.12 illustrates just a sampling of the different kinds of unstructured metadata.

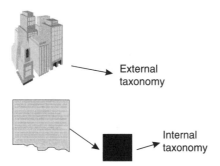

External
taxonomy

Internal
taxonomy

■ **FIGURE 4.11**   Where different taxonomies come from.

Unstructured
metadata

Taxonomies
internal
external
stop words
terminology
synonyms
homographs
alternate spellings
other

■ **FIGURE 4.12**   Some forms of
unstructured metadata.

Some other types of metadata that are common to the unstructured environment include:

- Stop words—words that are used in speech but which are not central to the meaning of the text. Typical stop words include a, and, the, was, that, which, where, to.

- Synonyms—words that mean the same thing but have different spellings, the *fur* and the *coat* of a cat, for example.

- Homographs—words that are spelled the same but have different meanings, for example the *bow* of a ship versus a *bow* and arrow.

- Alternate spellings—two or more acceptable ways of spelling the same word, for example, *color* and *colour*.

METADATA IN THE ARCHIVAL SECTOR

There is one anomaly in the DW 2.0 environment when it comes to metadata, and that is the metadata that is associated with the Archival Sector. The metadata that is associated with archival processing is stored with the archival data itself. The reason for storing the archival metadata with the archival data is that it is assumed that the metadata will be lost over time if it is collocated with its associated archival content data. Of course, it is possible to store a separate set of metadata with the archival environment, but the first place where historical metadata is most often sought and likely to be most useful is with the archival data itself.

Archival

■ **FIGURE 4.13** Metadata in the Archival Sector.

Figure 4.13 suggests that archival data should contain its own metadata.

MAINTAINING METADATA

One of the biggest challenges associated with metadata is not the initial creation of the metadata environment, but rather the ongoing maintenance of the metadata environment. Change is a constant and it affects metadata just as much as it does everything else.

Figure 4.14 shows that change occurs and that when the environment is an active metadata environment it is easier to keep up with change than in a passive environment.

It is much too easy to just ignore change with a passive metadata environment. Change occurs and the associated alterations to passive metadata tend to be put off. Then one day, someone wakes up and sees that normal, routine changes have not been reflected in the metadata environment for a long time, resulting in a passive metadata that is so far out of sync with the present that it is virtually useless, often coincidentally when it is most needed.

With an active metadata repository, changes need to be reflected regularly in the metadata to keep up with the normal evolution and maintenance of existing systems. Whenever the systems are changed, the metadata must be changed as well.

Using metadata is just as important as the storing and periodic update of metadata. Although there are many ways to use metadata, perhaps the most effective way is at the point of end-user interface—the point at which the end user is doing interactive processing.

USING METADATA—AN EXAMPLE

For an example of the usage of DW 2.0 metadata, consider the following scenario. An airline agent—P. Bruton—pulls up a screen with the flight details for a client—Bill Inmon.

Figure 4.15 shows the screen that she has pulled up.

P. Bruton is not familiar with the reservations made by Tiki Airlines. She sees a data field on the screen that interests her. She highlights the CONNECTIONS field on the Tiki Airlines screen, as shown in Figure 4.16.

MD
MD
MD
Change
Development
Query

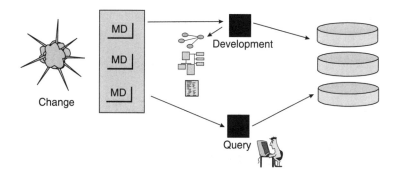

■ FIGURE 4.14 Where there is an active repository it is relatively easy to keep up with change.

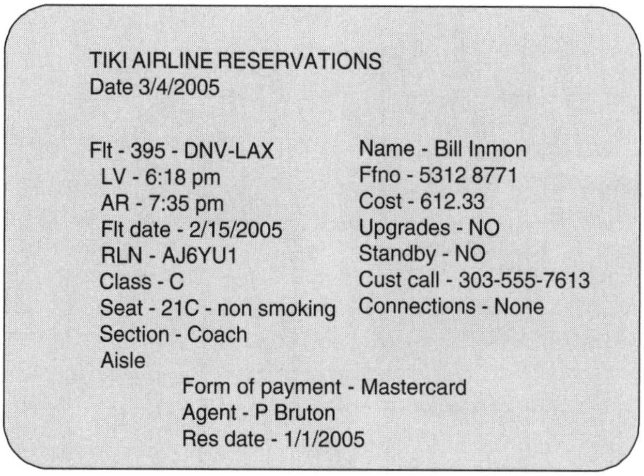

TIKI AIRLINE RESERVATIONS
Date 3/4/2005
Flt - 395 - DNV-LAX
LV - 6:18 pm
AR - 7:35 pm
Flt date - 2/15/2005
RLN - AJ6YU1
Class - C
Seat - 21C - non smoking
Section - Coach
Aisle
Name - Bill Inmon
Ffno - 5312 8771
Cost - 612.33
Upgrades - NO
Standby - NO
Cust call - 303-555-7613
Connections - None
Form of payment - Mastercard
Agent - P Bruton
Res date - 1/1/2005

■ FIGURE 4.15 An end user initiates a screen or report.

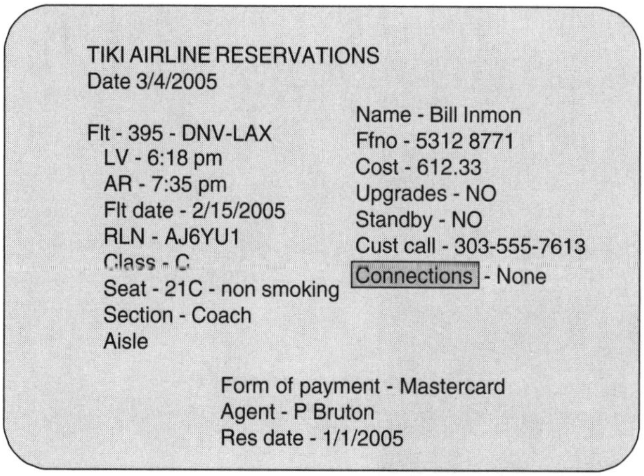

TIKI AIRLINE RESERVATIONS
Date 3/4/2005
Flt - 395 - DNV-LAX
LV - 6:18 pm
AR - 7:35 pm
Flt date - 2/15/2005
RLN - AJ6YU1
Class - C
Seat - 21C - non smoking
Section - Coach
Aisle
Name - Bill Inmon
Ffno - 5312 8771
Cost - 612.33
Upgrades - NO
Standby - NO
Cust call - 303-555-7613
Connections - None
Form of payment - Mastercard
Agent - P Bruton
Res date - 1/1/2005

■ FIGURE 4.16 The user selects a unit of data that is of interest.

Next, P. Bruton hits a Function key, and the popup menu shown in Figure 4.17 appears. The menu asks her to identify what aspect of CONNECTIONS she wants to see. The options on the menu are "AKA" (also known as), "definition," "formula," "where used," and "owned by." P. Bruton selects the definitions option.

Figure 4.17 shows the menu of types of metadata that are available.

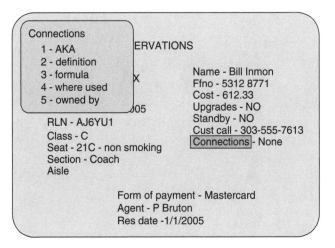

■ **FIGURE 4.17**   The system describes the possibilities of metadata that can be displayed.

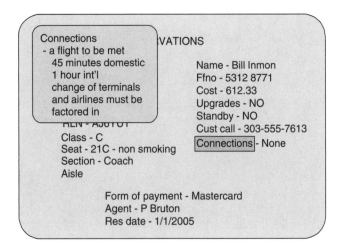

■ **FIGURE 4.18**   The desired metadata is displayed.

Now the system goes and searches its metadata information for a definition of CONNECTIONS. Upon finding the definition, the system displays a message showing the definition of CONNECTIONS.

Figure 4.18 shows the display of a metadata definition in an interactive mode.

Note that the accessing of metadata never entailed leaving the original screen. The display of metadata was done on top of an analytical process. The metadata was displayed interactively and became part of the analytical process.

FROM THE END-USER PERSPECTIVE

There are many purposes served by metadata in DW 2.0. Metadata serves to interconnect the different sectors of data. It serves as documentation for the environment. It serves as a road map for adding to the DW 2.0 environment. But the most important role metadata plays is as a guide to the contents and relationships of data found in DW 2.0.

It is the end user who needs a guide to the data and relationships that are found in DW 2.0. When the end user has a guide to what data already exists in the DW 2.0 environment, there is the possibility of the reuse of data. Stated differently, when there is no metadata in DW 2.0, the end user always has to invent every new analysis from scratch. The end user is incapable of seeing what analytical work has been done before. Therefore everything must be new.

The problem with every analysis being new is that in many cases the wheel gets to be reinvented over and over. But with metadata there is no need to reinvent the wheel. One analyst can build on the work of another analyst.

From the standpoint of the business user, there is another important role for metadata and that role is in showing the heritage of data. In many cases in which an analyst considers using a unit of data as part of an analysis, the business user needs to know where the data came from and how it was calculated. It is metadata that provides this very important function in DW 2.0.

There is yet another important role played by metadata in the eyes of the business user. On occasion there is a need for compliance of data. There is Sarbanes Oxley and there is Basel II. Metadata provides the key to the audit trail that is so vital to compliance in the analytical environment.

There are then some very pragmatic reasons metadata plays such an important role in the eyes of the business user in DW 2.0.

SUMMARY

Metadata is the key to reusability of data and analysis. Metadata enables the analyst to determine what has already been built. Without metadata, the analyst has a hard time finding out what infrastructure is already in place.

There are four levels of metadata:

- Enterprise
- Local
- Business
- Technical

There is metadata for both the structured and the unstructured DW 2.0 environments. A metadata repository can be either active or passive. As a rule, an active metadata repository is much more desirable and useful than a passive metadata repository. When development and analysis are used interactively with a metadata repository, the repository is considered to be active.

The system of record of data warehouse data is ideally defined in a metadata repository.

Unstructured metadata consists of taxonomies, glossaries, and ontologies. The forms of metadata may be internal or external.

Archival metadata is stored directly in the archival environment. By colocating the metadata with the physical storage of archival data it describes, a time capsule of data can be created.

5

Fluidity of the DW 2.0 technology infrastructure

There are many important aspects to the DW 2.0 architecture for the next-generation data warehouse—the recognition of the life cycle of data, the inclusion of unstructured data, and the inclusion of metadata as essential components. But one of the most challenging aspects of the DW 2.0 architecture is the placement of DW 2.0 into an environment in which the technology can be changed as fast as the business changes.

From the end user's perspective fluidity is very important because the business climate is always changing. At one moment a corporation needs to focus on profits. This means raising prices and expanding sales. The next year the corporation needs to focus on expenses. This means lowering expenses and stopping expansion. The next year the company needs to focus on new products and new channels of revenue. As each change in the business climate occurs, there is a need for new types of information. Furthermore, as the competitive, technological, and economic climate changes, there are constant new demands for information.

If a data warehouse is built on top of technology that is difficult to change, then the corporation will not be able to adapt its technology to the business climate. And that means that as important as the data warehouse can be to a corporation, it will always be less than optimal in terms of its value.

In first-generation data warehouses, the technology that housed the data resided on traditional information-processing technologies. As such, the data warehouse was cast in stone. Making significant changes to the data warehouse became very difficult to do. DW 2.0 recognizes and responds to the problems associated with casting the data warehouse in stone.

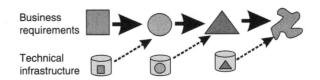

■ **FIGURE 5.1** Business requirements are constantly changing, whereas the technology infrastructure is rooted in concrete.

The story begins with Figure 5.1.

Figure 5.1 characterizes the ever-changing nature of business requirements. Constantly changing business requirements are simply inevitable—as inevitable as death and taxes. The only difference from one organization to the next is the rate and the extent of change.

THE TECHNOLOGY INFRASTRUCTURE

Sitting beneath the business is an infrastructure of technology. The problem arises as business requirements change. Because of the effort required to make changes to the technological infrastructure, the business is always ahead of the technical foundation that is supposed to support it.

There are lots of good reasons for the intransigency of the technical infrastructure. At the heart of the matter is the popular notion among systems vendors that when a definition of technology is given to their technology, that definition is permanent. This fundamental notion is revealed in many situations:

- by DBMS vendors, when the structure of the data is defined at the start of a project;
- by compilers, who have the notion that once processing and algorithms have been specified, that is the way they are going to remain indefinitely;
- by business intelligence vendors who think that once a query is written the same query will work way into the future;
- by management that thinks that when they make a lease or a long-term commitment the problem is solved and will not mutate into something else.

There are many more examples of the erroneous assumption that once requirements are defined, no more requirements will ever arise.

Figure 5.2 illustrates this assumption.

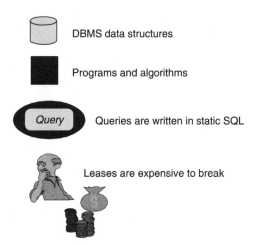

■ **FIGURE 5.2** Some of the many reasons the technology infrastructure is so difficult to change.

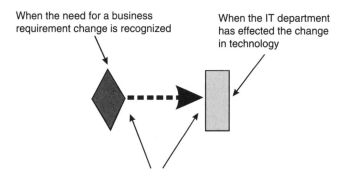

■ **FIGURE 5.3** The length of time that is required to make changes to the IT infrastructure.

But requirements are constantly changing and mutating. Consider the simple diagram in Figure 5.3.

The red diamond in Figure 5.3 indicates a change in business requirements. The blue box indicates that IT has adjusted the technology infrastructure in response to the change in business requirements. The black dotted line represents the length of time from the moment when a business requirement has changed until the time when IT has completed the necessary changes. The black dotted line is often very, very long. The situation depicted in Figure 5.3 is ubiquitous.

RAPID BUSINESS CHANGES

Next consider what happens when business changes come in faster than IT can respond. Figure 5.4 shows this circumstance.

Figure 5.4 depicts how business requirements change faster than the rate at which IT can respond to change. When the first change is identified, IT starts to design, plan, and build. But before they can finish, another set of business requirements starts to emerge. This set of new requirements has its own life cycle. A different group of people start to work on the new requirements. Things become complicated when both groups of people need to work on and change the same data and processes. To make matters worse, another new set of business requirements comes in before the first or second IT infrastructure changes are done. And things get to be really complicated when the first, the second, and the third groups of people all need to be working on the same data and the same process at the same time.

A great mess ensues.

THE TREADMILL OF CHANGE

What often happens is that the organization finds itself trapped in a vicious cycle. An eternal treadmill is created by the fact that new and changed business requirements are generated by the business faster than IT can respond. Figure 5.5 depicts this treadmill.

The long-term effect of the treadmill in Figure 5.5 is that the IT department is perceived as not being responsive to the business of

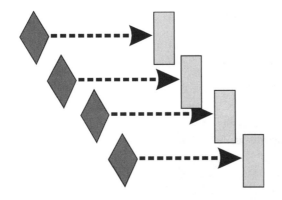

■ **FIGURE 5.4**   What happens when the rate of needed change is faster than the ability to make those changes.

■ **FIGURE 5.5**   IT is on a treadmill that it can never get off of.

the organization. Business and IT are perceived as heading in different directions.

Figure 5.6 shows this perceived divergence.

GETTING OFF THE TREADMILL

So what can be done about this dilemma? There are several possible solutions:

- Freeze business requirements: Unfortunately freezing business requirements is the equivalent to sticking one's head in the sand at the first hint of problems. It simply is not an acknowledgment of reality.

- Add IT resources: Throwing more IT people into the fray is expensive and often simply is not effective. (See *The Mythical Man Month* by Fred Brooks).

- Shorten IT response time: Reducing the length of time it takes IT respond to new and changing business requirements is often the only alternative.

■ **FIGURE 5.6** IT and business are seen as going in divergent directions.

In fact, only the third option is viable over the long haul.

REDUCING THE LENGTH OF TIME FOR IT TO RESPOND

Figure 5.7 suggests that reducing the length of time required for IT to respond to change is the only real alternative.

It is one thing to say that IT's response time for the accommodation of change must be shortened. Determining exactly how that should be done is another thing altogether.

■ **FIGURE 5.7** The only realistic plan is to shorten the length of time required for IT to respond to business changes.

SEMANTICALLY TEMPORAL, SEMANTICALLY STATIC DATA

One of the best and most effective ways to reduce the amount of time it takes IT to adapt the technology infrastructure to ongoing business changes lies in a most unlikely place—data that is semantically temporal and data that is semantically static. Figure 5.8 represents these two types of data.

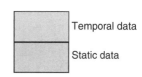

■ **FIGURE 5.8** In classical data base design, temporal data is freely mixed with static data.

The yellow box indicates data that is semantically temporal. The green box indicates data that is semantically static.

What is meant by semantically static and semantically temporal? Data can change in one of two ways. The content of data may change. For example, my bank account balance may go from $5000 to $7500. This is an example of the meaningful content of data changing. But there is another fundamental kind of change—semantic data change. Semantic change occurs when the definitions of data change, not when the content of data changes. As a simple example of semantic change, suppose the definition of an account holder's data is created. The definition includes such things as:

- Account ID
- Account holder name
- Account holder address
- Account holder birth date

This data is defined in the system when the example banking application is initially designed, built, and deployed.

Then modern times arrive and it is recognized that there are other types of data that should have been included with the account holder data. Perhaps the following types of data now need to be added to the definition of account holder:

- Cell phone number
- Fax number
- Email address

The addition of the new data elements is a semantic change.

Data can change either in content or in semantics. The remainder of the chapter addresses semantic change, not content change.

SEMANTICALLY TEMPORAL DATA

Semantically temporal data is data that is likely to undergo semantic change. Some forms of semantic data are particularly notorious for frequently changing. Some of these semantically unstable types of data are shown in Figure 5.9.

Organization charts change with stunning frequency. Every new manager thinks that it is his/her job to reorganize the company. Sales

Temporal data -
- org chart
- sales territories
- legislatively mandated
- management
- marketplace

■ **FIGURE 5.9** Temporal data.

territories are constantly reshuffled. Sales managers are constantly debating where Ohio fits—in the Eastern region or the mid-Western region. One manager wants Ohio in one place, and another manager wants Ohio in another place.

There are many other forms of data whose semantics are constantly in an uproar. Data is semantically temporal wherever there is a likelihood that the semantics of data will change.

SEMANTICALLY STABLE DATA

The reverse of semantically unstable data is semantically stable data. Semantically stable data is static data—data whose semantics are likely to remain stable for a long time. Basic sales data is a good example of semantically stable data.

Figure 5.10 depicts some semantically stable data.

Basic sales data typically includes information such as:

- Date of sale
- Amount of sale
- Item sold
- Purchaser name

While this basic sales data is certainly applicable today, it is probably fair to assume that merchants in the markets of ancient Rome were interested in exactly the same data as were merchants in the Chinese markets of Peking 4000 years ago, as is Wal-Mart today.

The truth is that this basic data is fundamental and was of interest long before there ever were computers. And it is predictable that this basic data will be of interest in 2100, just as it is today.

All of this leads to the conclusion that semantically stable data exists. It is called static data here.

So how do systems designers and data base designers treat semantically static data and semantically temporal data? They pay no attention to it at all. The semantics of data are not a major consideration in data base design. As a direct consequence, semantically static data and semantically temporal data are typically freely mixed at the point of database design.

Sales data -
- date of sale
- amount of sale
- item sold
- to whom sold

■ **FIGURE 5.10**   Static data.

MIXING SEMANTICALLY STABLE AND UNSTABLE DATA

Figure 5.11 shows the result of freely mixing semantically static data and semantically temporal data.

The top line of symbols in Figure 5.11 represents the constant change in business requirements over time. Every time business requirements change, the technical infrastructure that supports the business has to change. Semantically static and semantically temporal data are common components of the supporting technical infrastructure that must be adapted to constantly changing business requirements. Therefore, mixing semantically static and semantically temporal data together is a recipe for trouble.

Figure 5.12 shows that when semantically static and semantically temporal data are mixed, change is difficult to accommodate.

There are lots of good reasons there is such an upheaval whenever change occurs to data that has been mixed together. The most important reason is that a data conversion must be done. Consider what happens to semantically static data when change occurs. The semantically static data must be converted and reorganized even though nothing has happened that alters the actual content of the data. This situation is exacerbated by the fact that organizations typically have a lot of semantically stable data. And there are lots of other reasons change wreaks havoc on semantically static and semantically temporal data when they are mixed together.

SEPARATING SEMANTICALLY STABLE AND UNSTABLE DATA

So the question naturally arises, what would happen if semantically static data and semantically temporal data were separated? Figure 5.13 depicts this design practice.

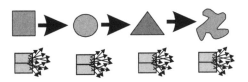

■ **FIGURE 5.11**   Every time there is a change in business requirements, the technology infrastructure goes haywire.

MITIGATING BUSINESS CHANGE

When semantically static data and semantically temporal data are separated, the devastation usually caused by changing business requirements is mitigated, as depicted in Figure 5.14.

Even though the phenomenon shown by Figure 5.14 is true, it is not at all intuitive why it is the case. There are several good reasons the separation of semantically static data and semantically temporal data has the very beneficial effect of insulating the IT technological infrastructure from constantly changing business requirements. Consider changing business requirements and semantically static data side by side.

Figure 5.15 shows that semantically static data is not affected much or at all by changes in business requirements. Semantically stable data is by definition and nature semantically stable data under any set of business requirements.

Now consider what happens to semantically temporal data when change occurs.

When semantically temporal data needs to be changed, no change is made at all. Instead a new snapshot of the semantics is created. Creating a new snapshot of semantics is much easier to do than opening up a database to convert and/or change the data it contains. Therefore, when business change occurs, just a new snapshot is made of semantically temporal data (Figure 5.16).

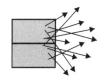

■ **FIGURE 5.12** Temporal and static data are hardwired together.

■ **FIGURE 5.13** What would happen if temporal and static data were separated?

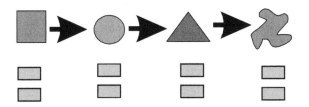

■ **FIGURE 5.14** When temporal and static data are separated, the friction and turmoil caused by change are greatly alleviated.

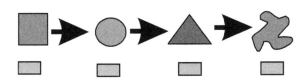

■ **FIGURE 5.15** Static data is stable throughout change.

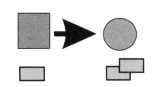

■ **FIGURE 5.16** When change occurs, a new snapshot is created.

CREATING SNAPSHOTS OF DATA

Figure 5.17 shows what happens over time to semantically temporal data as business requirements change.

Over time, a series of snapshots is made. Each snapshot is delimited by time—each snapshot has a *to* date and a *from* date. To determine which semantic definition is appropriate, the query has to be qualified by time, which is natural to do with any query.

Figure 5.17 shows that by taking snapshots of the new semantics of temporal data rather than trying to convert older data, managing change over time becomes a very easy thing to do.

A HISTORICAL RECORD

There is an interesting side benefit of managing change to semantically temporal data this way. That benefit is that a historical record of the semantically temporal data is created. This record is seen in Figure 5.18.

The value of historical records of the semantics of data is highlighted by the following example. Consider the information needed by an analyst interested in examining the changes that have been made to a company's organization chart over time. Suppose the analyst particularly wishes to look at the company's organization chart as it existed in 1990. With a historical record of the semantic data changes that have occurred over time, the analyst can easily locate and retrieve the firm's 1990 organization chart using the *from* and *to* dates included on every snapshot taken of the company's semantically temporal data.

When semantically static data and semantically temporal data are separated, and those forms of data are used as a basis for technological infrastructure, organizations can gracefully withstand change over time. The upheaval of systems that is caused by business change is mitigated, as depicted in Figure 5.19.

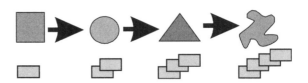

■ **FIGURE 5.17** Over time a collection of snapshots is made that reflects all the changes over time.

DIVIDING DATA

The next logical question is how to create such a division of data. The answer is that semantically static and semantically temporal data should be physically separate in all future database designs. Failing that, there are technologies that manage the DW 2.0 infrastructure as described.

Figure 5.20 represents how infrastructure management software manages the DW 2.0 data infrastructure holistically.

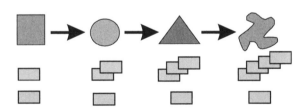

■ **FIGURE 5.18**   One of the benefits of keeping snapshots of data over time is that there is a historical record.

FROM THE END-USER PERSPECTIVE

The business user lives not in the world of technology, but in the world of business. And whatever else you can say about business, it is a fact that business changes. In some cases the changes are slower and in other cases the changes are faster. But change is a way of life to the business person.

The economy changes, legislation changes, new products come and go, competition changes, and so forth.

The business person needs to be able to have information adapt to those changes. If the information infrastructure does not adapt to the

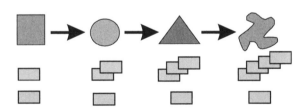

■ **FIGURE 5.19**   The effect of separating temporal data from static data in the face of changing business requirements.

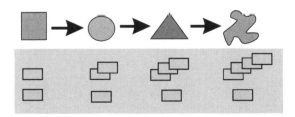

■ **FIGURE 5.20**   One way to manage static and temporal data is by technology such as Kalido.

changes then it becomes a millstone around the neck of the business user. Information becomes a liability rather than an asset. It is only when information is truly agile that it becomes a business asset.

The end user does not need to know what is going on "underneath the covers." The end user looks at the information infrastructure in the same way as most drivers look at their automobile. Most drivers know that there is an engine. Most drivers know that there is a need for gas and oil. But most drivers do not have a clue as to the inner workings of the engine. The best that can be said for most drivers is that when there is a malfunction beneath the hood of the automobile, the driver heads for a garage or repair station.

The same is true for the business analyst and DW 2.0. The business analyst is aware of the existence of DW 2.0. But the he/she does not know the detailed underpinnings of the infrastructure. All the business analyst knows is that when something goes amiss, it is time to find a data architect who does understand the underpinnings of DW 2.0.

SUMMARY

The foundation of technology that DW 2.0 is built upon needs to be able to change. When the technological infrastructure is immutable, the organization soon has business requirements that are not reflected in the data warehouse environment. Furthermore, the longer it takes to add new requirements to a data warehouse, the bigger and more intractable the problem of adapting the data warehouse to business change becomes.

There are two ways to create a technological infrastructure for the data warehouse that can change over time. One approach is to use technology that is designed for that purpose. Another approach is to separate semantically static data from semantically temporal data. By separating the semantically different types of data, the impact of change is mitigated.

Methodology and approach for DW 2.0

To be successful with DW 2.0, organizations need to adopt a spiral development approach in which numerous small iterations of data warehouse development are accomplished frequently. There should be a period of no longer than 3 months for each iteration of development. The spiral development approach to the building of a data warehouse is a standard practice that has proven its worth around the world as people build data warehouses.

So what is the spiral methodology all about? To describe the spiral methodology, it is necessary first to have a look at its exact opposite, the waterfall development methodology. The diagram in Figure 6.1 illustrates the typical waterfall development methodology life cycle.

The waterfall methodology has also been called "SDLC," which is short for "systems development life cycle." Waterfall methods have historically been very successful in delivering online transaction processing

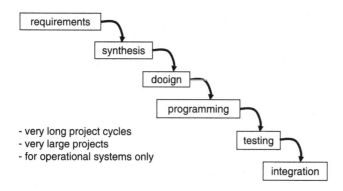

- very long project cycles
- very large projects
- for operational systems only

■ **FIGURE 6.1** Waterfall development methodology.

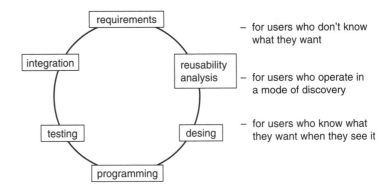

- for users who don't know
  what they want

- for users who operate in
  a mode of discovery

- for users who know what
  they want when they see it

■ **FIGURE 6.2**   Spiral development methodology.

systems. These operational systems normally have very long project cycles. They are very large projects, and all the requirements are typically documented up front. During the early days of data warehousing, DW 1.0, it was mistakenly thought that waterfall methodology could be applied to data warehouse projects.

SPIRAL METHODOLOGY—A SUMMARY OF KEY FEATURES

In contrast to the above, the spiral methodology, illustrated in Figure 6.2, is ideally suited to users who do not know what they want. Most of the time when a data warehouse project is undertaken, it is impossible to gather all the business requirements up front. This is not due to anyone's fault—it is not because the business cannot make up its mind, and it is not because the information technology group is too out of touch to be able to understand the business's needs. It is simply the nature of the beast. Business intelligence capability is normally developed in a mode of discovery. The members of the business community will ultimately know what they want when they see it—and as soon as they get what they want, they understand that they want and need something else.

The BI requirements goal posts are constantly changing, and it is understandable that this should be the case, because the business is constantly changing. In the development of an operational system, if the business asks for changes to be made to the system after it is deployed, it is seen as a mark of failure. In contrast, change is seen as a very good thing with data warehouse/business intelligence systems. A change request is a sign of success—it means the business is using the warehouse; it means the warehouse has stimulated thought, which has now resulted in a request for more or different information. If no requests for change occur, then the data warehousing initiative is a failure. In short, change is bad in a transaction processing system and change is good in a data warehouse environment.

Many people confuse the spiral methodology with the iterative approach that has its roots in the object-oriented disciplines. Although there are some similarities, the two methodologies are actually quite different.

Some of the hallmarks of the spiral development methodology are as follows:

- Spiral methodology makes extensive use of prototyping.

- Major tasks in spiral methodology can occur in any sequence.

- It is not necessary to wait for one task to finish before starting the next task.

- A different project management philosophy and mind-set are required.

- Culture change in both the business and the IT communities is required.

- Expectations must be managed, because the first iteration of data warehouse development is incomplete and subject to further refinement.

- A quarterly delivery cadence is typical, requiring strict scope discipline.

During the first generation of data warehousing, one voice consistently called for the use of spiral methodologies. Larissa Moss has written several books and given numerous public classes on using spiral methodology for building data warehouses. Organizations that have taken heed have benefited from her guidance. Organizations that have disregarded spiral methodology continue to struggle. As the era of DW 2.0 begins, it is imperative that the lessons of past mistakes be heeded.

Figure 6.3 illustrates Larissa Moss's "Business Intelligence Road Map" methodology.

At first glance, the major segments of work listed down the left-hand side of Figure 6.3 appear to be just like any waterfall methodology.

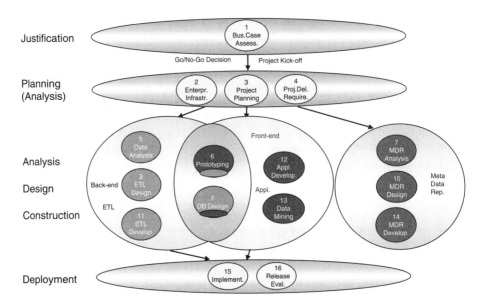

Justification

Planning (Analysis)

Analysis

Design

Construction

Deployment

■ **FIGURE 6.3** Larissa's three spiral parallel development tracks. Courtesy of Larissa T. Moss, Method Focus, Inc.

Indeed, many of the same things that people do on waterfall projects are equally applicable in spiral methodology. The diagram highlights, however, that there is a lot of concurrency happening in the analysis, design, and construction work segments. Put this together with the fact that work can begin at any point in the spiral development life cycle (e.g., it is common to start with construction and then work upward) and one can begin to see how vastly different this methodology is from conventional IT development methodologies.

Careful consideration must be given to team organization to achieve the concurrent tasks. The diagram in Figure 6.3 highlights three natural groupings of work: back-end work, front-end work, and metadata work. It shows the overlap of back-end and front-end work around prototyping and data base design. The metadata work, although shown off to the right-hand side, is in fact also highly interdependent on the other parallel work. It would probably be more accurate, but less readable, in the diagram to show the metadata work superimposed over the top of the back-end and front-end work. Project management must be able to recognize and manage these interdependencies.

It is important to note that although a data warehouse application iteration can start with construction, the iteration will not be complete unless and until justification, planning, analysis, design,

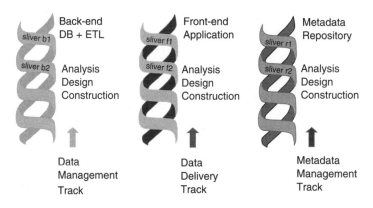

Back-end DB + ETL

Analysis
Design
Construction

sliver b1
sliver b2

Data
Management
Track

Front-end Application

Analysis
Design
Construction

sliver f1
sliver f2

Data
Delivery
Track

Metadata Repository

Analysis
Design
Construction

sliver r1
sliver r2

Metadata
Management
Track

■ **FIGURE 6.4**   Another illustration of Larissa's three parallel development tracks of spiral methodology. After Larissa T. Moss, Method Focus, Inc.

construction, and deployment have all been done. To build an application, it may take several passes through the three spiral work tracks. Although it is true that for each application all steps need to be done, there is normally no need to revisit "Justification" or even some of the other steps in each pass.

Figure 6.4 provides further insight into the three parallel spiral development tracks.

A spiral methodology produces an application by means of several interim deliverables, or "slivers." Note that each spiral sliver in Figure 6.4 addresses a very small, but meaningful, component of the overall application scope. The delivery is small and meaningful, but not completed all at once. The diagram shows two slivers per work track—in reality there may be several slivers per work track, and the back-end, front-end, and metadata repository work tracks seldom have equal numbers of slivers. Successive iterations, delivering successive slivers, ultimately deliver the working application.

The scope of each sliver must be kept extremely small. In addition, the scope must be managed very carefully so as to ensure no scope-creep occurs.

The goal of spiral methodology is to build an inventory of reusable assets. Larissa shows in Figure 6.5 how project constraints have to be reshuffled dramatically, with quality being maximized and scope being minimized.

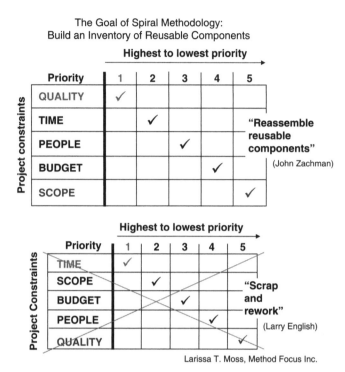

FIGURE 6.5 Project constraint reshuffling and component reuse. Courtesy of Larissa T. Moss, Method Focus, Inc.

Using the spiral methodology helps an organization move away from the death spiral of scrap and rework toward a culture based on a return on assets. This new way of thinking about things is designed to focus on reusable components that can be reassembled to meet the business's demand that things be done cheaper, faster, and better.

Second-generation data warehousing needs to move away from the conventional return on investment (ROI) approach. The return on investment approach has led many organizations to build successive "point solutions" (or data marts), with little or no attention given to the reusability of anything that has been delivered. The ROI imperative says: "get it in as quickly as possible and get some return." The fact that the initial success cannot be sustained, and the data structures prove to be brittle (not change-enabled), seems to escape the ROI mind-set.

In the world of DW 2.0, success is measured by ROA (return on assets). Has the data been reused? Has the metadata been reused? Have the structural business rules been reused? Is the ETL logic reusable and extensible? Are the components of the presentation layer reusable and flexible?

Introducing a spiral methodology is a critical step toward success in second-generation data warehousing. There are several things that an organization can and must do to make spiral development methodology a certain success. A whole new approach to enterprise data needs to be adopted. This approach is discussed in the remainder of this chapter, encapsulated in a tried and tested approach called the "seven streams approach."

THE SEVEN STREAMS APPROACH—AN OVERVIEW

The basic premise is that business intelligence initiatives should be seen as programs, not projects. Such business intelligence initiatives should be ongoing, becoming more and more honed and sophisticated as business needs change. To achieve and sustain this in a changing business environment requires more than any "data warehouse in a box" or 30- to 90-day "wonder cure" solution can provide.

What then are the various factors one needs to take into consideration to achieve sustained success in a business intelligence/data warehousing program? A highly summarized answer to this question is given in the pages that follow, starting with Figure 6.6, which illustrates the seven streams approach—a proven business intelligence planning and delivery framework.

The key thing to note about the seven streams approach is the fact that each activity stream marches to the beat of a different drum. Each stream is simultaneously in itiated, is concurrently driven, and needs to be coordinated and monitored. There is no implied sequence in the way the diagram is organized.

ENTERPRISE REFERENCE MODEL STREAM

The first activity stream addresses the creation and continued maintenance of a corporate data model (Figure 6.7). Of course, this is not done by saying, "stop the world while we build this great gargantuan corporate data model." This is a corporate data model that is built incrementally, subject area by subject area (e.g., customer, product, etc.).

ENTERPRISE KNOWLEDGE COORDINATION STREAM

The next activity stream, knowledge coordination, entails taking the various artifacts that come out of the three data discovery streams

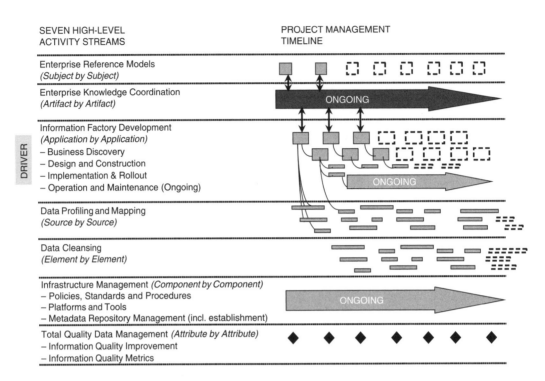

SEVEN HIGH-LEVEL
ACTIVITY STREAMS

PROJECT MANAGEMENT
TIMELINE

Enterprise Reference Models
(Subject by Subject)

Enterprise Knowledge Coordination
(Artifact by Artifact)

ONGOING

Information Factory Development
(Application by Application)
– Business Discovery
– Design and Construction
– Implementation & Rollout
– Operation and Maintenance (Ongoing)

ONGOING

Data Profiling and Mapping
(Source by Source)

Data Cleansing
(Element by Element)

Infrastructure Management *(Component by Component)*
– Policies, Standards and Procedures
– Platforms and Tools
– Metadata Repository Management (incl. establishment)

ONGOING

Total Quality Data Management *(Attribute by Attribute)*
– Information Quality Improvement
– Information Quality Metrics

DRIVER

■ **FIGURE 6.6** The seven streams approach to DW/BI projects.

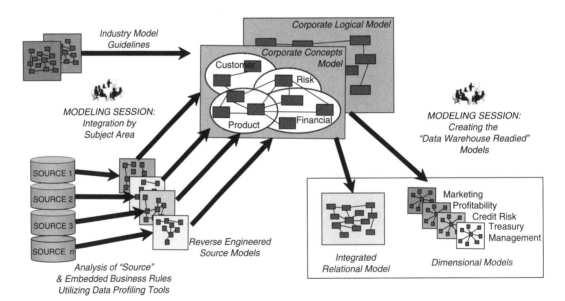

Industry Model
Guidelines

Corporate Logical Model

Corporate Concepts
Model

Customer

Risk

Product

Financial

MODELING SESSION:
Integration by
Subject Area

MODELING SESSION:
Creating the
"Data Warehouse Readied"
Models

SOURCE 1

SOURCE 2

SOURCE 3

SOURCE n

Reverse Engineered
Source Models

Analysis of "Source"
& Embedded Business Rules
Utilizing Data Profiling Tools

Integrated
Relational Model

Marketing
Profitability
Credit Risk
Treasury
Management

Dimensional Models

■ **FIGURE 6.7** The corporate data model stream.

(i.e., the corporate data modeling, information factory development, and data profiling streams) and making sense out of those findings, as follows:

- Corporate data modeling: Corporate data modeling usually entails analyzing the corporation's data top down—identifying the context, concepts, and high-level logical view of the enterprise's data. The corporation's enterprise data is discovered along the path from major business subject (the top) to corporate data entity attribution (the bottom).

- Information factory development: In the information factory development stream, build activities take place topic by topic or application by application. The business discovery process is driven by the "burning questions" that the business has put forward as its high-priority questions. These are questions for which the business community needs answers so that decisions can be made and actions can be taken that will effectively put money on the company's bottom line. Such questions can be grouped into topics, such as growth, profitability, risk, and so forth. The information required to answer these questions is identified next. Finally the data essential to manufacture the information that answers the burning questions is identified.

- Data profiling: The data profiling stream entails bottom-up data discovery. The actual detailed data in the company's existing systems is examined and analyzed. Data profiling identifies and helps resolve redundant data elements; it helps identify the correct data systems of record, as well as systems that should not be considered data warehouse sources; it enables data modelers to map data elements to data entities and fully attribute the company's major data entities. Chapter 18 has more detail on data profiling.

The above three sources of data discovery obviously all need to be tied together and resolved in some way, and that is what happens in the corporate knowledge coordination stream. Artifact by artifact, the output from the three data discovery streams is reconciled. A steady-state model is created that provides reusable knowledge about the organization's data and reliable information that can be delivered to stakeholders at the appropriate time.

It is best practice for knowledge coordinators to make use of the Zachman framework as a classification schema for the reusable artifacts

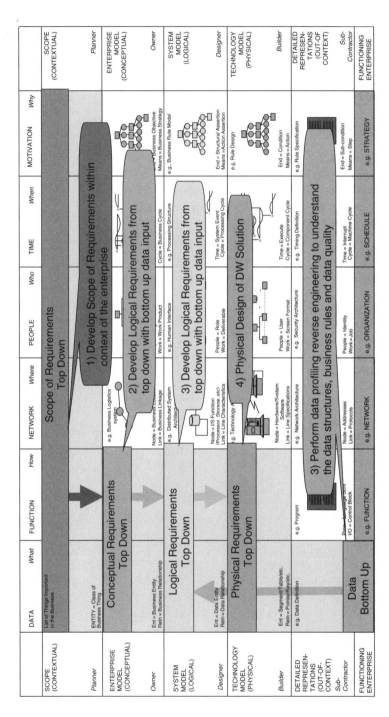

■ FIGURE 6.8 The knowledge coordination stream makes use of the Zachman framework as a classification schema. Published with permission from John A. Zachman, www.zachmaninternational.com.

under their custodianship. Figure 6.8 illustrates how top-down and bottom-up knowledge is coordinated, using the backdrop of the Zachman framework as a "thinking tool."

INFORMATION FACTORY DEVELOPMENT STREAM

The next stream is the information factory development stream. It is here that building of the information factory takes place. The factory is usually built topic by topic. Each topic contains several burning questions. Of course a topic, such as growth, often spans multiple subject areas, such as customer and product. Topics are often grouped into applications, e.g., an agent scorecard. The information factory development stream is the domain of the spiral methodology. This stream is the "driver stream" in that it sets the priorities for the other six streams.

DATA PROFILING AND MAPPING STREAM

The next activity stream is the data profiling and mapping stream. This is where the online transaction processing source systems are examined to understand what the data in those systems looks like in terms of its quality and its completeness. The output of the data profiling exercise enables the data modeler to map the source data to the various targets in the information factory. The data profiling stream is discussed further in Chapter 18.

DATA CORRECTION STREAM (previously called the Data Cleansing Stream)

The next activity stream is the data correction stream. This stream involves going attribute by attribute through the pertinent source systems and determining what data needs to be corrected, completed, or purged and what data correction rules need to be applied. This stream is also discussed further in Chapter 18.

INFRASTRUCTURE STREAM

The next activity stream is the infrastructure stream. This stream of activities addresses the supporting infrastructure for the scalability of the information factory, including consideration of people, resources, platforms, tools, policies, standards, and procedures, as indicated in Figure 6.9. The infrastructure stream is undertaken component by component.

- Custodians of BI policies, standards, and procedures
- Responsible for designing and implementing the optimal technology platform for the corporate information factory data bases and data base tools
- Design, implementation, and maintenance of the full BI infrastructure, including metadata repository, DQ tools, etc.
- Performance and usage monitoring
- Enhancements to the environment

■ **FIGURE 6.9** Infrastructure management stream components.

TOTAL INFORMATION QUALITY MANAGEMENT STREAM

Last but not least, the total information quality management stream concerns data quality monitoring and process improvement, which is achieved process by process. Specific data elements in the environment are examined and their quality is monitored and reported over time. The most comprehensive and rigorous method for addressing total information quality management has been developed by Larry English. His total information quality management methodology (TIQM), formerly called total quality data management (TQdM), consists of several major processes. The "assess information quality" process is shown in Figure 6.10.

Notice that the process is ongoing—see the recursive loop between P2.8 and P2.6 in Figure 6.10. In the world of DW 2.0, the organization should measure the quality of information on a regular basis to assure the process stays in control. It is, after all, a truism that "you cannot manage what you cannot measure."

After measuring the extent of information quality problems, including accuracy, completeness, and non-duplication, you should measure and calculate the costs of the poor quality information on the downstream processes, including costs to business intelligence processes. This provides the business case for process improvement to identify and eliminate the root causes of defects at the source and through the information value chain. This process is TIQM Process 3, "measure poor quality information costs and risks," illustrated in Figure 6.11.

At a minimum you should measure the direct costs of poor quality information following step P3.3. While the opportunity costs are considered "intangible," they can be dramatic in the form of missed customer revenue and lost customer lifetime value. These are very real costs that come with poor quality information, such as misspelling names, wrong addresses, duplicate customer records, incorrect billing, sending the wrong item on an order.

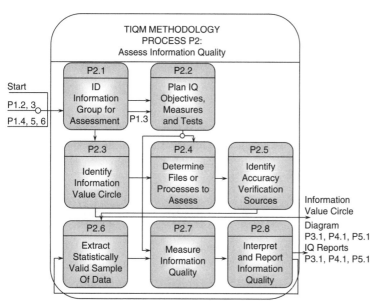

L. English, *Improving Data Warehouse and Business Information Quality*, p. 156.
Used with permission.

■ **FIGURE 6.10**   Information quality assessment in the total information quality management stream.
Courtesy of Larry P. English.

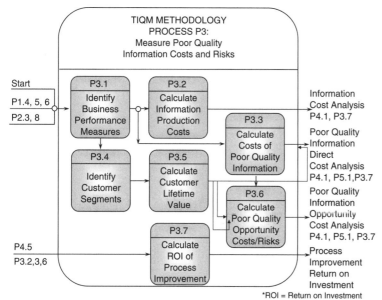

L. English, *Improving Data Warehouse and Business Information Quality*, p. 214.
Used with permission.

■ **FIGURE 6.11**   Measurement of the costs of poor quality information and the ROI of information
process improvements in TIQM. Courtesy of Larry P. English.

Understanding the costs of poor quality information enables you to focus on the high pay-off areas for process improvement, always taking a Pareto approach of most important to next-most important. The process "improvement cycle of plan-do-check/study-act" is illustrated in TIQM P4, "improve information process quality," illustrated in Figure 6.12.

Process 4 is the core competency process in TIQM, required to use the name "quality" in the "information *quality* management" label. For this is the process that eliminates the defects which cause business process failure and information scrap and rework. When this process becomes a habit within an organization, it puts that organization on the path to world-class status. Step P4.1 establishes an initiative for a process improvement based on the organization's project management guidelines. Step P4.2 first analyzes and identifies the root cause or causes of a broken process causing defective information. This step then defines process improvements that will eliminate the root causes and prevent or significantly reduce the information defects. Step P4.3 implements the improvements to study and assure

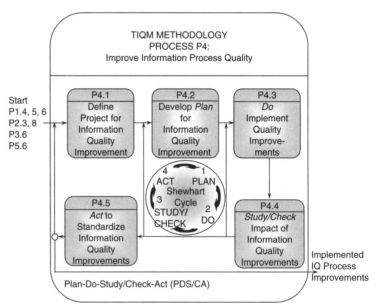

L. English, *Improving Data Warehouse and Business Information Quality*, p. 290. Used with permission.

■ **FIGURE 6.12**   The improve information process quality process in TIQM. Courtesy of Larry P. English.

they have achieved the improvement goals. Step P4.4 analyzes the results to assure the improvements worked and documents the lessons learned. Step P4.5 acts to roll out the improvements to all places where the process is performed, and puts the process in control.

For more information about these TIQM processes, see Larry English's *Improving Data Warehouse and Business Information Quality*, Chapters 6, 7, and 9, respectively. Please note that TIQM Process P4 "improving information process quality" is numbered P5. Mr. English is changing it to precede the process for data correction.

SUMMARY

Each of the seven streams in the DW/BI project approach focuses on a different aspect of the corporation's data architecture and is undertaken using a different and correspondingly appropriate work approach:

Stream 1—Enterprise reference modeling is done subject by subject.
Stream 2—Enterprise knowledge coordination is done artifact by artifact.
Stream 3—Information factory development is done topic by topic.
Stream 4—Data profiling and mapping are done source by source.
Stream 5—Data correction is done attribute by attribute.
Stream 6—Infrastructure management is done component by component.
Stream 7—Total information quality management is done process by process to improve and error-proof processes.

Each stream produces deliverables at different rates. The astute DW/BI program manager will recognize what these different rates and rhythms are, will synchronize the work priorities in each of these concurrent streams, and will use this information to define meaningful releases for the organization. DW/BI program management will produce an overall project road map such as the example shown in Figure 6.13.

The seven streams approach is a framework and tool for designing a DW/BI program that lends itself well to rapid spiral development. The interaction of the seven streams approach and spiral development methodology is graphically depicted in the next few diagrams.

Figure 6.14 illustrates the position of the spiral development methodology in the information factory development stream.

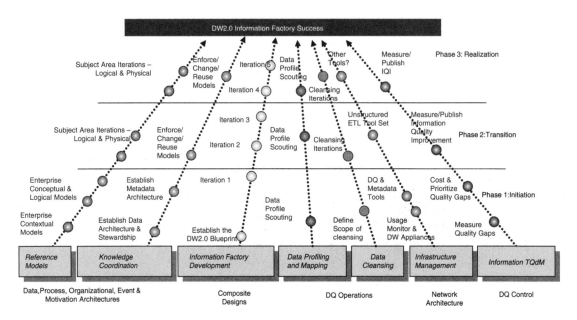

■ **FIGURE 6.13**   DW/BI project road map based on the seven streams approach.

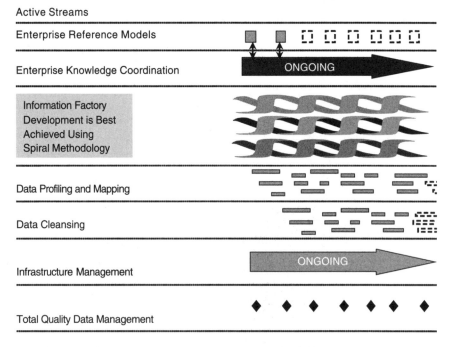

■ **FIGURE 6.14**   Spiral development methodology in the seven stream DW/BI approach. How do the spiral methodology and the seven streams approach fit together?

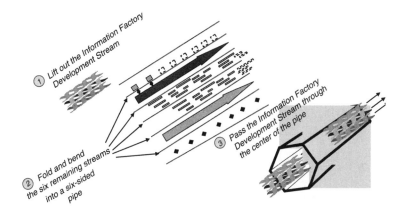

■ FIGURE 6.15   The seven streams approach—preparing the way for the spiral methodology.

Figure 6.15 illustrates the relationship between the seven streams approach and the spiral methodology.

The spiral methodology has proven most effective for data warehouse projects. The spiral methodology is further enhanced by implementing the seven streams DW/BI approach. Spiral DW/BI development iterations can be expedited if the correct level of attention is given to building the corporate data model, coordinating knowledge about the enterprise, doing proactive data profiling and mapping, doing proactive data cleansing, managing the infrastructure proactively, and establishing the correct culture for total quality data management. The combined impact of the method and the approach means that the development team will not hit as many roadblocks—data models, rules, and definitions will be there waiting for them, data quality anomalies will be known way ahead of time, and the appropriate infrastructure will be in place.

The benefit of spiral development and the seven streams approach is a regular cadence of delivery to the business based on quarterly releases. The challenge is the culture change required from both the IT and the business communities. The most successful organizations manage this culture change through a combination of training in spiral methodology and the seven streams approach, plus mentorship by people with deep skills and experience in both approaches. The combined DW/BI program method and approach must also be supported by the correct governance structure.

Statistical processing and DW 2.0

One of the most important functions of any data warehouse is the support of statistical analysis. If an organization has a data warehouse and there is no statistical analysis that is occurring, then a major function of the data warehouse environment is not being exploited. Traditionally, certain industries have made more of the capability of statistical analysis than other industries. While the insurance, manufacturing, and medical research industries have all made extensive use of statistical analysis, there is a place for statistical analysis in practically any industry.

From the end user's perspective, the kind of data that is revealed by statistical analysis is fundamentally different from information determined in other manners. For one example, statistically generated data is almost always used strategically. There are very few cases in which statistically generated data is used tactically.

Another reason why statistical analysis is different from other forms of analysis is that statistical analysis of necessity looks across broad vistas of data. Other forms of analysis look at much smaller sets of data.

And a third difference between analysis of statistical data and that of other data is that the vista of information examined by statistics is much longer than other forms of analysis. It is normal when doing statistical analysis to look across 5 years, 10 years, or even more.

DW 2.0 supports statistical analysis and processing just as it supports other forms of analysis. Depending on the type and frequency of statistical analysis, DW 2.0 can be used either directly or indirectly.

TWO TYPES OF TRANSACTIONS

The nature of the statistical analysis transaction lies at the heart of the DW 2.0 support of statistical analysis. Figure 7.1 illustrates the two

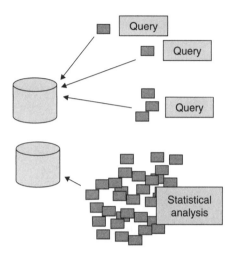

■ **FIGURE 7.1** The resources used by statistical analysis far exceed those used by other styles of transactions.

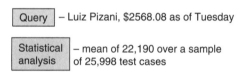

Query – Luiz Pizani, $2568.08 as of Tuesday

Statistical analysis – mean of 22,190 over a sample of 25,998 test cases

■ **FIGURE 7.2** The results of a query are quite different from the results of a statistical analysis.

basic transaction types common in data warehousing—a standard query or a statistical analysis.

Figure 7.1 shows that standard queries typically use only a few resources, because only a few units of data (i.e., records of data) are required. In contrast, statistical analysis typically requires many, many resources to satisfy the statistical query, and many, many records of data are required.

Another way of looking at this fundamental difference between query and statistical analyses is to compare the output of a typical query transaction and a typical statistical analysis, as shown in Figure 7.2.

Figure 7.2 represents a query that looks for a small amount of data and reports a small amount of data. In this example, the query has retrieved the record for Luiz Pizani and has found his bank balance. To satisfy the query, only one or two records of data were required for analysis.

In a statistical analysis, however, many records are required. In Figure 7.2 is it seen that the results of the query entailed computation of a statistical mean or an average, and to calculate that mean, nearly 26,000 records had to be accessed. Furthermore, the records accessed by the statistical query had to be accessed all at once. The mean value could not be calculated until all the records were available.

USING STATISTICAL ANALYSIS

There are many things that can be done with statistical analysis. One of the simplest statistical analyses that can be done is the creation of a profile of data. A profile of data is a statistical summary of the contents of a body of data. Typical questions answered by a statistical profile of data include: How many records are there? What values are the highest, the lowest? What is the mean, the median, and the mode? Are there values that are out of domain? Are there values that are in domain and appear to be outliers? What is the distribution of data values?

All these questions and more contribute to the creation of a profile of a body of data. The profile of the body of data allows the analyst to look at an overview of the data set—to examine the forest, not just the individual trees.

However, there are many other uses for the statistical analysis of data. One such use is the comparison of corporate data to external data. The development of corporate data is the first step in the comparison of corporate data to external data. Then, the external data is captured and put on a similar footing. Then a comparison is made.

To illustrate a typical comparison of corporate data to external data, Figure 7.3 depicts what might be shown when Coca Cola data is compared to industry-wide beverage sales.

Comparisons of the statistical peaks and valleys may be of particular interest to the beverage business analyst who wants to know, Are Coca Cola sales rising while general industry trends are falling? Are Coca Cola sales falling while industry trends are rising? Is there a general correlative pattern between the two beverage sales curves?

The ability to compare and contrast corporate information to external information can lead to truly valuable business insight.

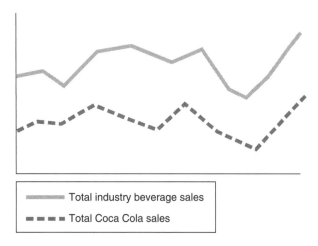

■ **FIGURE 7.3** Comparing industry information to corporate information.

THE INTEGRITY OF THE COMPARISON

The validity of data is one of the key issues in comparative statistical analysis. Conscientious statisticians routinely want to know if they are comparing the same thing—comparing apples with apples, or apples with oranges. Returning to Figure 7.3, for example, when industry beverage sales are compared to sales of Coca Cola, is the comparison valid? After all, if beverage sales include beer and wine coolers, is it fair and meaningful to compare Coca Cola sales to the sales of these beverages? What if Coca Cola includes such drinks as Minute Maid? Is it fair (or even smart) to compare sales of Minute Maid to sales of Pepsi Cola?

The comparison of external data to internal data introduces issues to be resolved before the statistical comparison can be considered a valid one.

There are, however, many important uses for statistical analysis other than the comparison of external to internal data. Another such usage for statistical analysis is to determine trends and patterns in data.

The business case for data warehouse support of statistical analysis is a strong one.

Even the act of analysis must be considered when pondering statistical analysis. When simple queries are made, the intent is to find data that satisfies an immediate need for information. But, when statistical analysis is done, it typically takes the very different analytical form known as heuristic analysis.

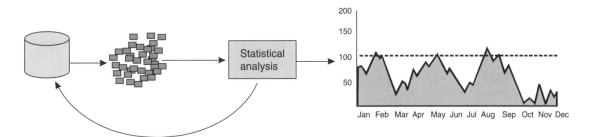

■ FIGURE 7.4 One of the essences of statistical processing is heuristic analysis.

Heuristic analysis is the kind of analysis that is done as a part of discovery. A thing is characterized as heuristic if it involves or serves as an aid to learning, discovery, or problem-solving. In an act of discovery, the analyst does not know what secrets the data holds. The analyst sets out to find or learn what the data contains or means, without knowing what the data contains or what the analyst is looking for ahead of time.

HEURISTIC ANALYSIS

The heuristic analyst has the attitude, "I don't know what I want, but I will know it when I see it." In heuristic analysis, the next iteration of analysis is determined by the results obtained from the current analysis. In a true heuristic analysis, it is not possible to plan how many iterations of analysis there will be or where the analysis will lead.

The heuristic analytical attitude is found everywhere in business. It usually is only the clerks who know exactly what they want.

Figure 7.4 depicts the general flow of analysis in a heuristic environment.

Statistical processing is associated with heuristic analysis. One of the unusual aspects of heuristic analysis is the need occasionally to "freeze" data. When data is frozen, no new data is ingested into the system. The reason for occasionally freezing data when doing heuristic statistical processing is the need to see if the results obtained by the analysis were caused by a change in algorithms or a change in data.

For example, an analyst runs a transaction against a body of data and finds that the data returns an average of 67 units. The analyst then changes the algorithm and reruns the analysis, yielding a new average of 98 units. The question then becomes, Is the change in results a function of the change in the algorithm or a change in the data? If the second analysis was run against a different set of data, the different results may be a function of operating against different data, rather than the result of changing the algorithm used in calculation.

FREEZING DATA

When fine distinctions like this are important, it is necessary to be able to freeze the data that has been used in a calculation. Freezing the data means that any change in results can definitely be attributed to algorithmic change and nothing else.

Figure 7.5 depicts data frozen to support heuristic processing and results analysis.

EXPLORATION PROCESSING

One of the essences of statistical processing is that it is often an exercise in exploration. In many forms of information processing, analysis is done on data whose content, form, and structure are well known. However, in other forms of information processing, analysis is done when the content, form, and structure of the data are not well known. It is this style of processing—exploration processing—to which statistical analysis is particularly well suited.

Figure 7.6 depicts exploration processing.

The challenge for the DW 2.0 data warehouse environment is how best to support statistical processing. Certainly DW 2.0 holds data that can be very useful in statistical processing. In fact, the DW 2.0 architecture includes the key ingredient for statistical analysis. However, there remain some issues relating to the usage of the data found in the DW 2.0 environment.

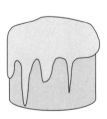

■ **FIGURE 7.5** On occasion data needs to be frozen.

■ **FIGURE 7.6** Exploration processing—finding out what the possibilities are.

THE FREQUENCY OF ANALYSIS

The frequency of statistical analysis is germane to the support of statistical processing by DW 2.0. Figure 7.7 shows that as the frequency of statistical analysis changes, the supporting DW 2.0 infrastructure also changes.

Figure 7.7 suggests that as the frequency of statistical analysis grows, the need for a separate exploration facility increases. If only one statistical analysis is done per year, the basic DW 2.0 infrastructure alone is able to support that level of processing. If statistical analysis is done once a quarter, then the DW 2.0 infrastructure can probably support that level of processing. If statistical analysis is to be done once a month, then maybe the DW 2.0 infrastructure can support that level of processing. But anything more frequent than once a month is unlikely to be able to be supported by the DW 2.0 infrastructure without some addition or enhancement. And certainly in organizations in which statistical analysis is done once an hour, a separate exploration facility needs to be included in the data warehouse environment.

THE EXPLORATION FACILITY

The exploration facility is a place where statistical processing can be done with no performance impact on the central DW 2.0 infrastructure. The exploration facility is located in a place that is physically apart from the DW 2.0 environment. They are physically separate places.

The exploration facility can be frozen for periods of time if necessary. It can include external data if warranted. The exploration facility typically contains subsets of data taken from the DW 2.0 environment. Only rarely is it a direct copy of the DW 2.0 environment, or even parts of the DW 2.0 environment.

The exploration facility takes in data at its lowest level of granularity. In addition, it typically takes in huge amounts of historical data. Both detail and history are needed to satisfy the requirements of the exploration analyst.

The data structure of the exploration facility is mixed. Some data is put in tables on disk storage. Still other data is flattened into a file. The flattened file is often optimal for doing statistical analysis.

Exploration facilities usually contain a large volume of fairly homogeneous data. There is often a low degree of data diversity and a large number of data records found in an exploration facility.

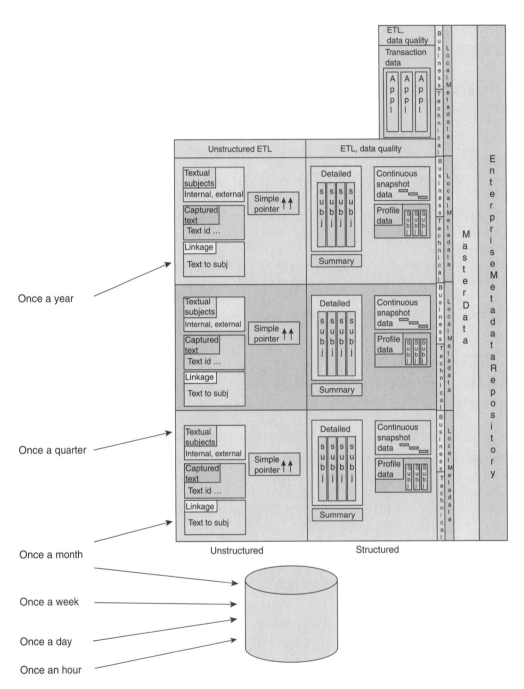

■ FIGURE 7.7 The frequency with which statistical analysis is done determines whether a separate exploration facility is needed.

THE SOURCES FOR EXPLORATION PROCESSING

The exploration facility can draw from many sources of data—from the Integrated Sector, the Archival Sector, and the Near Line Sector. Figure 7.8 shows that the exploration facility can draw from the Archival and Near Line Sectors. However, the DW 2.0 Integrated Sector is generally the primary source of data for the exploration facility.

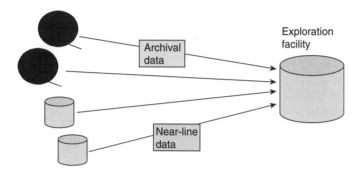

■ **FIGURE 7.8** Archival data and near-line data can also be sent to the exploration facility.

On occasion the exploration facility can draw data from the Interactive Sector. However, if it does draw data from that sector, then there are several cautions, the first being the disruption of service in the Interactive Sector. If exploration data is to be drawn from the Interactive Sector, it must be taken with great attention to the performance levels in that sector. The second caution is that if data is taken from the Interactive Sector into the exploration facility, it must be understood that the data is not auditable. For example, a unit of data taken from the Interactive Sector at 10:31 AM may not exist at 10:32 AM. If these cautions are considered, then the Interactive Sector can be used to provide data to the exploration facility.

REFRESHING EXPLORATION DATA

Figure 7.9 depicts the refreshment of exploration facility data with data from the DW 2.0 environment.

The refreshment cycle of data into the exploration facility is deliberate. In other parts of DW 2.0 data flows as rapidly as it is available. Data flows into the exploration facility only when the exploration analyst wants the data to flow. This may be daily, weekly, or monthly, depending on the needs of the exploration analyst.

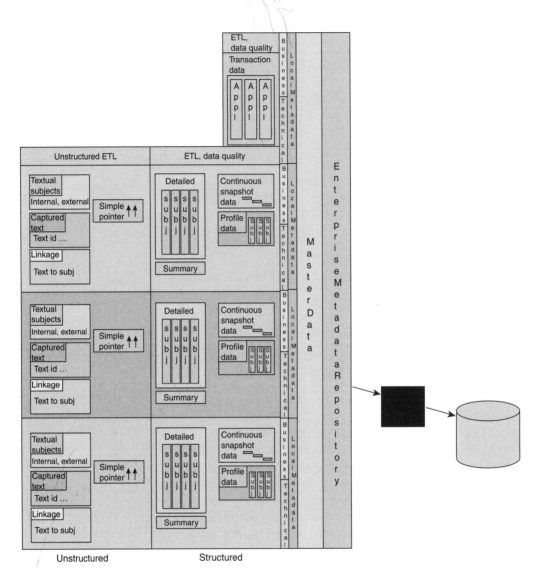

■ FIGURE 7.9 Periodically data is refreshed from the DW 2.0 environment to the exploration facility.

PROJECT-BASED DATA

Exploration facilities are project based as a rule. This usually means that a particular issue needs to be studied by management. Data relevant to the issue is gathered, an analysis is made, and then the results are sent to management. Once the results are sent to management and the study is finished, the data is either discarded or mothballed. The project-based exploration facility is not a permanent structure.

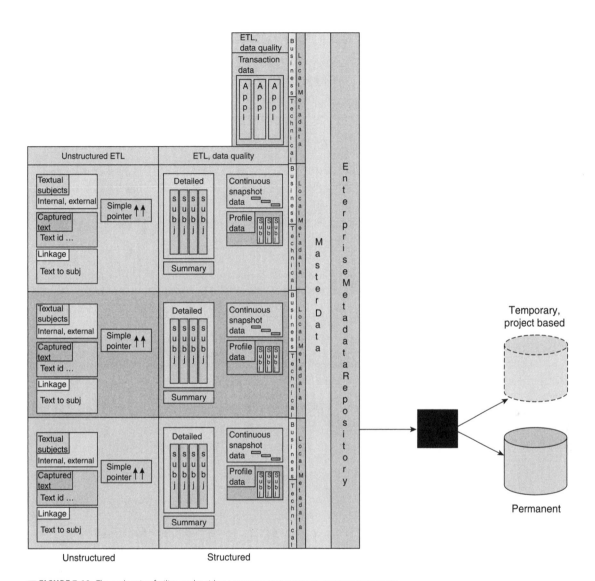

FIGURE 7.10 The exploration facility can be either a permanent structure or a temporary structure.

However, some organizations elect to have a permanent exploration facility. When this is the case, the exploration facility is available any time an analysis needs to be done. The detailed data is often changed inside the permanent exploration facility.

Figure 7.10 illustrates that the data in an exploration facility can be permanent or temporary.

DATA MARTS AND THE EXPLORATION FACILITY

Analysts often think that the exploration facility is the same as or very similar to a data mart. In fact, a data mart and an exploration facility are very different. Some of the major differences between a data mart and an exploration facility are:

- The exploration facility holds detailed data; the data mart holds summarized or aggregated data.
- The exploration facility is used for the purpose of discovery; the data mart is used for the purpose of easy dissemination of information.
- The exploration facility attracts mathematicians; the data mart attracts business analysts.
- The exploration facility is usually a flat file; the data mart is OLAP based.
- The exploration facility may be and often is temporary; the data mart is almost always permanent.
- The exploration facility is acted on by statistical software; the data mart is acted on by business intelligence software.

These are only the primary differences between an exploration facility and a data mart.

Figure 7.11 suggests that an exploration facility and a data mart are very different components of the architecture.

A BACKFLOW OF DATA

Another interesting issue is that of whether it is wise to let data flow from the exploration facility back into the DW 2.0 environment. Indeed it is permissible for data to flow from the exploration facility into the DW 2.0 environment, but there are certain conditions that must be met beforehand.

Some of the conditions are:

- The data that is output from the exploration facility needs to be used in multiple places throughout the corporate environment. If the output data is to be used in only one or two places, then it does not make sense to place it in the DW 2.0 environment.

- There needs to be an audit trail of data and calculations associated with any exploration facility data placed in the DW 2.0 environment.

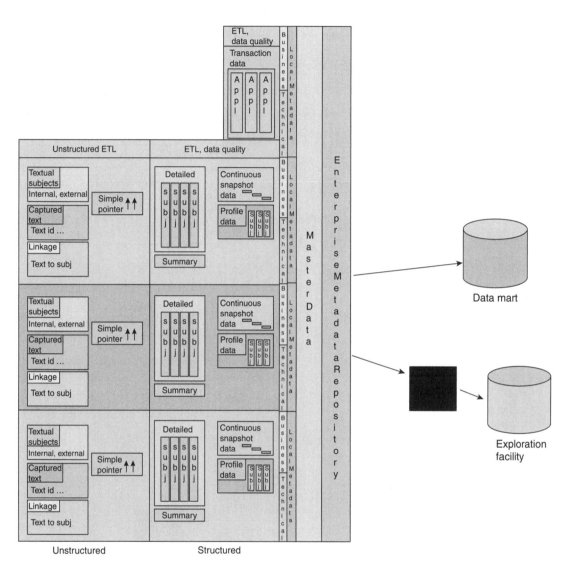

■ FIGURE 7.11 There are significant differences between a data mart and an exploration facility.

- If exploration facility data is to be placed in the DW 2.0 environment, and if the exploration facility is a project-based facility, then the expectation for the exploration data to be placed in the DW 2.0 environment must also be that it is a limited, one-time-only supply of data. In other words, if data is to be placed in the DW 2.0 environment from a temporary source, it is not reasonable to expect that source to become a permanent supplier of data to the DW 2.0 data warehouse.

Figure 7.12 depicts the potential feedback of data from the exploration facility to the DW 2.0 data warehouse, under the right circumstances.

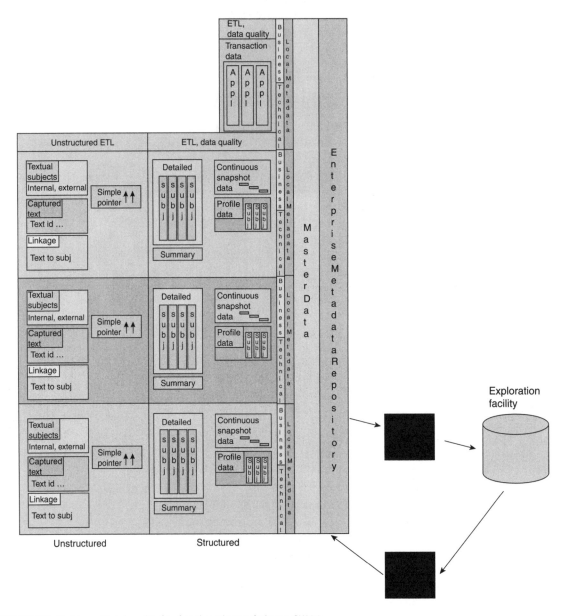

■ **FIGURE 7.12** It is possible to have data flow from the exploration facility into DW 2.0.

USING EXPLORATION DATA INTERNALLY

A word of caution about exploration facilities. In most cases, exploration facilities are used to produce analysis for internal consumption only. This is because the data that goes into the exploration facility normally is not subjected to the same rigorous ETL processing as the data flowing into and through the DW 2.0 environment. Therefore, when it comes to providing reports and data to auditors and examiners, it just does not make sense to use data from the exploration facility. Instead, only "official" data should be used as the basis for official reports. It is well worth remembering that information on reports often ends up also appearing in financial statements or even in the press. It is very unwise to allow reports based on exploration facility data to be used in a public manner, because these reports may not be calculated properly and may contain misleading data.

FROM THE PERSPECTIVE OF THE BUSINESS ANALYST

Many businesses do not take advantage of the statistical processing of the data that they own. As such they are not taking full advantage of their information resources. But there are some businesses that have long recognized the value of information and the statistical processing that can be done with the data. Typical of these businesses are insurance actuaries and research engineers.

The truth of the matter is that, in insurance and in engineering product development, statistical processing plays a very important role. Furthermore that role is recognized by the businesses that employ these types of people.

For a company that traditionally has not used statistical analysis widely to start to do so, there needs to be some obvious successes. These successes do not happen magically. Usually these statistical analyses happen as the result of "skunk-work" projects. Because there has been no past success, the business is loath to fund a statistical analysis. So one or two interested and experimental workers get together and do a "see what happens" project. These projects are almost always small because they are not formally funded.

Assuming that the analysts find something interesting and useful, the skunk-work project then makes its way into the corporate mainstream. Once established, the statistical analysis function grows thereafter.

The type of individual who conducts these types of projects must have some sort of mathematical background. The background may be formal or informal, but to do statistical analysis properly requires a way of thinking that entails an understanding of mathematics.

SUMMARY

There are two types of queries—analytical queries and exploration queries. Exploration queries access large amounts of data and can take a long time. Exploration queries require granular and historical data. Exploration processing typically makes use of statistical techniques.

Occasionally exploration data needs to be frozen. The freezing of exploration data occurs when heuristic processing is being done. In heuristic processing, the next step of analysis depends entirely on the results obtained from the most current level of analysis.

An exploration facility can be built exclusively for the purpose of supporting exploration processing. Whether or not there is a need for an exploration facility depends entirely on the frequency of statistical analysis. If only infrequent statistical analysis is occurring, then there is no need for a separate exploration facility. If there is frequent statistical analysis that occurs, then there may be a need for a separate exploration facility.

Exploration facilities are built on a project-by-project basis. There is no need to keep the exploration facility after the project that required it is completed.

8

Data models and DW 2.0

The world of DW 2.0 is a complex one. There are many aspects and many facets. It is very easy to become entwined in details and quickly lose your direction. It is important to keep one's perspective when dealing with DW 2.0.

AN INTELLECTUAL ROAD MAP

To that end, an essential part of DW 2.0 is the data model. The data model acts—in many ways—as an intellectual road map to the many parts of DW 2.0. Figure 8.1 shows the role of the data model in DW 2.0.

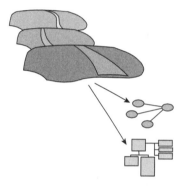

■ **FIGURE 8.1** A data model serves as an intellectual road map.

There are many reasons for a road map in DW 2.0. But perhaps the best reason is that DW 2.0 is not built all at once. Instead DW 2.0 is built a step at a time, over a long period of time. In addition DW 2.0 is built by many people, not just a single person.

To coordinate the efforts of these people over time and across different audiences, it is mandatory that there be a road map—a data model—that describes how the different parts of DW 2.0 fit together. Without a data model the DW 2.0 development efforts are scattered and disjointed, resulting in a mess.

THE DATA MODEL AND BUSINESS

The data model is built from the business itself. It mimics the different components of the business.

Figure 8.2 shows that the data model is built from the business.

157

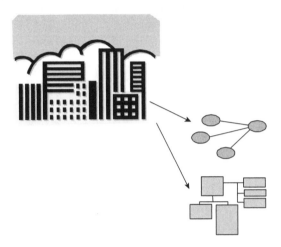

■ **FIGURE 8.2** The data model is derived from the business itself.

■ **FIGURE 8.3** The first step in building the data model is to define the scope of integration.

THE SCOPE OF INTEGRATION

The first step in the building of the data model is the definition of the scope of integration. The scope of integration is the statement of what is to be in the data model and what is not to be in it. The scope of integration is necessary because without it the data model can go on endlessly. It can be extended to include the universe. And when the data model includes the universe, the model is never finished.

Figure 8.3 shows that the definition of the scope of integration is the starting point for the data model.

The data model is based on the data found in the corporation. And in most organizations there is ample data. If the analyst is not careful, the data model will go on endlessly even when the scope of integration is defined, unless there is a distinction made between granular data and summarized or aggregated data. Granular data is data at its lowest level of meaning. A person's name is granular. A person's date of birth is granular. The salary of a person at a moment in time is granular.

Summarized data is data such as the ending transaction volume for a day, the amount of revenue for a month, the number of employees in a year, the gross national product for a quarter, and so forth.

MAKING THE DISTINCTION BETWEEN GRANULAR AND SUMMARIZED DATA

The reasons there needs to be a distinction made between granular data and summarized data are that

- there is much more summarized data than granular data;
- summarized data changes faster than it can be modeled;
- summarized data carries with it an algorithm describing how the summarization is to be made.

If summarized or aggregated data is included in the data model, the model will never be finished.

Figure 8.4 shows that granular data is the fiber of the data model.

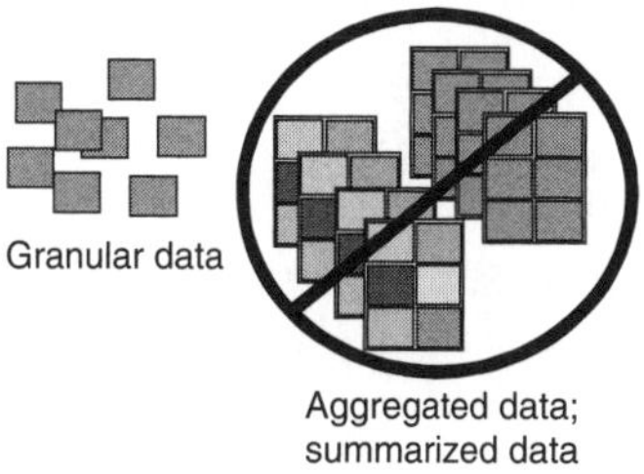

Granular data

Aggregated data; summarized data

■ **FIGURE 8.4** The data model focuses on granular data, not aggregated or summarized data.

LEVELS OF THE DATA MODEL

There are different levels of the data model. In a standard data model there are

- the ERD—entity relationship level—the highest level of the data model;
- the midlevel mode—the dis, or data item set;
- the low-level model—the physical model—the lowest level of data modeling.

The ERD is at a high level and can be constructed quickly. The ERD shows the major subject areas of the business of the corporation, and the relationships between those subject areas. The midlevel model—the data item set—shows the keys, attributes, and relationships of the details of the data model. The low-level model shows the physical characteristics of the data model, such as physical attributes of data, indexes, foreign keys, and the like.

The lower the level of the model, the greater the level of detail. The higher the level of the model, the more complete the model.

Figure 8.5 shows the different levels of the data model.

The fact that there are multiple levels of modeling for something as complex as DW 2.0 is not a new or strange technique. Consider maps of the world, as seen in Figure 8.6.

In Figure 8.6 it is seen that there is a map of the United States, a map of Texas, and map of how to get to a house in Dallas, Texas. Each map has a relationship to each of the other maps. Texas can be found inside the United States. Dallas can be found inside Texas. So there is a relationship between each of the maps.

There is a different level of detail found on each map. The U.S. interstate highway system is found on the map of the United States. Texas 285 is found on the map of Texas. And Grapevine road in Denton is found in the city map of the Dallas vicinity. So the level of detail goes downward with each map.

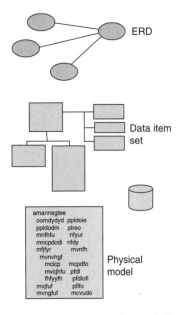

■ **FIGURE 8.5** There are different levels of the data model.

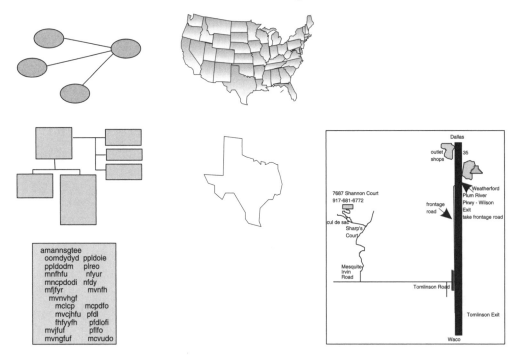

■ **FIGURE 8.6** How the different levels of the data model relate.

Correspondingly, the completeness of each map goes down with each level. The map of the United States shows the United States but does not show Brazil. The map of Texas shows Texas but does not show Arizona or Tennessee. The map of Dallas shows downtown Dallas but does not show Sanderson or Del Rio.

The different levels of mapping are knitted together so that there is an order to the entire globe.

In the same fashion, the data model is knitted together so that there is meaning and order to all of the systems that constitute the DW 2.0 environment. Figure 8.7 shows the data model and the order it brings to information systems.

There are many different models that are found in the DW 2.0 environment. It is a mistake to think that there is one model for DW 2.0.

DATA MODELS AND THE INTERACTIVE SECTOR

The first set of models is found in the applications that are in the Interactive Sector. As a rule there is a separate data model for each application. The application data models are shaped by the application requirements. One major consideration of the application data models is the need for performance. Throughout the application environment, especially where there are OLTP transactions, the data models are shaped by the need for performance. When performance considerations are applied to a data model, the result is a streamlined

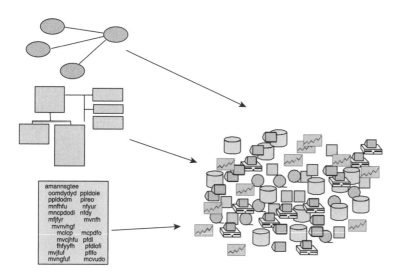

■ **FIGURE 8.7** The data model is used to bring order out of chaos.

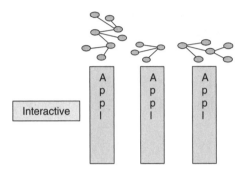

■ **FIGURE 8.8** An application data model shapes each of the applications.

data model, in which high performance is achieved by a streamlined flow through the system. And a streamlined flow though the system is abetted by a model that positions data together.

Figure 8.8 depicts applications and their models.

In Figure 8.8 it is noteworthy that there are different application models for each application.

THE CORPORATE DATA MODEL

But there are other data models as well. The next data model is the corporate data model. The corporate data model is the model that shows how data coming from the application-oriented environment is to be shaped into corporate data.

The corporate data model sits between the interactive layer and the integrated layer. It is *the* data model of the DW 2.0 environment, if there is such a thing.

The corporate data model depicts all the data of the corporation in an integrated manner.

As a simple example of the need for integration at the corporate level, suppose there are three applications. Application A has data at the daily level, where dollars are U.S. dollars, and the gender of people is M/F. Application B has information stored at the weekly level, where dollars are Canadian, and the gender of people is stored as MALE/ FEMALE. Application C has data stored by the hour, where dollars are stored in Australian dollars, and where gender is designated as X/Y.

The corporate view is at the daily level, where dollars are stored in euros, and where gender is specified as MEN/WOMEN.

The data model reflects the true corporate view of information, which is a unified view of information.

A TRANSFORMATION OF MODELS

Figure 8.9 shows that a fundamental transformation of data is made as data passes from the Application/Interactive Sector to the Integrated Sector.

It is noteworthy that as data passes into the Integrated Sector it is stored by subject area.

As data passes into the Near Line Sector, there is no transformation or change of data models. Because the near-line environment needs to mimic the interactive environment as much as possible, the data model for the near-line environment is exactly the same as the data model for the Interactive Sector.

Figure 8.10 shows that the data model does not change as data passes into the Near Line Sector.

Finally data passes into the Archival Sector. As it does so, there may or may not be a change of data models. In some cases data passes

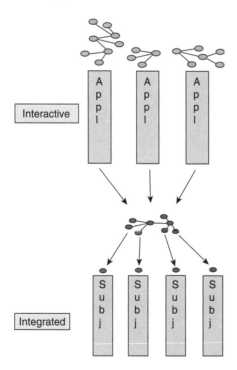

■ FIGURE 8.9 A fundamental transformation of data is made as data passes from application data to corporate data. The corporate data model is used to guide the transformation.

■ **FIGURE 8.10** As data passes from the Integrated Sector to the Near Line Sector, no changes are made at all to the data model.

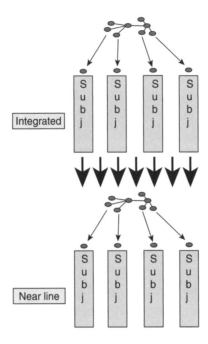

into the Archival Sector in exactly the same state as it was in the Integrated Sector. In this case there is no change of data models.

But on other occasions, data undergoes a fundamental change as it passes into the Archival Sector. In this case data passes into what can be termed an inverted list format. When data passes into an inverted list format, it is fundamentally rearranged into a series of simple lists.

The archival analyst may want such a transformation, because it can make the data in the archival environment easier to find and analyze.

And of course, data in the archival environment can be placed in *both* a corporate data model format and an inverted list format.

Figure 8.11 shows this movement of data into the archival environment.

DATA MODELS AND UNSTRUCTURED DATA

Data models are appropriate for and useful to the structured side of DW 2.0. But there is some applicability of data models to the unstructured side of DW 2.0. It is not surprising that the data model does not play as big a role in the unstructured world as it does in the structured world.

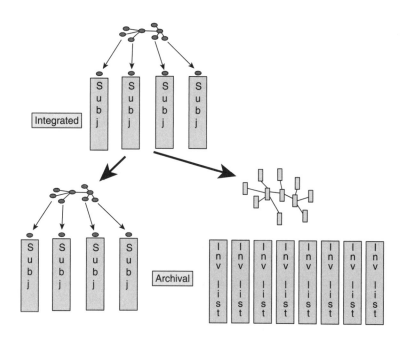

The first place where a data model is found in the unstructured component of DW 2.0 is in terms of external taxonomies. External taxonomies are used to group and classify data during the process of terminology normalization or rationalization.

Figure 8.12 shows that data models can be used to shape an external taxonomy.

The second place where data models can be found in the unstructured environment is in the creation of an internal data model. An internal data model is used to describe the contents of and the structure of a body of text, usually a large body of text.

First the unstructured data is gathered. Then the unstructured data is organized into themes. From the themes an SOM (Self-Organizing Map) can be created. Once the SOM is created, the major themes of the unstructured text and the relationships between those themes are formed. From that basic information, an internal data model can be created.

Figure 8.13 shows the creation of an internal data model from the themes that occur in the body of unstructured text.

■ **FIGURE 8.12** An external data model is used to shape the external taxonomies found in the unstructured environment.

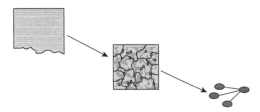

■ **FIGURE 8.13** A document can be reduced to internal themes. In turn the internal themes can be used to create an internal data model.

FROM THE PERSPECTIVE OF THE BUSINESS USER

The business user is essential to the data modeling process. Indeed, from an intellectual standpoint, the data model is the embodiment of how the end user perceives the data found in DW 2.0.

Stated differently, if the data model comes from any other source than the end user—or if the end user does not at least look at and acknowledge the validity of the data model—then the contents of DW 2.0 are shaped inappropriately.

The implication here is that the end user needs to be involved from the beginning, because it is at the beginning of the building of DW 2.0 that the data model is built. Building the data model at the beginning and then showing the data model to the end user at a later point in time risks having major aspects of DW 2.0 built incorrectly.

In some cases it is necessary to have very formal procedures in place as the data model is built and the input from the end user is recorded. The comments of the business person can be written down and the end user asked to sign off on what was and what was not said. This may be necessary when the end user is forgetful or in a large organization in which one business person speaks for a wide body of users. At a later moment in time it may become quite useful to have a written transcript of what the end user did or did not say.

The end user does not have to become an expert in data modeling techniques. (Ironically some end users become enamored of the modeling process and do—in fact—become experts in data modeling.) Instead the data modeling process is usually handled by an outsider who is a professional in data modeling.

Over time the business model will change. The business user is as involved in the changes to the data model as he/she was in the original creation of the business model.

SUMMARY

Data models form the intellectual road map for the DW 2.0 environment. DW 2.0 is large and complex and will be built over a period of time by a large number of developers. It is the data model that allows one development effort to be connected to another development effort.

The data model is shaped from the business requirements of the corporation. It is built for the most granular of data, not summarized data or aggregated data.

There are three levels of the data model—the ERD level, the midlevel (or the dis level), and the low level (or the physical level).

The Interactive Sector is shaped by an application model. The Integrated Sector is shaped by the corporate data model.

There are data models that can be applied to unstructured data. In particular, external taxonomies can have a data model built for them. In addition, an internal data model can be created by the themes that are generated out of text.

Monitoring the DW 2.0 environment

The DW 2.0 environment is complex and dynamic. There are many complex interactions between the various components. Data flows from one component to another, transactions are executed, and transformations of data are done.

In many ways the DW 2.0 environment is like a black box. Data is put in one place and taken out of another, and mysterious things happen in between. Unfortunately, if the DW 2.0 environment is treated like an opaque black box, it is a good bet that over time, things will happen inside the black box that are untoward—data starts to collect where it shouldn't, transaction response time turns bad, data is not placed where it ought to be placed, or worse.

The DW 2.0 environment should not be like a black box. There needs to be periodic "checks underneath the hood" to ensure that the DW 2.0 environment is operating as it should be.

MONITORING THE DW 2.0 ENVIRONMENT

To that end it is strongly recommended that regular monitoring of the DW 2.0 environment be conducted. At the very least, a stethoscope should be inserted into the black box to find out what is going on. When adjustments need to be made to the DW 2.0 environment or any of its components, those adjustments can be made proactively rather than reactively.

THE TRANSACTION MONITOR

There are at least three types of monitoring that need to occur in the DW 2.0 environment. The first is monitoring of the transactions that

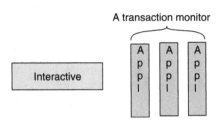

■ **FIGURE 9.1** A transaction monitor is one form of monitoring found in the DW 2.0 environment.

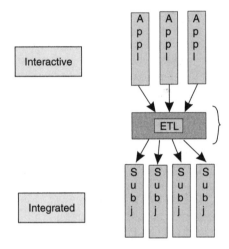

■ **FIGURE 9.2** A data quality monitor at the moment of ETL is also found in the DW 2.0 environment.

are run in the Interactive Sector of DW 2.0. A transaction monitor ensures that there is good and consistent response time.

Figure 9.1 depicts a transaction monitor.

MONITORING DATA QUALITY

The second type of monitoring that needs to occur in the DW 2.0 environment is ETL monitoring for data quality. There needs to be a monitor that is dedicated to verifying the quality of data passing through the transformation components of DW 2.0. If low-quality data is being passed into DW 2.0, then the data analyst needs to be alerted, at the very least.

Figure 9.2 depicts a data quality monitor.

■ **FIGURE 9.3**   A data warehouse monitor is an essential component of DW 2.0.

A DATA WAREHOUSE MONITOR

The third type of monitor that needs to be a part of the DW 2.0 environment is a data warehouse monitor. This monitor looks at the data in the data warehouse. While the data warehouse monitor serves many different purposes, its main purpose is to measure the usage frequency of data. From the usage frequency of data, it can be determined if any data has gone dormant. The management of dormant data is one of the most important aspects of the management of the DW 2.0 environment. Figure 9.3 illustrates the data warehouse monitor.

Each of these types of monitors for the DW 2.0 environment will be addressed in greater depth.

THE TRANSACTION MONITOR—RESPONSE TIME

The primary purpose of the transaction monitor is to ensure that there is good, consistent response time. Unfortunately, there are many aspects to system processing that have an effect on system performance.

When system performance is mentioned, it is usually a reference to response time. Response time in the 2- to 3-second range is normally considered acceptable. There may be a few periods during the course of the day when response time starts to drift higher, but as long as those periods are short and infrequent, and as long as the response times do not drift too high, then the system will be deemed to be running in a satisfactory manner.

Usually acceptable response time parameters are defined in a Service Level Agreement.

Some of the characteristics and features of a transaction monitor include:

- Transaction queue monitoring: The transaction queue is the place where transactions are stored prior to execution. When the system becomes very busy, transactions can become stalled in the transaction queue awaiting execution. If the system

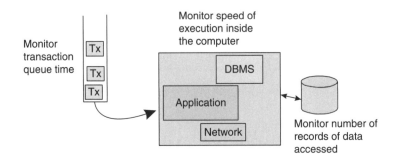

■ **FIGURE 9.4** The basic activities of a transaction monitor.

becomes really busy, this wait in the transaction queue can become the single largest obstacle to performance.

■ Application monitoring: Applications that process transactions inside the computer need to be monitored. When a transaction goes into execution, it occupies system resources. The length of time those resources are dedicated to running the code that constitutes the transaction being executed is the single most important measurement of system throughput and performance.

■ Transaction record monitoring: The number of records needed to complete a transaction also impacts system performance. Often many resources are consumed by a single business transaction. But the most revealing indicator of transaction processing performance is the number of records the transaction needs for execution. Simply stated, a transaction that requires a few records will execute much more quickly than a transaction that entails processing many records.

There are other measurements of performance, but these measurements are the most important.

Figure 9.4 illustrates some of the components to which transaction monitors can be applied for maximum benefit.

There are many outcomes of transaction monitoring. Some of the more salient outcomes of transaction monitoring are discussed next.

PEAK-PERIOD PROCESSING

One important metric that comes from the monitoring of transactions is the measurement of how close the system comes to having all of its resources consumed during peak-period processing.

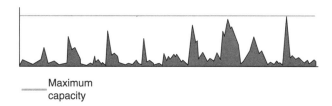

Maximum
capacity

■ **FIGURE 9.5** The burning question—When will capacity used reach maximum capacity and what will happen when that point is reached?

There are periods of low activity and periods of high activity in every transaction processing environment. The periods of high activity are called the "peak periods."

The system operates smoothly as long as there is capacity for all processing. But during peak periods, if the system's demand for resources starts to exceed the resources that are available, then the system starts to slow down, in most cases dramatically. Therefore, it behooves every organization to monitor how closely peak-period processing comes to exhausting the available system resources. If the resources used in peak periods are steady, then there is no need to add capacity. If or when there is a steady increase in the resources needed for peak-period processing, that is a warning sign that more system resources are needed, or a different allocation of resources is called for.

Figure 9.5 shows the tracking of peak-period resources.

Another important parameter typically tracked by the transaction monitor is the rate of growth of the system. Typical indicators of system growth that can be tracked over time are the number of transactions and the volume of data in the system.

The number of transactions is a good indicator of the rate at which a system is growing and its capacity is being consumed. By extrapolating and projecting the number of transactions a system processes, the systems analyst can determine when a hardware upgrade will be needed. The objective is to predict when an upgrade will be needed and to enable the organization to respond in a proactive manner before performance problems begin. Operating in a reactive manner invariably means that the organization will suffer periodic "meltdowns." Meltdowns cause an untold amount of grief due to their negative impact on the operations of the company.

Figure 9.6 illustrates the typical result of tracking transaction volume and data quantity growth over time.

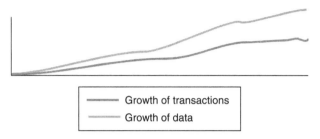

■ FIGURE 9.6 Tracking the growth of data and the growth of transactions.

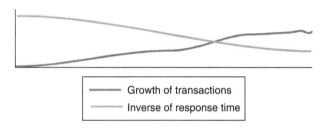

■ FIGURE 9.7 Tracking the growth of transactions matched against the inverse of response time.

There are many other aspects of the operations of transaction processing that can be monitored. For example, the juxtaposition of transaction volume growth and associated response time degradation over time can reveal and forecast when it will become critical for the organization to increase its transaction processing capacity. Figure 9.7 depicts this kind of comparative performance measurement.

THE ETL DATA QUALITY MONITOR

The ETL data quality monitor examines data as it passes from one DW 2.0 sector to another or as the data initially enters the system. The purpose of the ETL data quality monitor is to evaluate the quality of data as it is being transformed.

The ETL data quality monitor looks at many aspects of data. Among other things, it examines

- Domain of data: Suppose gender is defined as "M/F." If gender data is entered as "MALE," the ETL data quality monitor registers a discrepancy.
- Unmatched foreign key: For example, a foreign key is presumed missing and unmatched if there is a reference to "John Jones" in the data, but the customer data base has no John Jones.

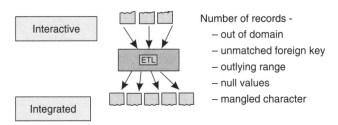

FIGURE 9.8 The data quality monitor.

- Outlying range: The normal age of a customer is between 15 and 80. If a customer comes into the system attributed with an age of 234 years, there is obviously an age range data quality problem that needs to be detected and reported.

- Null values: Every data key that is specified needs to be present. If a record is passed to the data warehouse with no key, it must be detected and reported.

- Mangled character: A name spelled "Mar[++*]" could find its way into an ETL routine. Unless the person has a really unusual name, like the Artist Formerly Known as Prince, there is a good chance that there is a quality discrepancy in this data.

These are just a few examples of many data quality conditions that need to be detected and reported by an ETL data quality monitor.

One of the most interesting data quality questions is what to do once an error condition has been detected. One option is to reject the data, but this is generally a bad solution because

- other parts of the record are rejected when they may be perfectly fine;
- some means of correction will be needed. Manual correction is absolutely the last choice, because manually correcting large amounts of incorrect data can take an enormous amount of time and significantly delay project progress.

Another solution is to create default data. Although this works well, the data that has been determined to be incorrect is permanently lost to the system. Yet another solution is to let the bad data pass into the system and flag it as being incorrect. Flagging incorrect data warns the end user that there is a problem with the data.

Figure 9.8 depicts the place and role of an ETL data quality monitor.

THE DATA WAREHOUSE MONITOR

The data warehouse monitor is a software tool that monitors what data in the data warehouse is being used and what is not being used. If a unit of data goes long enough without being used, it is considered "dormant" data. Good data warehouse monitors are designed to detect and report dormant data.

The normal way that data warehouse data monitoring is done is through the interception of SQL code submitted to the data warehouse system. By gathering the SQL passed into the system, the analyst can determine what data is being accessed inside the data warehouse and what data is not being accessed. Usually the SQL is intercepted as a result of "sniffing" the lines of communications. One way to arrange a sniffer is by placing it outside the data warehouse computer. Figure 9.9 depicts a sniffer located outside the computer that manages the data warehouse.

The other place the sniffer can be located is inside the computer where the data warehouse is being managed. Figure 9.10 depicts the placement of a sniffer inside the data warehouse computer.

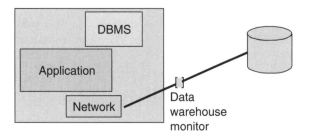

■ **FIGURE 9.9** The data warehouse monitor is placed outside the computer on the network.

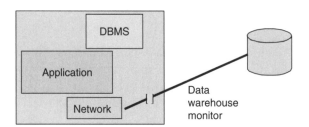

■ **FIGURE 9.10** The data warehouse monitor is placed inside the computer.

As a rule, it is much more efficient to sniff SQL code from outside the computer that hosts the data warehouse. The overhead of sniffing can become a large factor when the sniffer is allowed to be part of or interact directly with the data warehouse DBMS.

DORMANT DATA

There are lots of reasons for having a dormant data monitor in the data warehouse. The primary reason is that when data goes dormant, it needs to be moved to alternate storage. Alternate storage is much less expensive than high-performance disk storage. In addition, dormant data "clogs the arteries" of high-performance disk storage.

There are two good reasons that moving dormant data to an alternate form of storage makes sense:

- It saves money—potentially lots of money.
- It improves performance.

Dormant data creeps into a system silently. Figure 9.11 shows how dormant data grows inside a data warehouse.

Newly built and implemented data warehouses typically do not contain a lot of data and therefore do not contain much dormant data. As the volume of data grows in a data warehouse, the percentage of data that is dormant grows as well. When there is a significant amount of data in a data warehouse, there is almost always a significant amount of data that has gone dormant.

One alternative is simply to leave the dormant data in the data warehouse, but doing so is expensive and slows down the system considerably. The other alternative is to move the dormant data to either near-line storage or archival storage. Figure 9.12 depicts the periodic transfer of dormant data to near-line or archival storage.

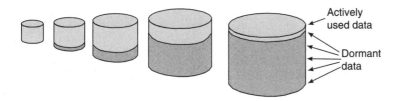

■ **FIGURE 9.11** As the volume of data increases, the percentage of dormant data grows.

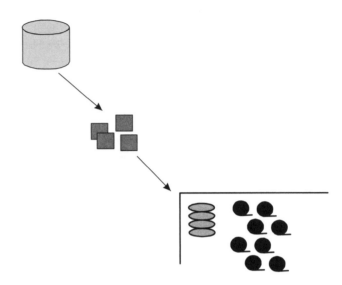

■ **FIGURE 9.12** There is a burning question—What data needs to be placed into near-line storage?

The data warehouse monitor is used to tell when data has gone dormant.

FROM THE PERSPECTIVE OF THE BUSINESS USER

The monitoring of data is a technical exercise. As such the business user is not directly involved in monitoring. However, the business user definitely sees the results of monitoring.

To use an analogy, the business user sees that the oil light has gone on. He/she pulls over into a garage and half an hour later is on his/her way. This time when driving down the road the oil light is no longer flashing.

The same is true of monitoring the DW 2.0 environment. In the DW 2.0 environment the business user notices a slowdown in performance. Or the end user notices that upon making a query too much data is being returned. The business person goes and discusses the symptoms with the data architect. The data architect then employs a monitor and effects a cure.

It is noteworthy that using a monitor and effecting a cure is not a half-hour exercise. In the best of circumstances, there is a considerable period of time between the noticing of symptoms of a problem and the curing of that problem.

SUMMARY

Three types of monitors are needed in the DW 2.0 environment:

- Transaction monitor
- Data quality monitor
- Data warehouse monitor

The transaction monitor addresses the Interactive Sector and is focused on transaction response time and capacity planning. The transaction monitor is especially concerned with data warehouse activity that occurs during peak processing periods. The transaction monitor examines workloads, queues, and resource utilization.

The data quality monitor looks at data domains and data ranges as data is moved from one part of the DW 2.0 data warehouse environment to another.

The data warehouse monitor is focused on the Integrated Sector of the DW 2.0 data warehouse and addresses dormant data. It looks at data and determines what data is being used and what is not being used.

The best data warehouse monitors are those that operate outside of the data warehouse DBMS. The use of SQL sniffers is the least obtrusive and the least time-consuming technology for monitoring the activity that goes on inside the data warehouse.

10

DW 2.0 and security

There are no information systems built today that can ignore the issue of security. The DW 2.0 next-generation data warehouse is no different from any other type of system in this regard. Given the sweeping nature of data warehousing—covering transaction processing systems to archival systems—it is no surprise that the security measures take many different forms and address security from many different perspectives in the DW 2.0 environment.

PROTECTING ACCESS TO DATA

There are many ways to address security of data and security of systems. Figure 10.1 suggests one of the simplest ways to protect data.

Figure 10.1 represents the barriers that may be put up to prevent people from gaining unwanted or unauthorized access to data. These barriers take many different forms, such as passwords, special transactions, and software intervention.

Barriers are useful throughout the DW 2.0 environment—from the Interactive Sector to the Integrated Sector, the Near Line Sector, and the Archival Sector.

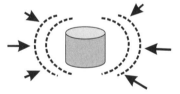

■ **FIGURE 10.1** One way to protect data is to be very careful who has access to it.

ENCRYPTION

There are other ways to protect data. Figure 10.2 depicts another technique.

When data is encrypted it is rewritten in a form that is different from its original form. While anyone may be able to access encrypted data, only those who know how to decrypt the data can make sense of it. The protection of data by encryption does not lie in protecting it

■ **FIGURE 10.2** Another way to protect data is to encrypt it.

181

Access

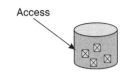

■ **FIGURE 10.3** When data is encrypted, the person accessing the data must be aware of the encryption prior to conducting a search.

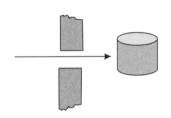

■ **FIGURE 10.4** A basic form of protection for online security is the firewall.

from access. Encryption protects data by restricting the decryption mechanisms to only authorized people. Encryption is useful in some cases in the DW 2.0 environment, but due to the disadvantages of encryption, very careful use of it must be made in DW 2.0.

These two security techniques—protection from the access of data and data encryption—are found in different places in different forms throughout the DW 2.0 environment.

DRAWBACKS

There are drawbacks to both types of security. Protecting data from unauthorized access requires a technological infrastructure all its own. There is an administrative cost to keeping the protective infrastructure up to date.

There are also definite costs associated with data encryption. When data is encrypted, the encryption disables several important aspects of the data warehouse system. Encrypted data cannot be indexed effectively. It requires that the person accessing the data encrypt the parameters in the query before the query can be executed. And, it cannot be used for logic or numerical calculations or comparisons.

In short, there are many disadvantages to the encryption of data. Figure 10.3 illustrates one such disadvantage.

Because of the disadvantages of both types of security, no one type is sufficient for the DW 2.0 data warehouse. Instead, a mixture of security types is found in the DW 2.0 environment.

THE FIREWALL

Perhaps the most well-known type of security is the firewall. Firewalls are used where the Internet connects the outside world to the systems of the corporation. Figure 10.4 depicts a firewall regulating the transactions that are entering from the Internet.

It is worth noting that firewall protection applies only to access to the Interactive Sector, because the Interactive Sector is the place in the DW 2.0 architecture where active transaction processing occurs.

MOVING DATA OFFLINE

Figure 10.5 shows that it is only the Interactive Sector that has an interface with the Internet environment.

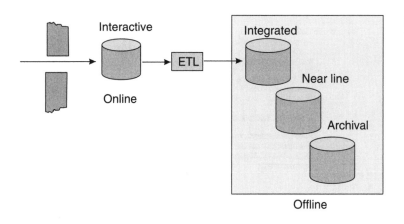

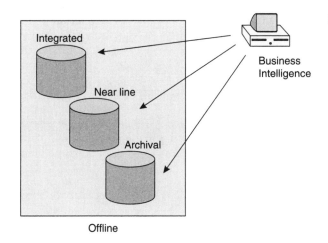

■ **FIGURE 10.5** A basic form of protection is to keep the noninteractive data in DW 2.0 offline.

■ **FIGURE 10.6** Offline data is accessed by a separate network.

This figure shows that the Integrated Sector, the Near Line Sector, and the Archival Sector of the DW 2.0 data warehouse must not interface directly with the Internet. Completely insulating these key data warehouse sectors from the Internet means that even the best hacker cannot get to the data contained in their data bases. Only the interactive data is at risk. This is a very simple yet very effective security measure.

The only Interactive Sector data that is allowed to pass to the Integrated Sector must first be processed through the DW 2.0 ETL interface.

Data in the Integrated, Near Line, and Archival Sectors can still be accessed; however, to access them requires offline processing or authorized access to the organization's internal network.

Figure 10.6 shows that DW 2.0 data can still be accessed offline.

■ FIGURE 10.7 One approach is to encrypt only part of the data in a record.

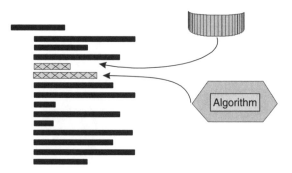

■ FIGURE 10.8 The way encrypted data is accessed.

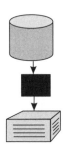

■ FIGURE 10.9 One way to bypass all security is to do a system dump.

Data in the DW 2.0 environment can in fact be encrypted. However, because it is not practical or effective to encrypt huge amounts of data, only selected pieces of data should be encrypted.

LIMITING ENCRYPTION

Figure 10.7 depicts encryption of only a few fields of data inside a record.

Even though it is technically possible to index encrypted data, data is not easy to retrieve after it has been encrypted. By encrypting only a small part of the data in a record, the disadvantages that come with encryption are minimized.

There needs to be a means by which the actual values that have been encrypted can be restored. Figure 10.8 shows that actual values represented by the encrypted data can be determined by either going through an index or by passing data into an algorithm.

The techniques of encryption are best used in the DW 2.0 environment in the Integrated Sector. If they are used at all, encryption techniques should be used sparingly, due to the disadvantages that accompany encrypted data. When encryption techniques are used in the Interactive Sector, special attention should be paid as to whether performance will be negatively and severely impacted. It is questionable if encrypted techniques should be used in the Archival Sector.

A DIRECT DUMP

As effective as barriers to unauthorized data access are, security protection can be bypassed by simply doing a system dump of the data and then reading the data manually. Figure 10.9 depicts a system dump of a DW 2.0 data base.

After the system data dump is done and the data is free of any protection other than encryption, the dump can then be read manually, as indicated by Figure 10.10.

Reading a dump manually is not something that most people would do, either for pleasure or for work. There is also an arcane set of rules that need to be followed if a dumped data set is to be read in its entirety. However, textual data contained in a data base dump can easily be read without the aid of special skills or tools. Even a nontechnician can read a data dump if all that is required is picking out text that the dump contains.

■ **FIGURE 10.10** After the dump is made, the data is read manually.

Because reading a dump bypasses all other forms of protection, at least some form of encryption is encouraged. This protection is especially encouraged for DW 2.0's Integrated Sector.

THE DATA WAREHOUSE MONITOR

The data warehouse monitor is a standard recommendation for the DW 2.0 environment. The monitor is recommended for the reasons described in Chapter 9. But there is another good reason the data warehouse monitor should be used, namely to determine who is looking at what data. Identifying who is sending queries and to what data bases is one of the most useful things that a data warehouse monitor can do.

Data warehouse monitors and the transaction monitor both produce transaction logs. A transaction log is just a register of the activity that has been detected by the monitor.

Figure 10.11 shows a DW 2.0 environment that has been monitored, resulting in the creation of a transaction log. It is a fairly simple matter to read the log after it has been generated by the monitor. The analyst can tell who has been querying what data by reading the access transactions logged by the data warehouse monitor.

This form of security is passive, because it does not prevent an unauthorized access to the data warehouse data bases. But it is security nevertheless, and if there have been unauthorized accesses they will show up in the log.

SENSING AN ATTACK

Detecting an attack coming from outside the DW 2.0 environment before it becomes a serious problem, or better yet before it happens, is

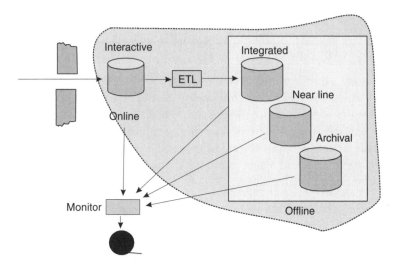

■ **FIGURE 10.11** The access log can be used to see who is looking at what data.

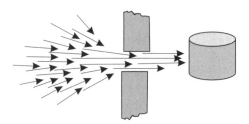

■ **FIGURE 10.12** If too many unsuccessful access requests come through the firewall in rapid succession, the system senses that an attack may be occurring.

another good way to protect and secure the data warehouse. Prompt identification of invalid or unauthorized access enables the organization to sense and stop an attack. For example, occasionally a system will want to enter another system without knowing the password. A fairly effective way to overcome this problem and carry out an unauthorized access is to flood the system with many different passwords. As soon as the assault yields a password that grants entry to the system, the attacking routine stores the good password for future use.

This kind of attack can be sensed by keeping track of the unacceptable passwords that are sent to the system for authorization. If there is a sudden flurry of passwords that are invalid, the system senses an attack. The system can then selectively shut down until the attack is over.

This kind of attack is most likely to happen in the Interactive Sector of DW 2.0 as transactions flow in via the Internet.

Figure 10.12 depicts a password flooding attack.

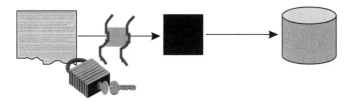

■ **FIGURE 10.13** If documents are protected they are not entered into the unstructured data base.

Security protection on the unstructured side of the DW 2.0 data warehouse mimics the security of the structured side, but there is an added twist. If incoming documents are protected and the system detects that protection, then the documents are never brought into the DW 2.0 environment at all. This ensures that external protection mechanisms are honored and data that has been protected by others never even enters the unstructured side of DW 2.0.

Figure 10.13 shows that external security is honored at the point of entry into DW 2.0.

SECURITY FOR NEAR LINE DATA

The Near Line Sector is the environment that requires the least protection. The Near Line Sector is merely an extension of the Integrated Sector. Therefore, any security measures that apply to the Integrated Sector also apply to the Near Line Sector. Stated differently, under normal operating procedures, the Near Line Sector cannot be accessed by itself; it consequently requires the least protection.

Finally there is protection of archival data. Archival data can be protected in the standard ways—through access authorization and through encryption. However, because archival data is often placed on storage media other than disk storage, there are usually even more possibilities for protecting it.

Many archival environments include check-in/check-out processing. If a unit of data is to be protected, not allowing the data to be checked out is a good approach that adds an extra level of protection.

Figure 10.14 shows that archival data offers even more opportunities for security.

FROM THE PERSPECTIVE OF THE BUSINESS USER

Security is an absolute necessity in the eyes of the business user. The business user simply takes for granted that data is somehow safe.

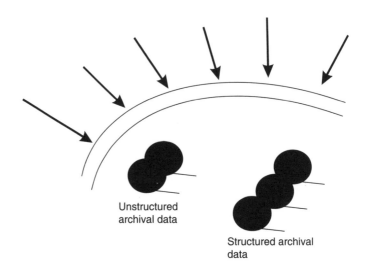

Unstructured
archival data

Structured archival
data

■ **FIGURE 10.14** Oftentimes the archival environment can have its own separate levels of security.

Most end users are not experts in security. Most business users want security to be there but do not want to see any manifestation of security.

That can be a problem. Some types of security are very cumbersome and do have an impact on the everyday usage of the system. It is like a line waiting for customs as a person enters a country. People expect to wait a little bit. On occasion people expect to wait more than a little bit. But people do not expect to wait for hours and hours each time they enter a country.

There is the same attitude with security in DW 2.0. People expect for there to be overhead. But the overhead had better not be prohibitive consistently.

SUMMARY

Security is a requirement for the entire DW 2.0 environment. The diversity and complexity of the DW 2.0 environment calls for different forms of security throughout the environment.

There are two basic types of security: (1) barrier security, in which blocks are placed in front of people to prevent unauthorized access; and (2) data encryption security, in which anyone can access the data, but only authorized people can make sense of the data.

There is passive security, in which no attempt is made to stop people from accessing data, but a log record is maintained of all data that is accessed. Upon sensing that an unauthorized hacking has occurred, the passive monitor reports what data has been accessed and by whom.

The raw data base dump is a form of security breach that bypasses all security measures when raw data is downloaded, and the data is examined in a raw state.

One technique for protecting data is to move as much data offline as possible. This prevents access to the data from online hacks.

Another form of security is an attack monitor that checks to see if an unusual number of unauthorized accesses to protected data are being made.

Time-variant data

One of the essences of the DW 2.0 environment is the relationship of data to time. Unlike other environments where there is no relationship between data and time, in the DW 2.0 environment all data—in one way or another—is relative to time.

ALL DATA IN DW 2.0—RELATIVE TO TIME

Figure 11.1 shows that all data in DW 2.0 is relative to time.

This fact means that when you access any given unit of data, you need to know at what time the data is accurate. Some data will represent facts from 1995. Other data will represent information from January. And other data will represent data from this morning.

In DW 2.0 then, whether it is explicit or implicit, all data has a moment in time that depicts its accuracy and relevancy. The data structure at the record level that is commonly used to make this depiction is seen by Figure 11.2.

In Figure 11.2 there are two record types. One record type is used for a snapshot of data at a single moment in time. This record type—on

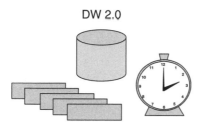

DW 2.0

■ **FIGURE 11.1**   In one way or another, all data in the DW 2.0 environment is relative to time.

Key structure

Key
Key   Key
DATE   FROM
TIME   TO
attr A   attr A
attr B   attr B
attr C   attr C
....

■ **FIGURE 11.2** Time shows up as part of the key structure of the data.

Interactive sector

■ **FIGURE 11.3** In the Interactive Sector, data is correct as of the moment of usage.

the left—has DATE and TIME as part of the key structure. The other type of record is shown on the right. It is a record that has a FROM date and a TO date. The implication is that a block of time—not a point in time—is being represented.

Note that in both cases the element of time is part of the key structure. The key is a compound key and the date component is the lower part of the compound key.

TIME RELATIVITY IN THE INTERACTIVE SECTOR

In the Interactive Sector, the time relevancy of data is somewhat different. In this sector, data values are assumed to be current as of the moment of access. For example, suppose you walk into a bank and inquire as to your balance in an account. The value that is returned to you is taken to be accurate as of the moment of access. If the bank teller says to you that you have $3971 in the bank, then that value is calculated up to the moment of access. All deposits and all withdrawals are taken into account.

Therefore, because interactive data is taken to mean accurate as of the moment of access, there is no date component to interactive data.

Figure 11.3 shows a banking transaction occurring in which interactive, up-to-the-second data is being used.

But in all other sectors of DW 2.0—in the Integrated Sector, the Near Line Sector, and the Archival Sector—data explicitly has a moment in time associated with the data.

DATA RELATIVITY ELSEWHERE IN DW 2.0

Figure 11.4 shows that each record in the Integrated Sector, the Near Line Sector, and the Archival Sector represents either a point in time or a span of time.

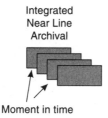

Integrated
Near Line
Archival

Moment in time

■ **FIGURE 11.4** In all other sectors of DW 2.0, each record represents a moment in time.

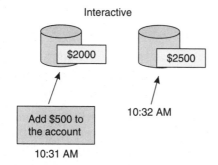

Interactive

$2000

$2500

Add $500 to
the account

10:31 AM

10:32 AM

■ **FIGURE 11.5** In the Interactive Sector, the value of data is changed as a result of an activity.

This notion of data being relative to time produces some very different ways of doing processing. In the interactive environment, update of data is done. In this case the update of data refers to the actual changing of the value of data. Figure 11.5 shows that a banking transaction is done and the value of the data is changed in the interactive environment.

At 10:31 AM there is $2000 in an account. A transaction adding $500 to the account occurs. The transaction is executed against the data in the data base and at 10:32 AM, the bank account has a balance of $2500.

The data has changed values because of the transaction.

TRANSACTIONS IN THE INTEGRATED SECTOR

Now let us consider a similar scenario in the Integrated Sector. At 10:31 AM there is a value of $2000 sitting in the integrated data base. A transaction is executed. At 10:32 a new record is placed in the data base. Now there are two records in the data base showing the different data at different moments in time.

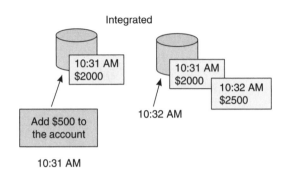

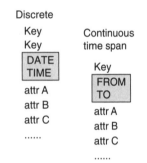

■ **FIGURE 11.7**   The two common forms of time-variant data.

Figure 11.6 shows the execution of a transaction in the Integrated Sector.

The different data found in Figures 11.5 and 11.6 make it clear that because of the difference in the way data relates to time, the content of data in the different environments is very different.

There are terms for these different types of data. Figure 11.7 shows those terms.

Where there is just a point in time, the data is called discrete data. Where there is a FROM date and a TO date, the data is called continuous time span data.

These two types of data have very different characteristics.

DISCRETE DATA

Discrete data is good for lots of variables that quickly change. As an example, consider the Dow Jones Industrial average. The Dow Jones is typically measured at the end of the day, not when a stock that is part of the Dow is bought or sold. The variables that are captured in the discrete snapshot include variables that are measured at the same moment in time. Other than that one coincidence, there is nothing that semantically ties the attributes of data to the discrete record.

Figure 11.8 shows some of the characteristics of the discrete structuring of data.

CONTINUOUS TIME SPAN DATA

Continuous time span data has a different set of characteristics. Typically, continuous time span data has very few variables in the

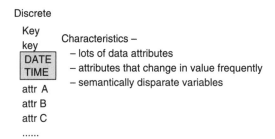

Discrete

Key
key
| DATE |
| TIME |
attr A
attr B
attr C
......

Characteristics –
– lots of data attributes
– attributes that change in value frequently
– semantically disparate variables

■ **FIGURE 11.8**   Some characteristics of discrete time-variant data.

record. And the variables that are in the record do not change often. The reason for these characteristics is that a new continuous time span record must be written every time a value changes. For example, suppose that a continuous time span record contains the following attributes:

Name
Address
Gender
Telephone Number

A new record must be written every time one of these values changes. Name changes only when a woman marries or divorces, which is not often. Address changes more frequently, perhaps as often as every 2 to 3 years. Gender never changes, at least for most people. Telephone Number changes with about the same frequency as Address changes. Thus it is safe to put these attributes into a continuous time span record.

Now consider what would happen if the attribute Job Title were put into the record. Every time the person changed jobs, every time the person was promoted, every time the person transferred jobs, every time there was a corporate reorganization, it is likely that Job Title would change. Unless there were a desire to create many continuous time span records, it would not be a good idea to place Job Title with the other, more stable, data.

Figure 11.9 shows some of the characteristics of the continuous time span records.

Great care must be taken in the design of a continuous time span record because it is possible to create a real mess if the wrong elements of data are not laced together properly. As a simple example,

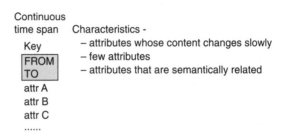

■ **FIGURE 11.9** Some characteristics of continuous time span time-variant data.

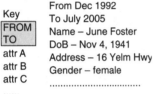

■ **FIGURE 11.10** The implications of a continuous time span record.

■ **FIGURE 11.11** A series of records are combined to form a continuous record over time.

Figure 11.10 shows some typical attributes that have been placed in a continuous time span record.

Figure 11.10 shows that the attributes Name, Date of Birth, Address, and Gender have been placed in a continuous time span record. These elements of data are appropriate because

- they are slow to change in terms of content;
- they all relate to descriptive information about an individual.

Whereas a single continuous time span record is useful, multiple continuous time span records can be strung together to logically form a much bigger record of continuity. Figure 11.11 shows several continuous time span records strung together.

A SEQUENCE OF RECORDS

The records form a continuous sequence. For example, one record ends on January 21, 2007, and the next record begins on January 22, 2007. In doing so, the records logically form a continuous set.

As a simple example, June Foster's address was on Yelm Highway until July 20, 2002. One record indicates that value. Then June moved to Apartment B, Tuscaloosa, Alabama, and her official move date was July 21, 2002. A new record is formed. Together the two records show the date and time of her change of addresses and show a continuous address wherever she was at.

Although continuous time span records are allowed to form a continuous record, they are not allowed to overlap. If there were an overlap of records, there would be a logical inconsistency. For example, if two records had address information for June Foster and they overlapped, they would show that June lived in two places at once.

NONOVERLAPPING RECORDS

Figure 11.12 shows that continuous time span record overlap is not allowed.

■ **FIGURE 11.12** Overlapping records are not allowed.

Although continuous time span records are not allowed to overlap, there can be periods of discontinuity. In 1995, June Foster sailed around the world. During that time she had no mailing address. The records of her address would show an address up until the moment she sailed and would show an address for her when she returned from her sailing voyage, but while she was on the voyage, there was no permanent address for her.

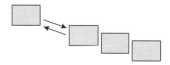

■ **FIGURE 11.13** Undefined gaps of time are allowed.

Figure 11.13 shows that gaps of discontinuity are allowed if they match the reality of the data.

When it comes to adding new records, the new record is added as of the moment in time when the business was transacted or concluded. Depending on how the records are constructed, it may be necessary to adjust the ending record.

Figure 11.14 shows the update of a new record into a sequence of continuous records.

BEGINNING AND ENDING A SEQUENCE OF RECORDS

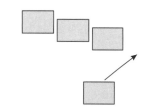

■ **FIGURE 11.14** When it comes time to update a set of time span records, a new record is added.

There are a variety of options for beginning and ending the sequence of continuous time span records.

For example, suppose that the most current record is from May 1999 to the present. Suppose there is an address change in April 2007. A new record is written whose FROM date is April 2007. But to keep the data base in synch, the previous current record has to have the TO date adjusted to show that the record ends on March 2007.

To that end, a sequence of records can begin and end anywhere. The FROM date for the first record in the sequence may have an actual date. Or the FROM date may be minus infinity. When the FROM date is minus infinity, the implication is that the record covers data from the beginning of time. Where there is a FROM date specified for the first record in a sequence, for any time before the FROM date, there simply is no definition of the data.

The ending sequence operates in much the same manner. The ending record in a continuous time span sequence may have a value in the

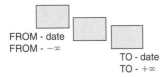

FROM - date
FROM - −∞

TO - date
TO - +∞

■ **FIGURE 11.15** There are several options for start date and stop date.

■ **FIGURE 11.16** With discrete data, there are no implications of continuity.

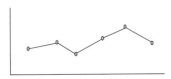

■ **FIGURE 11.17** With continuous time span data, there are definitely implications of continuity.

TO field, or the TO value may be plus infinity. When the value is plus infinity, the implication is that the record contains values that will be applied until such time as a new record is written.

For example, suppose there is a contract whose TO value is plus infinity. The implication is that the contract is valid until such time as notification is given that the contract is over.

Figure 11.15 shows some of the options for starting and stopping a sequence of continuous time span records.

CONTINUITY OF DATA

One of the limitations of discrete data is that there is no continuity between two measurements of data. For example suppose the NASDAQ closes at 2540 on Monday and at 2761 on Tuesday. Making the assumption that the NASDAQ was at a high of 2900 sometime on Tuesday is an assumption that cannot be made. In fact, *no* assumptions about the value of the NASDAQ can be made, other than at the end of the day when the measurements are made.

Figure 11.16 shows the lack of continuity of the discrete measurements of data.

Continuous time span data does not suffer from the same limitations. With continuous time span data you can make a judgment about the continuity of data over time.

Figure 11.17 shows the continuity of data that can be inferred with continuous time span data.

Whereas discrete data and continuous time span data are the most popular forms of data, they are not the only forms of time-variant data in DW 2.0. Another form of time-variant data is time-collapsed data.

TIME-COLLAPSED DATA

Figure 11.18 shows a simple example of time-collapsed data.

In time-collapsed data, there are several forms of measurement of data. When data enters the system it is measured in hours. Then at the end of the day, the 24 hours are added up to produce a recording of a day's worth of activities. The 24-hour measurements are then reset to zero. At the end of a week, the week's totals are created. Then the daily totals are reset to zero. At the end of the month, the month's

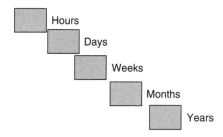

■ FIGURE 11.18   Time-collapsed data—another form of time-variant data.

totals are created. Then the weekly totals are reset to zero. At the end of the year, the year's totals are created. Then the monthly totals are reset to zero.

When this is done there is only one set of hourly totals, one set of daily totals, one set of weekly totals, and so forth. There is a tremendous savings of space.

The collapsing of time-variant data works well on the assumption that the fresher the data the more detail there needs to be. In other words, if someone wants to look at today's hourly data, they can find it readily. But if someone wants to find hourly data from 6 months ago, they are out of luck.

In many cases the assumptions hold true and collapsing of data makes sense. But where the assumptions do not hold true, then collapsing data produces an unworkable set of circumstances.

TIME VARIANCE IN THE ARCHIVAL SECTOR

The last place where time variance applies to the DW 2.0 environment is in the Archival Sector. It is a common practice to store data by years. One year's worth of data is stored, then another year's worth of data is stored. There are many good reasons for the segmentation of data in this way. But the best reason is that the semantics of data have the habit of varying slightly each year.

One year a new data element is added. The next year a data element is defined differently. The next year a calculation is made differently. Each year is slightly different from each preceding year.

Figure 11.19 shows that each year there are slight changes to the semantics of data.

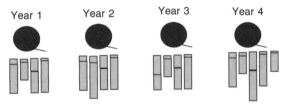

■ **FIGURE 11.19**   Archival data is stored on a year-by-year basis. Note that the data from one year to the next is never quite the same semantically.

FROM THE PERSPECTIVE OF THE END USER

Time variance is natural and normal to the business user of DW 2.0. When a business user wishes to look for data that is related to a moment in time, the end user supplies the time as a natural part of the analytic processing.

And when a business user wishes to look for the most current data, no date is supplied and the system understands that it needs to look for the most current unit of data.

So from the standpoint of a query and business user interaction, time variance is as normal and natural as making the query itself.

The business user is endowed with far greater analytical possibilities in DW 2.0 than he/she ever was in a previous environment.

The structure of DW 2.0 may require the end user to be aware that data of a certain vintage resides in one part of the DW 2.0 environment or the other. DW 2.0 may require separate queries for archival processing and against integrated data, for example.

However, the business user enjoys the benefits of performance that are gained by removing older, dormant data from the Integrated Sector. So there is a trade-off for sectoring data in DW 2.0.

SUMMARY

In one form or another, all data in DW 2.0 is relative to some moment in time.

Interactive data is current. It is accurate as of the moment of access. Other forms of data in DW 2.0 have time stamping of the record.

Time stamping takes two general forms. There is data that has a date attached. Then there is data that has a FROM and a TO field attached to the key. The first type of data is called discrete data. The second type is called continuous time span data.

Continuous time span data can be sequenced together over several records to form a long time span. The time span that is defined by continuous time span records can have gaps of discontinuity. But there can be no overlapping records.

There are other forms of time relativity in the DW 2.0 environment. There is time-collapsed data. Time-collapsed data is useful when only current data needs to be accessed and analyzed in detail. Over time the need for detail diminishes.

The other form of time relevancy in the DW 2.0 environment is that of archival data. As a rule archival data is organized into annual definitions of data. This allows for there to be slight semantic changes in data over time.

The flow of data in DW 2.0

There are many components of the DW 2.0 architecture. A next-generation DW 2.0 data warehouse includes many technologies. Building a DW 2.0 data warehouse environment is not like building a house. It is not even like building a town. It is much more like building a megalopolis.

Because of the enormity and complexity of DW 2.0's scope, it is easy to get lost. It is easy to focus in on and dwell on just one aspect of DW 2.0. If this is done, the larger picture of the architecture becomes lost. It sometimes is useful to stand back from the details of the architecture and look at the larger picture.

THE FLOW OF DATA THROUGHOUT THE ARCHITECTURE

There is a flow of data throughout the DW 2.0 architecture. In many ways, this flow is as important as the flow of blood in the human body. The flow of data feeds everything else that is accomplished by DW 2.0.

The flow of data begins as data is sent to the interactive environment. Data can be entered directly into the Interactive Sector, or data can flow into the sector through an ETL process. Exactly how data enters the Interactive Sector depends entirely on the application or applications that are found in DW 2.0.

ENTERING THE INTERACTIVE SECTOR

Data enters the Interactive Sector as application-oriented data. After it has found its way into the Interactive Sector, data is sent to the Integrated Sector. Figure 12.1 shows the basic flow of data entering the DW 2.0 environment.

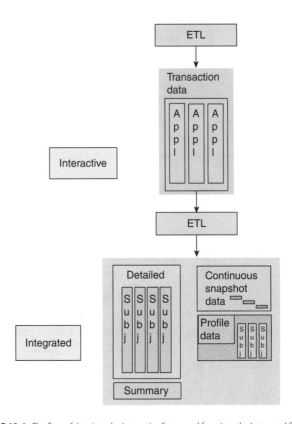

■ **FIGURE 12.1** The flow of data into the Interactive Sector and from it to the Integrated Sector.

One of the interesting aspects about the flow of data is the speed and volume at which the flow is realized. Data flows into the Interactive Sector quickly, sometimes just milliseconds after it has been transacted in the external application environment. Incoming transaction data of this nature can be considered real-time data. And of course, if transactions are executed directly from the Interactive Sector, the data has no latency.

In other cases, it may be an hour or a day before the external application transaction data enters the interactive environment. The amount of time the data is delayed in entering the interactive environment is determined entirely by the business requirements for the data. If there is a legitimate business case for having the data enter the interactive environment immediately, then the data should be entered immediately. If there is no legitimate business case for the speedy entry of data into the Interactive Sector, then the entry of the data should not be hurried.

It is important to point out that the faster the data needs to be entered into the Interactive Sector, the more complex and the more expensive the technology that is required to accomplish the goal of rapid data transfer will be.

THE ROLE OF ETL

The data coming from the external applications normally enters the Interactive Sector by means of ETL processing. It is possible, but not very common, for data to be placed in the Interactive Sector by means of a simple file transfer. It is much more likely that the data will enter through standard ETL technology.

Data passing into the Integrated Sector comes from the Interactive Sector. It is possible to have data enter the Integrated Sector directly, without passing through the Interactive Sector. Normal processing occurs as data passes into the Integrated Sector from the Interactive Sector. The normal way that data enters the Integrated Sector is through ETL processing. The ETL process reorganizes the data from an application-oriented structure into a corporate data structure.

DATA FLOW INTO THE INTEGRATED SECTOR

The flow of data into the Integrated Sector is more relaxed in terms of speed compared to the flow of data to the Interactive Sector from the Integrated Sector. Data flows into the integrated environment on a periodic basis—overnight, weekly, monthly, or even quarterly in some cases. Figure 12.2 depicts the speed of the flow of data into the Integrated Sector.

Data flows into the Interactive Sector in small, fast spurts. Data records enter this sector one at a time. It is not normal for an entire file or large set of records to be passed into the Interactive Sector all at once. Data enters the Interactive Sector like a rainfall, not a flood.

The event that sets the stage for the entry of data into the Integrated Sector is the execution of a transaction. As soon as a transaction is completed, the data it contains is ready to be entered into the Integrated Sector. Of course, transaction records can be batched together and entered en masse. But the gathering and queuing of the transactions prior to entry into the Interactive Sector slow transaction immeasurably and defeat one of the goals of the interactive process.

The trigger for the transfer of data into the Integrated Sector is simple: the passing of time. In some cases, data needs to be entered into

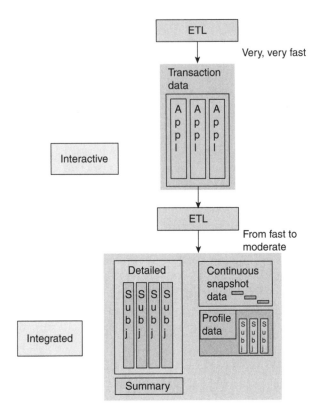

■ FIGURE 12.2 The rates of flow.

the Integrated Sector quickly, on an hourly basis. In other cases, data can wait to be transferred on an overnight basis. As a rule, if the data required for a report needs to be up to the second, the report should be created using the data found in the Interactive Sector. Normally it is a mistake to generate reports or analyses that require immediacy or real-time data from the Integrated Sector. Reports and analyses based on integrated data are of a strategic nature and should not depend on up-to-the-second data accuracy. Therefore, the movement of data from the Interactive Sector to the Integrated Sector can be done on a somewhat more relaxed schedule.

Figure 12.3 shows the triggers that cause movement of data from external applications to the Interactive Sector and from the Interactive Sector to the Integrated Sector.

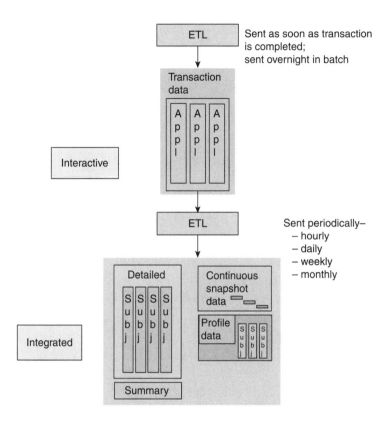

■ **FIGURE 12.3** The triggers that determine when data moves to different sectors.

DATA FLOW INTO THE NEAR LINE SECTOR

As important as the flow of data from the external applications to the Interactive Sector and that from the Interactive Sector to the Integrated Sector are, they are not the only major data flows in the DW 2.0 data warehouse. The flow of data from the Integrated Sector to the Near Line Sector is another important data flow in the DW 2.0 environment. This flow is optional and occurs when

- there is a lot of data in the Integrated Sector;
- some portion of the data in the Interactive Sector is dormant;
- where there is a desire for access to data in the Integrated Sector.

If data in the Integrated Sector does not meet these criteria, then there is no need for moving it to the Near Line Sector. In many ways, the Near Line Sector acts like a cache for the data in the Integrated Sector. Data is placed in the Near Line Sector when it is not likely to be needed very frequently.

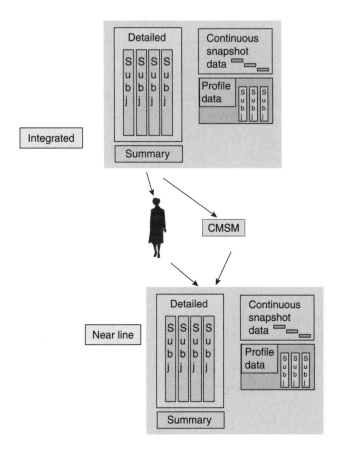

■ **FIGURE 12.4** The flow of data from the Integrated Sector to the Near Line Sector.

The Near Line Sector is based on nondisk storage. Consequently, near-line data storage is able to be stored much less expensively, and this sector is capable of holding vast amounts of data.

Figure 12.4 illustrates the flow of data from the Integrated Sector to the Near Line Sector.

The flow of the data from the Integrated Sector is slow. Data is generally removed from the Integrated Sector only in large chunks, periodically—once a month, once a quarter.

A decrease in the probability of data access is the sole criterion for moving data from the Integrated Sector to the Near Line Sector. Moving data to the Near Line Sector reduces the volume of data in the Integrated Sector. This lowers the cost of the data warehouse environment and improves performance. Ridding the integrated environment of data that is not accessed very often frees disk storage in the integrated environment for data that has a high probability of access.

DATA FLOW INTO THE ARCHIVAL SECTOR

Data also moves from the Integrated Sector to the Archival Sector. There is a key difference between data being moved from the Integrated Sector to the Archival Sector and integrated data being moved to the Near Line Sector.

When data is moved to the Near Line Sector, the structure and format of the data are preserved. This means data can be moved quickly and smoothly back to the Integrated Sector from the Near Line Sector when necessary. The Near Line Sector is designed to support access of data in the Integrated Sector.

In contrast, when data is moved to the Archival Sector, there is no intention of quickly moving the data back to the Integrated Sector. The purpose of the Archival Sector is to preserve data for a long period of time. At some point in the future, data may need to be retrieved from the archival environment and restored in a place for a special analysis, or may even be sent back to the integrated environment, but there is no intention of immediate and detailed support of the integrated environment by the archival environment. Immediate and exclusive support of the Integrated Sector is the role of the Near Line Sector.

Data is removed to the Archival Sector for the purpose of eliminating data that has a low probability of access. Figure 12.5 illustrates the movement of data from the Integrated Sector to the Archival Sector.

The speed of data flow from the integrated environment to the Archival Sector is slow. Integrated data is typically retired to the Archival Sector on a quarterly or even annual cycle.

THE FALLING PROBABILITY OF DATA ACCESS

The trigger for the movement of data from the Integrated Sector to the Archival Sector is when the probability of access of the integrated data has dropped. There are two basic ways to determine that the probability of data access has fallen. One way is based on date. For example, all data older than 3 years is removed from the Integrated Sector.

Another way to determine the probability of data access is by using a data warehouse monitor. Data warehouse monitors examine the accesses made to data in the Integrated Sector.

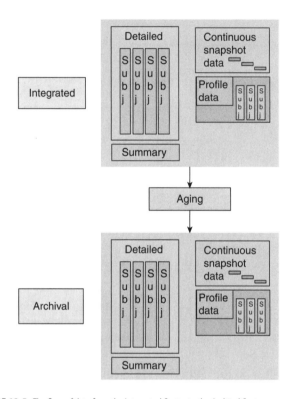

■ **FIGURE 12.5** The flow of data from the Integrated Sector to the Archival Sector.

Between the two approaches to determine the probability of access, the usage of a data warehouse monitor is by far the most accurate approach.

While the data movements that have been discussed can be considered the normal day-to-day migration of data in the DW 2.0 data warehouse environment, two other types of data movement are worthy of note.

EXCEPTION-BASED FLOW OF DATA

The next two movements of data in the DW 2.0 environment are executed only on a limited need-for-data basis.

The first nonnormal movement of data is the transfer of data from the archival environment back to the Integrated Sector. In this case there is data that, for whatever reason, has been deemed to be of use in standard analytical processing. This means, among other things, that the probability of access of the data has been elevated, and because the probability of access is high, the data properly belongs in the Integrated Sector.

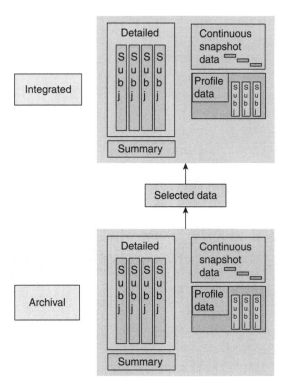

■ **FIGURE 12.6** Occasionally there is a need to move data from the archival environment to the integrated environment.

Usually data is moved to the Integrated Sector from the Archival Sector as a large block, not a few records at a time. In all cases, the transfer of archival data back to the Integrated Sector is done on an on-demand basis.

Figure 12.6 depicts the movement of data from the Archival Sector to the Integrated Sector.

The other nonnormal movement of data occurs when data from the near-line environment needs to be returned to the integrated environment. This data transfer can be accomplished in two ways. The CMSM software that sits between the two environments can be used to manage the relay of individual records of data. The CMSM tool places single records in the Integrated Sector, and the records are made to appear as if they have always resided in the Integrated Sector. The exchange is done so quickly that there is no serious degradation of system performance. The end user makes a query, and the system automatically senses that some of the requested data is in near-line

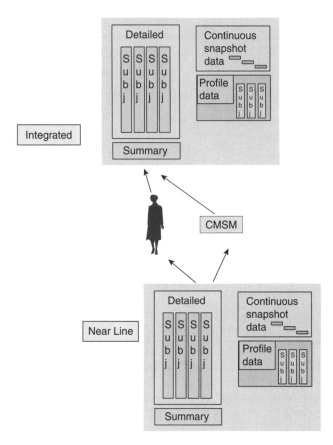

■ **FIGURE 12.7** The movement of data into the Integrated Sector from the Near Line Sector.

storage. The system uses the CMSM tool to find, fetch, and place the data in integrated storage, and then the query is fulfilled.

The second nonnormal movement of data, from the Near Line Sector to the Integrated Sector, occurs in bulk batch mode, when whole sections of data are moved. In this case the data may be moved either by the CMSM software or manually. In any case, the older data is moved back to the integrated environment because the anticipated probability of access has risen. Figure 12.7 depicts the movement of data to the Integrated Sector from the Near Line Sector.

There is one final movement of data in the DW 2.0 environment that is worthy of discussion—the movement of data from the Integrated Sector to the Interactive Sector, also known as a data "back flow."

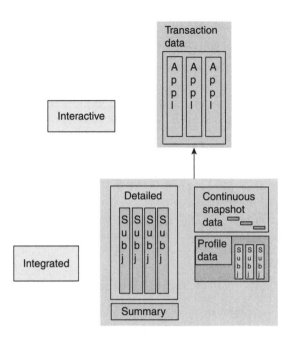

■ **FIGURE 12.8** Back flow of data to the Interactive Sector.

The movement of data from the Integrated Sector to the Interactive Sector occurs infrequently. Usually the volume of data involved is not large. When this back flow occurs, it must be done without disruption of the online performance that is an essential part of the interactive environment. Figure 12.8 depicts the back flow of data from the Integrated Sector to the Interactive Sector.

FROM THE PERSPECTIVE OF THE BUSINESS USER

The flow of data throughout the DW 2.0 environment is a natural and normal feature. The business user must be aware of such a flow, but he/she does not have to partake in any of the mechanics of the flow.

There is only one circumstance in which the business user is involved in the flow of data throughout DW 2.0 and that case is when the business user needs to alert the system administrators that there is a need to pull data from the archival environment or the Near Line Sector back into the Integrated Sector. This request is often called a staging request. Before a query is submitted, there is a staging request. The staging request tells what data parameters are needed to select the data from near-line or archival processing. In addition the staging request tells the system how long the data needs to remain in integrated storage.

Some data is part of a large study and needs to be placed in integrated storage for a long period of time. Other data is needed for only a short duration. Once this data is placed in integrated storage and is used, it can then be safely removed from the Integrated Sector.

But other than these brief interactions, the flow of data inside DW 2.0 continues at a rate unknown to the business user.

The flow of data throughout DW 2.0 is like the flow of gasoline in the combustion engine. The driver knows that a flow is occurring but trusts the combustion engine to operate properly.

SUMMARY

Data flows throughout the DW 2.0 environment.

Data enters the Interactive Sector either directly or through ETL from an external application. Data flows to the Integrated Sector through the ETL process, coming from the Interactive Sector.

Data flows from the Interactive Sector to the Near Line Sector or the Archival Sector as it ages.

On a limited basis, data may flow from the Archival Sector back to the Integrated Sector, and occasionally data flows from the Near Line Sector to the Integrated Sector.

13

ETL processing and DW 2.0

One of the most important processes in the DW 2.0 environment is ETL—extract/transform/load processing. ETL processing gathers, cleanses, and integrates data as it enters the Interactive Sector or as it passes through the Interactive Sector to the Integrated Sector. ETL processing is fundamental to the day-to-day operation of the DW 2.0 environment.

CHANGING STATES OF DATA

ETL is representative of something even more powerful than the mere flow of data. ETL is the mechanism by which data changes its state. As data passes through and is transformed by ETL processing, it undergoes a fundamental change in state. It evolves from an application state to a corporate state. This fundamental change lies at the heart of the rationale and existence of the DW 2.0 environment.

ETL does not just accomplish the collection and movement of data. ETL processing is the profound act of changing the state of data, and that is why ETL is an essential component of DW 2.0.

WHERE ETL FITS

Figure 13.1 illustrates where the ETL processing fits in DW 2.0.

ETL processing does a lot. It gathers old legacy data from technologies that have not been used as a primary DBMS technology for years, such as IMS, VSAM, CICS, IDMS, Model 204, and Adabas. Gathering the old legacy data is a nontrivial act, as each interface to a legacy application environment requires its own technology.

After the legacy data is gathered, the real work of data transformation begins. The problem with older legacy systems is that they were never

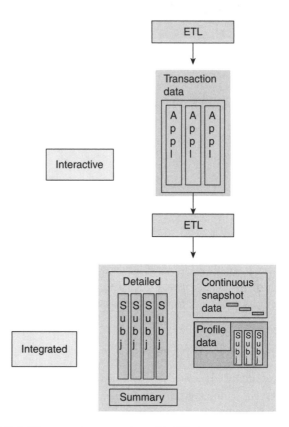

■ **FIGURE 13.1** ETL processing is an essential part of the DW 2.0 environment.

designed to work together. There are differences in structure, format, calculations, definitions of data, and other semantic differences. In short, the old legacy application data needs a lot of work before it is fit for the corporate data environment, and it is the job of ETL to make the necessary major corrections to the legacy data.

FROM APPLICATION DATA TO CORPORATE DATA

Figure 13.2 depicts the transformation of application data to corporate data by ETL.

ETL processing can operate in two basic modes: online, real-time processing and batch processing.

ETL IN ONLINE MODE

When ETL processing is done in an online mode, the length of time from the moment of execution of the legacy transaction until the

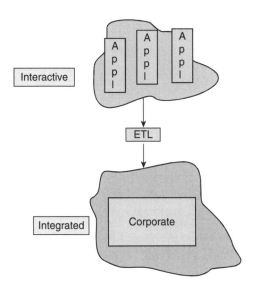

■ **FIGURE 13.2**   The real function of ETL is to convert application data to corporate data.

transaction is reflected in the DW 2.0 environment is measured in very small units of time, such as milliseconds. For example, a transaction is executed by a bank teller at 11:32 AM in the legacy systems environment. ETL captures the fact that the transaction has been executed, and at 11:32 AM and 10 milliseconds the transaction finds its way into the DW 2.0 environment. The transaction has been sent to the DW 2.0 environment so quickly that the transaction seems to appear simultaneously in the legacy environment and the DW 2.0 environment. In reality, the transaction has not been transacted and processed through ETL simultaneously, but it has happened so fast that for practical purposes it has happened simultaneously.

The problem with real-time ETL is that speed is generally considered the main success factor. Because speed is the main factor of success, not much transformation can be done to the data coming into DW 2.0.

ETL IN BATCH MODE

The other mode of ETL processing is batch mode. In batch mode, transactions in the legacy environment are stored and batched together. Then, at a convenient time (perhaps overnight), the batch of legacy transactions is run through the ETL process. This means that from the time the transaction has been processed in the legacy environment until DW 2.0 is aware of the transaction 24 hours or more may have elapsed. One of the advantages of batch ETL is that there is plenty of time for significant data transformation processing.

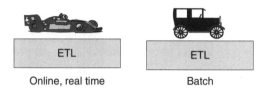

Online, real time   Batch

■ **FIGURE 13.3** There are two modes that ETL operates in.

As a rule, real-time ETL is expensive and not much transformation processing can be done. Batch ETL processing does not move the data through the system as quickly, but is much less expensive and it supports much more data transformation.

Whether to use batch or real-time ETL processing is more of a business decision than a technology decision. Some data—simple transaction data, such as a bank withdrawal—often can be done in real time. But more cumbersome, more complex data cannot be done in real time. However, in the case of batch ETL transactions, there often is no business justification for a speedy movement through the ETL process. It is more important to take the time to do the transformation properly than it is to do it quickly.

Figure 13.3 depicts the two modes of ETL processing.

SOURCE AND TARGET

The analyst determines what ETL logic must be applied to source operational data before it enters the data warehouse by building a source-to-target data map. The mapping is simply a statement of what data must be placed in the DW 2.0 environment, where that data comes from, and the logic or calculation or reformatting that must be done to the data. The source of the data—the operational application systems environment—is called the "source." The place where the data lands in the DW 2.0 environment is called the "target." The source system in which the data originates is also called the "system of record."

The following questions must be answered during the source-to-target mapping of each unit of data destined for the DW 2.0 environment:

- What specific units of data in what source system will constitute the data warehouse data?
- How should multiple sources of the same data be resolved?
- What must be done if default values of data are needed?
- What logic must be used to adjust the data to a corporate state?

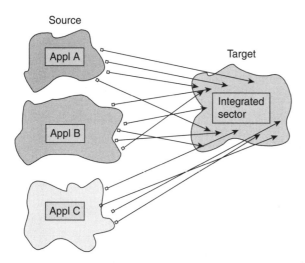

■ **FIGURE 13.4**   A mapping from the source to the target.

- What calculations must be applied to reconstitute the data into a corporate state?
- What restructuring or reformatting must be done to create corporate data?

The source-to-target data mapping needs to be complete before the ETL process design commences.

AN ETL MAPPING

Figure 13.4 depicts an ETL data source-to-target mapping.

One of the essential components governing the data that is mapped into the DW 2.0 environment is business rules. Business rules have a profound effect on the data that is sent to DW 2.0. Business rules reveal the correctness or quality of data. But, they often are different for different legacy systems. The ETL processing must therefore act like a referee and determine which business rule has precedence over all other business rules for each unit of data.

Figure 13.5 indicates that business rules are also necessary input to ETL specifications, along with source-to-target mapping.

CHANGING STATES—AN EXAMPLE

Data changes states as it passes through ETL processing. ETL processing transforms data from an application state to a corporate state.

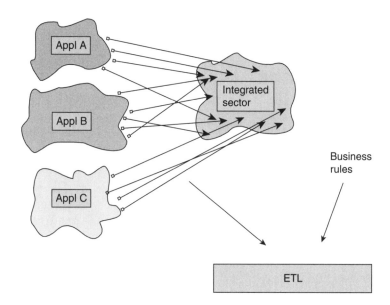

■ **FIGURE 13.5** The mapping and business rules are used to determine how ETL processing should be done.

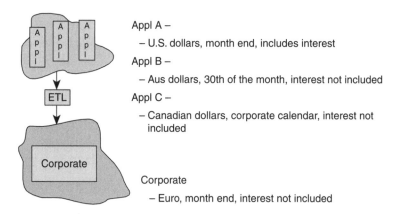

Appl A –
– U.S. dollars, month end, includes interest

Appl B –
– Aus dollars, 30th of the month, interest not included

Appl C –
– Canadian dollars, corporate calendar, interest not included

Corporate
– Euro, month end, interest not included

■ **FIGURE 13.6** Although there will be some similarity of data between the Interactive Sector and the Integrated Sector, the data is not identical and is not redundant.

To the uninitiated it is not apparent that anything unusual is happening here. Indeed, in many cases data is merely passed from one environment to the next, because there is no difference between its operational and its corporate state. But in other cases, a significant transformation of data is necessary.

Figure 13.6 illustrates some simple transformations.

This figure illustrates that application data for the same thing can exist in different forms. There are different kinds of dollars, there are different calculations of interest, and there are different closing dates for accounting. To achieve a corporate understanding of this data, all of these differences must be reconciled. The organization's business rules might dictate that in the corporate data state, cash is measured in terms of euros, the last day of the month is the closing date for all accounting activities, and interest is not included in certain calculations. It is the ETL process that will make these adjustments as the source data is passed into the data warehouse environment.

In some cases people say—"I can't trust DW 2.0 data because I ran an operational report last week, then I ran the same report from the DW 2.0 environment. I got different answers, so that means that DW 2.0 data can't be trusted." This confusion happens when people do not understand the difference between corporate and application data. The truth is that reports coming from these different sources ought to be different.

To understand why that is the case, imagine that the closing date used in a corporation's accounting system is the 28th of the month. A report is run from this application showing the closing balance as $108,076. Now the transaction is run through the ETL process. Suppose the corporate accounting close date is the 31st of the month. Now suppose that a transaction occurred on the 29th of the month. In the application, the transaction will show up in one month's total. In the corporate data the transaction will show up in another month's total.

There indeed are differences in data, but the differences are caused by the transformation from application data to corporate data.

MORE COMPLEX TRANSFORMATIONS

The data transformations depicted in Figure 13.6 are actually easy transformations. Transformations become difficult when data keys have to be transformed. Usually when keys have to be transformed, one application is selected as having the proper designation for keys and all other applications have to conform to the key structure. Whereas most key transformations are resolved by selection of one key style and structure, occasionally data keys need to be completely converted to or replaced with an entirely new key format during ETL processing. Regardless of the approach, the rules for data key transformation must be specified during the design of the ETL routines.

ETL AND THROUGHPUT

Data throughput is another concern with ETL processing. Even with the simplest of ETL processing involving only the execution of a single process, if throughput is a problem, the ETL process can be parallelized.

When an ETL job stream is parallelized, part of the data passes through one ETL process, and another part of the job stream passes through another copy of the same ETL process. The ETL process and job streams are replicated as many times at it takes to achieve satisfactory ETL throughput. The creation of parallel ETL throughput streams greatly reduces the elapsed time for the execution of the entire data ETL process.

Figure 13.7 suggests that the ETL process can be parallelized.

From a theoretical perspective, there are a lot of transformation activities that have to be accomplished by ETL processing. Any one transformation activity is usually not terribly complex, but the fact that *all* of the transformations have to be accomplished in a single pass of the data makes ETL processing truly complex.

Figure 13.8 illustrates some typical transformations that have to be done by ETL processing.

This figure illustrates the many detailed types of data transformation that may occur inside of an ETL process, including:

- Summarization processing
- Adjustment of date formats

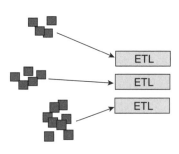

■ **FIGURE 13.7** If throughput is an issue, ETL processing can be parallelized.

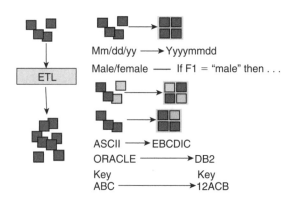

■ **FIGURE 13.8** The primary purpose of ETL is transformation.

- Specification of logic—such as conversion of "Male/Female" to "M/F"
- Aggregation of data
- Provision of default values
- Conversion from ASCII to EBCDIC
- DBMS conversions
- Restructure or creation of keys

This short list contains just a *few* of the transformation activities that need to be accomplished by ETL processing.

ETL AND METADATA

Although the primary purpose of ETL is to create corporate data from application data, ETL processing has a separate and secondary purpose. ETL can also be used to create an auditable record of the transformation of the data—a data transformation audit trail that needs to be placed into metadata. Metadata then becomes an important secondary by-product of ETL processing, as suggested in Figure 13.9.

Metadata is a natural by-product that is easily produced by ETL processing. The source-to-target data mapping that the analyst creates during ETL design is itself a metadata design. In fact, all source-to-target data mapping really is nothing but a data transformation audit trail and therefore is metadata. Source-to-target data mapping is "data about data," specifically data about how data is to be transformed on its way into the data warehouse, and therefore the design for ETL data transformation tracking.

The ETL data transformation metadata can be a very useful analytical tool for the decision support analyst. End users often want to find out more about the data used in an analysis. The metadata by-products of ETL data transformation processing can be a handy first step toward satisfying the end user.

ETL AND AN AUDIT TRAIL

Just as it is important as capturing and making available metadata when source data passes through ETL processing, there is also a need for an audit trail of ETL processing.

Figure 13.10 depicts the audit trail that can be left by metadata passing through an ETL process. The audit trail is very similar to metadata. However, the audit trail contains much more detailed data

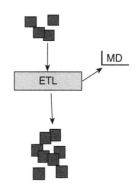

■ **FIGURE 13.9** Metadata is a by-product of ETL processing.

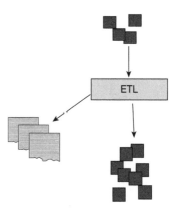

■ **FIGURE 13.10** An audit trail is often left by ETL processing.

concerning the passage of data through the ETL process. Typically data transformation audit trail records include:

- Number of records processed in a day
- Successful job completion indicators for a batch run through the ETL process
- Number of ETL failures in a day
- Reasons for any ETL failures
- Description of how the failures will be resolved
- Amount of new records added to the DW 2.0 environment
- Number of records read into the ETL process
- Length of time the ETL process was up and running

ETL AND DATA QUALITY

As data passes through the ETL process, there is an opportunity to do some basic data quality examination and even editing. Because source data must pass through ETL processing in any case on its way to the data warehouse, only a few additional resources are required to assess data quality along the way. For example, the following data quality checks are easily done as part of ETL processing:

- Domain checks
- Range checks
- Reasonability checks

It should be noted that any data quality assurance done during ETL processing is limited to processing that can be done with one record in hand. In other words, if data quality requires multiple records to determine the validity or quality of data, that type of data quality verification/checking is hard to do with ETL.

Figure 13.11 suggests that data quality checking can be done as part of ETL processing.

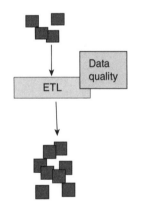

■ **FIGURE 13.11** ETL provides an excellent opportunity for data quality checks.

CREATING ETL

There are two basic ways that ETL programs can be created. One method is to create ETL programs from scratch using a programming language or tool such as VB.Net, C, or C++. The other approach is to purchase a third-party vendor's software package designed to enable ETL process development, such as Ascential, Informatica, or Talend. There are pros and cons to both approaches.

The advantage of ETL processing with home-grown software is that it can perform any kind of logic that is desired and specified by the organization. Anything that can be programmed can be included in an ETL program. The disadvantage of home-grown code is that most ETL programs are very standard routines that do not require any special processing. Furthermore, maintaining code over time can be an undesirable, expensive, resource-consuming approach.

The advantage of third-party software is that ETL processes based on third-party software can be created much more quickly than home-grown software. In addition, third-party software can be maintained much more easily than home-grown code. The problem is that almost always a few special data transformation algorithms are needed that are so complicated that they are difficult to incorporate into any pre-programmed third-party technology.

A good solution is to build 95% of the needed ETL transformation programs using a third-party tool and build the remaining 5% or less of the required ETL programs with home-grown code.

CODE CREATION OR PARAMETRICALLY DRIVEN ETL

Some ETL operates on the basis of code creation, and other ETL code operates on the basis of a parametrically fed program that does not generate special code. Figure 13.12 depicts the choices in the way ETL is to be implemented.

ETL AND REJECTS

One of the major challenges of ETL processing is how to handle rejected data. What happens when a source system record contains a value that is incorrect? There are several approaches for handling of this circumstance. Each approach has its advantages and disadvantages.

The first approach is not to let rejected data pass into the data warehouse environment at all. Although this approach maintains pristine data in the data warehouse, it can prevent the inclusion of other data that might be correct and useful. For example, suppose a transaction has 10 elements of data. If one element of data is incorrect, does that warrant exclusion of the other nine valid pieces of data from the data warehouse?

A second approach is to supply default values for data that is known to be incorrect. This approach allows all of the accompanying valid

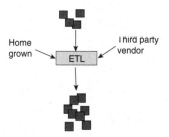

■ FIGURE 13.12 ETL can be home-grown, from a third-party vendor, or both.

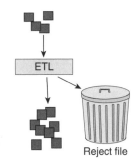

■ **FIGURE 13.13** Reject files must be handled carefully.

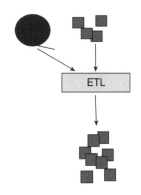

■ **FIGURE 13.14** Changed data capture logs are sometimes very useful.

data to be entered into the data warehouse. The important caveat is that this approach may produce very irregular or questionable results if/when data summaries are made or other data analysis is done.

The third approach is to place invalid data in the data warehouse and then flag it so analysts know that the data is invalid.

A fourth approach is to create a reject file. This is a good approach as long as the reject file can be reconciled in an automated manner. But if the reject record has to be reconciled manually, then this is usually a very poor approach and is not recommended.

Figure 13.13 depicts the creation of a reject file.

CHANGED DATA CAPTURE

A special form of data input into the DW 2.0 Interactive Sector is "changed data capture," or CDC. CDC is done when a log tape is created as a result of making transactions. It is much more efficient and accurate to capture transaction activities off of a log tape than it is to search a file looking for possible activities.

But there are several problems with using log tapes for this purpose. The first problem is that operations is often unwilling to part with what amounts to one of their essential cornerstone technologies. Log tapes are needed during backup and recovery. Should operations lose one of these tapes, the results could be disastrous.

The second problem is that backup log files are created for the purpose of data recovery, not for input to the data warehouse environment. The format of log tapes is arcane, at best, and is difficult to decipher.

Figure 13.14 depicts the usage of a log tape as input to the ETL process.

ELT

Extract/load/transform (ELT) processing is closely related to but not the same thing as ETL. The difference between ETL and ELT is that in ETL, data is extracted, transformed, and then loaded into the data warehouse, whereas in ELT processing data is extracted and loaded into the data warehouse and then transformed. In other words, with ELT, the data is not transformed until after it actually arrives in the data warehouse. There are some fundamental problems with ELT.

The first problem is the cleanliness of data. It is entirely possible to extract and load data and then forget to do the transformation process. This, of course, is not acceptable.

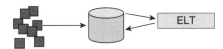

■ **FIGURE 13.15** Another form of ETL is ELT.

The ELT approach also invites data integrity problems when data transformation is done after the data has been loaded into the data warehouse. At one moment in time there is a value of 100 for some unit of data. At the next moment there is a value of 35. At this point the data warehouse has lost its credibility. Stated differently, with ELT there is no integrity of data in the data warehouse environment.

Figure 13.15 depicts an ELT process.

Because of its inherent problems, ELT processing is not a good architectural choice.

FROM THE PERSPECTIVE OF THE BUSINESS USER

ETL is a part of the DW 2.0 environment that the business user does get involved in. In most other aspects of DW 2.0 the business user is a casual observer. In most other cases he/she is aware of what is happening inside the system but is not actively involved.

Not so with ETL. The business user needs to become involved with ETL because it is through ETL that the transformation from application data to corporate data is made. And in many cases it is only the business user that knows how that transformation is to be done properly.

Stated differently, the business user has the final right of approval for determining how the transformation is to be done. Therefore the business user needs to be actively involved in the creation of the requirements for transformation.

Usually the business user does not actually execute the ETL procedures. Instead he/she tells the technician how the transformation should be made.

As a rule it is a good idea to have the specifications for transformation written down. The act of writing down the specifications can be very important. In the case in which there is a question after the fact, having the specifications written down is a good way to determine where the error has been made. But there is another case in which writing down the specifications is important, and that is where the specifications are converted into metadata.

Once the transformation specifications are converted into metadata, they are then available to the analyst who wants to look at the heritage of data. Answering the question, "Where did this data come from and what does this data mean?" becomes easy to do with metadata that reflects the transformation process.

Business users are selected as the authority for transformation based on their knowledge of the data. The business users are often called data stewards. In an ideal world each unit of data in the DW 2.0 environment has exactly one and only one data steward. In other words there is no overlap between data stewards, and each data element has one data steward.

The process of data stewardship is an ongoing process. While it is important to have data stewardship at the start of the DW 2.0 environment, it also needs to be recognized that data stewardship is necessary throughout the life of the DW 2.0 environment.

The data steward is not responsible for the day-to-day care and tending of a data base. If the load of a data base fails it is the job of the system administrator to mend the error. Instead the data steward is responsible for the care and tending of the data found in the tables. For example, if a person's age is listed as 1000 years, unless the person's name is Methuselah the data steward is responsible for correcting the error and determining how the error got into the data base in the first place.

SUMMARY

ETL is the process used to change the state of data. Data changes from an application state to a corporate state after passing through ETL. ETL processing occurs as data passes into the Interactive Sector and again as data passes from the Interactive Sector to the Integrated Sector.

ETL can be run in an online mode or a batch mode. When it is run in an online mode the emphasis is on the movement of data. When it is run in a batch mode, the emphasis is on the transformation of the data.

The place where data comes from is called the source. The place where data goes to is called the target. The logic that shows how to get from the source to the target is called the mapping. The collective source of the data for all data is called the system of record.

ETL processes can be run in a parallel manner if there is a lot of data that needs to go into the target.

A by-product of ETL is metadata describing the movement of data. Another by-product of ETL processing is an audit trail.

In addition to doing transformation, simple data quality checks can be done as part of ETL processing.

ETL can be done with home-grown processing or with third-party vendor software.

On occasion when dealing with a source that consists of a lot of transaction processing, a log file can be used as input into ETL processing. When a log file is used this way, it is commonly called changed data capture, or CDC.

DW 2.0 and the granularity manager

Nearly all of the data that passes from external sources to the Interactive Sector, or occasionally directly into the Integrated Sector, passes through an ETL process, for good reason. But on rare occasions, there is need for another type of process to move data from external sources.

THE GRANULARITY MANAGER

This type of processor is called a granularity manager. The granularity manager does something quite different from what an ETL program does.

Consider what an ETL process does. Figure 14.1 depicts normal ETL processing at a conceptual level.

Figure 14.1 represents the customary storage of different kinds of data by subject area following normal ETL processing. ETL reads a source record and then sends different parts of the record to different destinations based on the subject area to which they relate. For example, suppose a transaction is executed and produces a record about the sale of an item. The item sales data reaches the ETL process as a single record. However, in the record are elements of information about

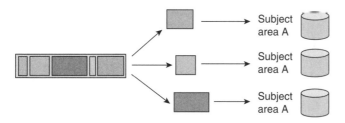

■ **FIGURE 14.1**   The normal progression of data.

very different kinds of data, such as information about revenue, about products, and about a customer. The ETL process knows that these different types of information need to be sent to different destinations. The ETL process turns the sales application transaction data into corporate, subject-oriented data when it grooms the source data to be loaded into the target data warehouse. This is one of the primary, most important functions of ETL processing.

RAISING THE LEVEL OF GRANULARITY

Data granularity management is quite different. Instead of separating data contained in a single record into subject-oriented units of data, a granularity manager actually brings data together. The need to combine or unify data does not occur very often, but it does occur. Data needs to be unified on the rare occasions when the source data state is at too low a level of detail in the external world. Click-stream data produced during Internet processing is a good example of when there is a need for a granularity manager.

When web site processing is tracked, every movement of the cursor, every movement to another page, and every entry into a new area on the screen generates a click-stream record. The activity that occurs on the web site is tracked down to the lowest level of detail. The problem with this very low-level click-stream data tracking is that most of it has no business value whatsoever.

It has been estimated that more than 90% of the data that ends up as click-stream data is useless. The nature of click-stream data tracking is that it generates a lot of this data and the data gets in the way. The useless data found in the click-stream data can create an enormous and totally unnecessary overhead.

Another example of source data at too low a level of granularity occurs when manufacturing data is collected by an analog computer. Most of the analog data is specious, but some of the analog data is really important. The important data is at too low a level of granularity, but it is needed in the DW 2.0 environment, so it must be processed by a granularity manager before entry.

FILTERING DATA

Figure 14.2 illustrates a large volume of data entering the work stream through a mechanism such as click-stream processing and then being "filtered," aggregated, or summarized.

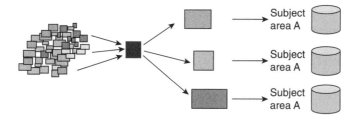

■ **FIGURE 14.2**   There are some types of data the granularity of which is too low for the data warehouse.

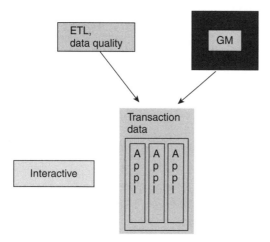

■ **FIGURE 14.3**   One place the granularity manager fits.

The granularity manager can be located when needed in several places in the DW 2.0 environment. Figure 14.3 illustrates one place where the granularity manager may be found as data enters the Interactive Sector.

A second place where a granularity manager may be required is where data enters the Integrated Sector directly. This is the case when there is no reason for data to reside in the Interactive Sector before it enters the Integrated Sector. Figure 14.4 depicts a data granularity manager positioned to process data that passes directly into the Integrated Sector.

There is one other place where the granularity manager is occasionally used, and that is when data is passed into the archival environment.

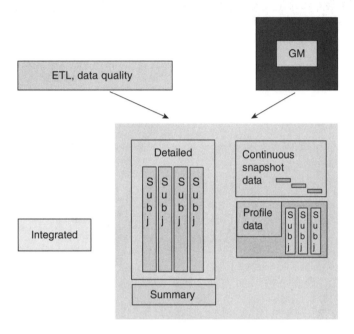

■ **FIGURE 14.4** Another place the granularity manager fits.

Figure 14.5 depicts the granularity manager's role as data enters into the archival environment.

The need for a granularity manager as data enters the archival environment is a rare occurrence. It makes sense to use a granularity manager here only when massive amounts of transactions occur in the Integrated Sector and the details of those transactions are never going to be needed for analysis.

THE FUNCTIONS OF THE GRANULARITY MANAGER

The functions that a granularity manager accomplishes are very straightforward. The granularity manager does, at the least, the following:

- Eliminate unneeded data: Records in the input stream that will have no future value to the corporation are discarded. This may be as much as 90% of the incoming data.

- Summarize: Data that will have future value to the corporate analysts can often be summarized from multiple records into a single record.

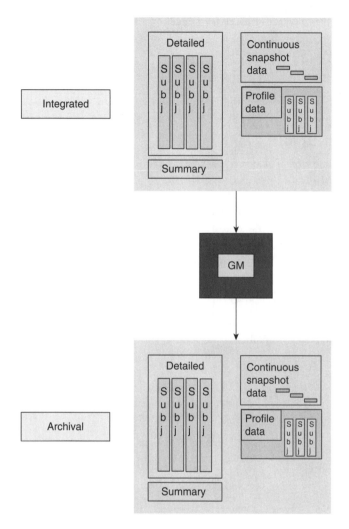

■ **FIGURE 14.5**   Yet another place the granularity manager is found.

- Aggregate: Occasionally aggregation of different kinds of data into a single record makes more sense than data summarization.

- Recast data: When data is recast it enters as input in one format and structure and exits in a different format and structure. Recasting data that originates at too low a level of granularity is a very common thing to do.

These are the activities that are accomplished by a granularity manager. The net result is a tremendous compaction of data and a weeding out of useless data. Figure 14.6 illustrates the functions of granularity management.

HOME-GROWN VERSUS THIRD-PARTY GRANULARITY MANAGERS

The data granularity management module may be created by third-party software vendors or may be home grown. There is a strong case for using third-party ETL software. The rationale for using a third-party granularity management software package is not nearly so strong. There are far fewer cases in which granularity management will be needed compared to when ETL will be needed. Customized processing requirements for granularity management are very common. Consequently, it is not unusual for home-grown software to be used for granularity management.

Figure 14.7 illustrates the home-grown and third-party options for granularity management.

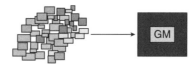

■ **FIGURE 14.6**   Granularity manager functions: eliminate, summarize, aggregate, recast.

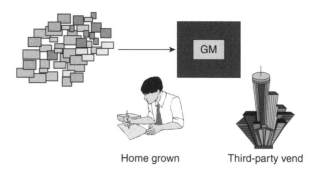

Home grown   Third-party vend

■ **FIGURE 14.7**   There are two basic ways the granularity manager is created.

PARALLELIZING THE GRANULARITY MANAGER

On occasion there will be *huge* amounts of data that will need to be processed by a data granularity manager. It is possible to run granularity management software in a parallel fashion to accommodate a large processing load. By running two or more instances of the data granularity management software in parallel, the elapsed time needed for processing can be dramatically reduced.

Figure 14.8 depicts data granularity management routines running in parallel.

METADATA AS A BY-PRODUCT

In addition to compacting data into a meaningful and useful size, granularity management can also be used for the production of metadata. Figure 14.9 depicts metadata as a by-product of granularity management.

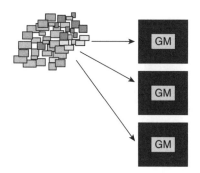

■ **FIGURE 14.8**   If warranted, the granularity manager can be run in parallel.

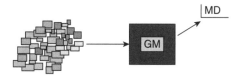

■ **FIGURE 14.9**   It is useful to produce metadata as a by-product of processing in the granularity manager.

The metadata by-products of data granularity processing may include information about the following:

- What data has been discarded
- What data has been summarized and what the summary record looks like
- What data has been aggregated and what the aggregate record looks like
- How data has been recast and what the recast record looks like

The metadata summarizes the results of granularity management processing.

FROM THE PERSPECTIVE OF THE BUSINESS USER

From the business user's perspective there is little direct interaction between the granularity manager and the end user. The only interaction is in the specification of the transformation made by the granularity manager.

The end user assumes the same responsibility for transformation specification for the granularity manager activity that the business user assumes for the specification of ETL.

SUMMARY

On occasion data exists outside of DW 2.0 at too low a level of granularity. When this is the case the data needs to be passed through a granularity manager to raise its level of granularity before it is loaded into the data warehouse.

The data granularity manager weeds out, summarizes, aggregates, or otherwise restructures data as it passes into or between the DW 2.0 sectors.

Data granularity managers can be run in parallel. The granularity manager can be home-grown software or third-party software.

Metadata is a by-product of processing data through a granularity manager.

15

DW 2.0 and performance

An information system that does not yield adequate performance is an abomination. Most people abhor waiting, especially when waiting is unnecessary and unproductive. Peoples' attitudes toward waiting are no different in the DW 2.0 environment.

An information system that does not provide good performance is simply ineffective. If performance is bad enough, the information system is useless. It is simply assumed that good performance is a feature of a good information system.

Yet good performance is not a feature that can simply be added into a system like a new function. Good performance has many facets and must be holistically designed and built into the system from the start.

GOOD PERFORMANCE—A CORNERSTONE FOR DW 2.0

Good performance is essential for an effective DW 2.0 data warehouse, and it is necessary throughout the DW 2.0 environment.

There are different kinds of performance applicable to the DW 2.0 environment. In the Interactive Sector there is online response performance, or OLTP—online transaction processing performance. OLTP performance is measured in seconds. In the Integrated Sector there is analytical performance. Depending on the analytical activity, response time may be measured in seconds or minutes. In the Archival Sector response time may be measured in terms of days. Response time is relative. Depending on what is being done and where, there is a different set of response-time measurement and expectations. Yet response time is important throughout the DW 2.0 environment.

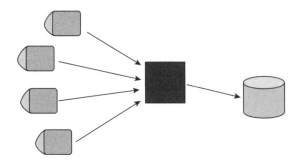

■ FIGURE 15.1   Transaction response time—2 to 3 seconds consistently.

ONLINE RESPONSE TIME

The normal expectation for online response time is 2 to 3 seconds. Online response time is often called real-time response time. Online response time is achieved in the Interactive Sector.

Figure 15.1 depicts online response time.

Online response time is measured from the moment the user presses the key that sends the transaction to the computer until the first of the response is returned to the user. A lot of processing happens from the time the transaction is entered until the first of the response is returned. The transaction is delivered to the network. The network then passes the transaction into the system. After passing through security protocols, the transaction enters a queue. It waits in the queue until system resources are available for its execution. The transaction then enters the application area of the computer where the transaction is processed. Computer code is executed and calls to the data base are done through the DBMS. The data is gathered from the data base(s) and returned to the application area. The application performs logic using the transaction, makes decisions, and may write more data into the data base. Finally, when the transaction is complete, it leaves the application area, and the final results are sent back through the network where they are displayed to the user who initiated the transaction. All of these activities must be completed in seconds to achieve good response-time performance.

The enemies of good transaction performance include:

- Lengthy activities, such as traveling up and down a network
- Input/output (I/O) into and out of a data base

- Wait times in queues or elsewhere
- Large volumes of competing transactions

ANALYTICAL RESPONSE TIME

The other type of performance consideration for the DW 2.0 environment can be called the analytical performance measurement. The analytical performance issues are relevant to the Integrated Sector, the Archival Sector, and occasionally the Near Line Sector.

Analytical response-time expectations are generally in the 10 seconds to 1 hour time range. Given the large amounts of time that performance is measured in for analytical processing, it is often assumed that performance in the analytical environment is easy to achieve. That is not the case at all.

The analytical environment is very different from the transaction environment. In the analytical environment

- the decisions being made are much more strategic than tactical;
- there is often *much* more data needed for analytical processing than is needed for transaction processing;
- there is a much less predictable flow of data throughout the day.

These fundamental differences between the transaction environment and the analytical environment allow for a much more relaxed approach to analytical response-time performance.

THE FLOW OF DATA

The flow of data through the system is generally the same as that described for transactional processing. There are two places where there are key differences in data flow:

- The volume of data required by analytical processing is significantly greater than that needed for transaction processing. Gathering large amounts of data for analysis requires lots of data input/output activity. I/O activity slows the computer down significantly, because I/O operates at mechanical speeds instead of electronic speeds like other operations inside the computer.

- The queue time for an analytical transaction is dependent on the other analytical activities that are in the queue waiting to be

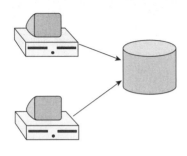

■ FIGURE 15.2 Analytical response time—15 seconds to 24 hours.

executed. In the case of analytical activities, the queue time is both unpredictable and potentially long.

Response time for analytical activities are therefore often long and unpredictable.

Figure 15.2 illustrates analytical activities being done against data.

Any discussion of performance must address the impact of poor performance. The impacts of poor performance on transactional processing and analytical processing are quite different.

QUEUES

When the performance of transactional processing goes bad, there is an impact on the business of the corporation, at the place where customers meet the corporation. Waiting queues form. Consider a bank or an airline check-in counter. Under normal operation, when customers arrive at the bank or the airport, there may be a few people in line in front of them—on a good day there will be just two or three people in line. On a bad day at the bank or airport, there may be 20 people in line. The speed with which customers move up in the line and receive service is a function of the length of the waiting line and their position in it.

To achieve smooth operations, the bank clerk or the airlines reservation clerk must have good response time as the clerk is transacting the business of the customer. Response time must be almost immediate and must be consistent. When transaction response time is good, the clerk can serve each customer in a short amount of time, and the customer waiting line advances at a steady, reasonable rate.

But consider what happens when the bank or the airline clerk does not get good system-response time. It takes a long time to serve any single customer, which is bad for the customer who has the clerk's attention. But it is even worse for the customers who are waiting in line. The queue builds and builds until there is an unacceptably large number of people in the waiting line.

So the real negative impact on transaction response time is not the execution of any given transaction, but rather the cumulative effect on the transactions that build up in the queue waiting to reach the position of execution. The worst part of poor transaction performance and long queue times is the negative impact that is felt directly by the customers of the enterprise.

Figure 15.3 illustrates the intolerably long queue that can form when basic transaction processing goes bad.

Poor performance in the analytical environment has an equally negative impact. It affects the productivity of the analyst preparing information for management.

HEURISTIC PROCESSING

The negative impact of poor performance on the analytical community is related to the way in which analytical processing is done. Figure 15.4 depicts the heuristic nature of analytical processing.

When processing is done heuristically, there can be very little planning of the analytical activity, because each step in a heuristic analysis depends entirely on the results achieved in the previous step.

An organization sets out to do heuristic analysis. The first results are obtained. The results are analyzed. Only then does it become clear what the next step of analysis needs to be. The second step is done and more results are achieved. Now the results of the second step are analyzed, and the activities for the third step of analysis become clear. The process continues until the final results are achieved.

The fact is that in heuristic analytical processing, there can be no organized, planned path through the analysis.

ANALYTICAL PRODUCTIVITY AND RESPONSE TIME

The speed with which heuristic analysis can be done depends entirely on how fast an analytical process can be done. Stated differently, the faster analytical processing can be done, the faster the final results can be achieved.

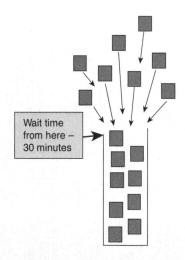

Wait time from here – 30 minutes

■ **FIGURE 15.3** There is a very negative impact on the business when OLTP response time goes bad.

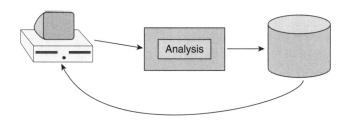

Analysis

■ **FIGURE 15.4** Heuristic processing is the essence of analytic processing.

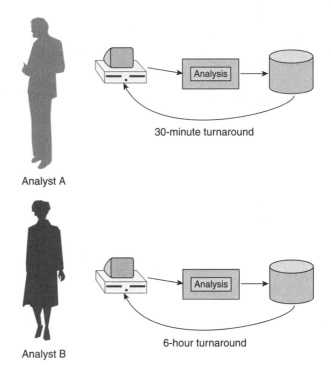

■ **FIGURE 15.5** Consider the productivity of two analysts whose only difference is in the speed of their analytical turnaround.

Figure 15.5 contrasts the performance of two analysts.

The only real difference between the two analysts shown in Figure 15.5 is the speed with which analysis can be done. Analyst A is able to turn his heuristic analysis around in 30 minutes. Analyst B needs 6 hours to turn her heuristic analysis around.

There is another major difference in poor performance between transactional processing and analytical processing. In transactional processing poor results are felt by the customers of the corporation. In contrast, poor analytical results are felt internally, by the analysts of the corporation. Poor transaction processing response times are much more devastating in the short term for the corporation.

MANY FACETS TO PERFORMANCE

There are many facets to achieving good performance. A holistic approach to performance is required. Performance must be addressed on many fronts, all at the same time. The following sections describe what needs to be done to achieve good long-term performance in the DW 2.0 environment.

INDEXING

One of the simplest design solutions for data warehouse performance is to create an index of the data. If this is done, the system does not have to do a sequential search of all of the data to locate and retrieve requested information.

Figure 15.6 depicts an indexing of data.

A data base without an index is shown at the top of Figure 15.6. When a person accesses this data base, the entire data base must be searched to find a record.

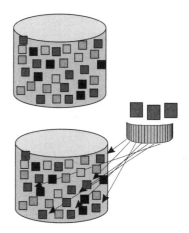

■ **FIGURE 15.6**   Searching for data without an index and with an index.

The data base on the bottom of Figure 15.6 has an index. Now when a person wants to find something in the data base, the index is consulted first. If the data can be found in the index, it is accessed directly. The result is a tremendous savings in the time required for the access of data.

It would seem then that indexing all data in a data base is a good thing to do. There is, however, a cost of indexing data. The index requires space, and if the data is constantly being updated in the data base, the indexes have to constantly be adjusted. When an online transaction occurs, the overhead of adjusting a lot of indexes can become prohibitive.

Therefore, there is a trade-off to be made. Although indexes can save tremendous time in accessing data, additional processing and data storage overhead are associated with the creation and maintenance of the indexes as well.

REMOVING DORMANT DATA

A second great way to enhance data warehouse performance is to remove dormant data. Dormant data is data that is no longer accessed or that has a very low probability of being accessed. Dormant data affects performance negatively by clogging up the machinery. It acts like cholesterol in the body. The more cholesterol there is in the body, the harder the heart has to pump just to keep the body alive. The less cholesterol there is, the more efficient the circulatory system is.

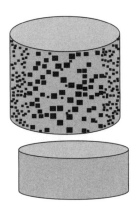

■ **FIGURE 15.7** Accessing a data base with no dormant data is much more efficient than accessing a data base with dormant data.

Every computer system has some amount of dormant data in it. It is only when there becomes an overwhelming amount of dormant data in the system that performance is hurt.

Figure 15.7 depicts two data bases. The data base on top contains a lot of dormant data. The data base on the bottom contains very little dormant data. It is *much* more efficient to access the data base on the bottom than it is to access the data base on top, with all of the dormant data in it.

It is then a very good practice to remove dormant data from the data base environment. Whereas the removal of dormant data is applicable to the Interactive Sector, the removal of dormant data is especially relevant to the Integrated Sector.

END-USER EDUCATION

There is another very simple idea that can produce really good results in the enhancement of performance. That idea is to educate the end users before they are allowed to use the data warehouse. There are two aspects to the end-user education that should be emphasized:

- What data is in the data warehouse, and what the structure and format of the data are?
- How to create efficient data queries?

A little end-user education goes a long way toward ensuring efficient data warehouse use and processing performance.

End-user education is applicable throughout the DW 2.0 environment, but is especially applicable to the Integrated Sector and the Archival Sector.

MONITORING THE ENVIRONMENT

Another technique for achieving good performance throughout the DW 2.0 environment is to monitor the environment. It is amazing how many people have important data bases and technology infrastructures that go unmonitored. A performance monitor is an excellent tool for detecting and diagnosing problems when they happen, as they inevitably will. If a problem cannot be diagnosed, then the necessary cure is only a guess.

There are two kinds of monitors that are relevant to the DW 2.0 environment: a transaction monitor for the Interactive Sector and a data warehouse monitor for the Integrated Sector.

The transaction monitor examines the speed of transaction processing, the resources used during transaction processing, and transaction queue wait times. The data warehouse monitor looks at dormant data and at the data users are accessing. Figure 15.8 depicts the monitoring of data warehouse activity and data.

CAPACITY PLANNING

Capacity planning naturally accompanies transaction performance and data usage monitoring. The objective of capacity planning is to predict proactively when performance may go bad so that remedial steps can be taken before it happens.

Without capacity planning, performance is great until, one day, the end of the capacity is reached. Acquiring new equipment and upgrading the technology are not things that can be done quickly, so the entire organization suffers when performance goes bad and until more capacity can be acquired and implemented. Therefore it is in the organization's best interests to be proactive, before the end of the data warehouse's capacity is reached.

Whereas capacity planning is important across the DW 2.0 environment, it is especially relevant to the Interactive Sector. Figure 15.9

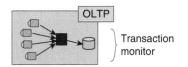

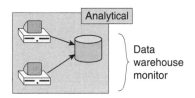

■ **FIGURE** **15.8** Monitoring the environment is a fundamentally good way of enhancing performance.

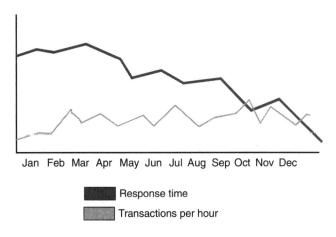

■ **FIGURE 15.9** Capacity planning puts the organization in a proactive stance when it comes to performance.

illustrates how data warehouse performance monitoring can provide predictive information that is extremely useful for proactive capacity planning purposes.

Capacity planning invariably raises the issues of hardware and software upgrades. There are occasions when the capacity of the hardware and/or software running a part of the DW 2.0 environment is simply exceeded. When this happens, more raw horsepower needs to be added to the environment. Data warehouse hardware capacity upgrades may involve many facets of the hardware environment, such as:

- More main memory
- More caching
- Faster internal speeds
- Parallelization of storage management
- Additional data storage

Increasing the capacity of a data warehouse may also involve software upgrades as well as hardware upgrades. Some typical features of software upgrades include:

- Support for newer and faster operating systems
- Support for parallelized software
- Support for new features in later releases of the software

There are plenty of reasons that upgrading both hardware and software can enhance the performance of a system. The task of keeping hardware and software on current releases is relevant across all sectors of DW 2.0. System upgrades are a regular part of the strategy for maintaining good data warehouse performance.

METADATA

A solid metadata infrastructure is an essential component of good data warehouse performance. The metadata infrastructure describes where data resides in the DW 2.0 environment.

Figure 15.10 depicts metadata in the DW 2.0 environment.

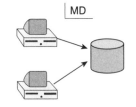

■ **FIGURE 15.10** The metadata infrastructure is essential to the performance of a system.

It may not be obvious that metadata has a relationship to performance, but it turns out that metadata has a very real and positive relationship to performance. Metadata is the key to reusability. Without reusability, everything must be built from scratch every time a problem or a question arises. With reusability, when an organization has already produced a result or done an analysis, it can reuse it rather than recalculating or redeveloping it. There is absolutely *nothing* that enhances performance like *not* having to do a major amount of work over again. If a major analysis does not have to be done because it has already been done, a huge amount of data warehouse resources are saved.

The reuse of existing analysis applies across the sectors of DW 2.0, but applies especially to the Integrated and Archival Sectors.

BATCH PARALLELIZATION

Parallelization of processing is a really good way to enhance performance. Suppose a job stream takes 12 hours to run. If two computers can be used to do the processing, then as few as 6 hours are required. If three computers can be used, then as few as 4 hours may be required.

By parallelizing a job stream, the elapsed time required to do the job is decreased. The decrease is proportional to the number of processors. If two processors are used to do the job, then the decrease in the elapsed time is $1/2$. If 10 processors are used to do a job, then the decrease is $1/10$. If there are n processors that the job stream can be spread across, then the maximum elapsed time benefit is $1/n$.

Note that, whereas many job streams can be parallelized, there are some job streams that cannot be parallelized.

Parallelization of job streams occurs as an approach to performance enhancement across the DW 2.0 environment. Figure 15.11 depicts parallelization to reduce elapsed processing time in the DW 2.0 environment.

The parallelization that is shown in Figure 15.11 applies to parallelization across multiple unrelated machines. This certainly is a way to achieve strong throughput, but there are other forms of parallelization that may also be useful.

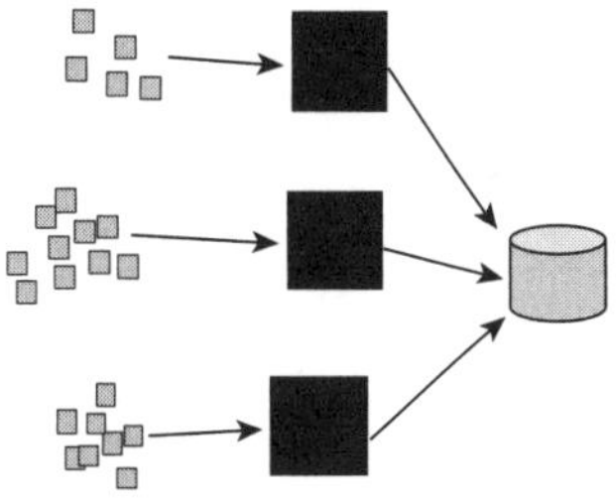

■ **FIGURE 15.11** Parallelization of a batch job stream reduces elapsed time.

PARALLELIZATION FOR TRANSACTION PROCESSING

Parallelization works for transaction processing, not just for job stream processing. When parallelization occurs for transaction processing, the transactions are gathered and managed centrally, while the data and processing power needed to handle the processing are managed separately. The operating systems that manage this type of processing are called "shared-nothing environments." In a shared-nothing

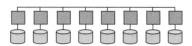

■ **FIGURE 15.12** Parallelization of storage management is another approach.

environment, each processor has and manages its own data. Each transaction is managed entirely separately from the execution of all other transactions. The result is really fast throughput. This form of parallelization is traditionally found in the Interactive Sector of DW 2.0. Figure 15.12 shows a shared-nothing transaction processing environment.

WORKLOAD MANAGEMENT

The workload that passes through a system is an important factor when it comes to good and swift performance. To understand how performance relates to the workload running through the system, consider a roadway and the cars that run on the roadway. Now consider a question—how fast can a Porsche go on the roadway? With rare exceptions, the answer is not 185 miles per hour. The Porsche can only go as fast as the vehicle in front of it. If the roadway is in Mexico City and it is rush hour, then the Porsche can go about 2 miles per hour. If the roadway is the German Autobahn, then the Porsche may be able to go 185 miles per hour. But if there is a lot of traffic and there are a lot of semitrailers on the roadway, then the speeds that are achievable by all types of vehicles are not very high.

Transaction processing streams work the same way. The types of transactions, the sizes of the transactions, and the numbers of transactions that share the same processing routes all have a direct bearing on the overall data warehouse speeds that are achievable.

In the Interactive Sector, only very small transactions are allowed to execute. This means that there are fast execution times. In the Integrated Sector there is a mixture of various sizes of transactions that are typically allowed to execute. This means that mixed response time is generally expected for the Integrated Sector. Archival Sector transactions are typically very large, so response-time performance in the archival environment is often poor.

Figure 15.13 illustrates how the makeup of the workload relates to response time.

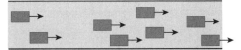

Small, homogeneous workload – very good performance

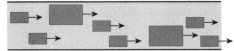

Mixed workload – erratic, inconsistent, poor performance

■ **FIGURE 15.13**   The makeup of the workload is a big factor when it comes to achieving good and consistent performance.

From a strategic standpoint, the movement of data to a data mart can greatly enhance performance.

DATA MARTS

A data mart is a collection of data that is used to satisfy the analytical needs of a group of users. Usually data marts are built along organizational lines, for example, financial, sales, and marketing data marts. Data marts are usually designed to serve a discrete group of people who all have fundamentally the same way of looking at the data.

By creating a data mart, the analytical processing can be shifted from one environment to the next. In other words, when a data mart is created, the amount of processing that is done against the DW 2.0 environment is reduced, and some of the processing load transfers to the data mart.

Creation of a data mart introduces the opportunity to do something else that is very beneficial for data warehouse performance. Moving data mart processing to a physically separate processor can significantly reduce the cost of processing in the enterprise data warehouse. Given the amount of processing that occurs in the DW 2.0 environment, the processor(s) that may be required to support it can be very expensive. Moving analytical cycles out of the DW 2.0 enterprise data warehouse environment can reduce processing costs because data marts usually require significantly less hardware support. So there are other powerful motivations for building data marts than just the enhancement of performance of the DW 2.0 environment.

Building of data marts applies almost exclusively to the Integrated Sector of the DW 2.0 environment. Figure 15.14 depicts the creation of data marts as an approach to the enhancement of performance.

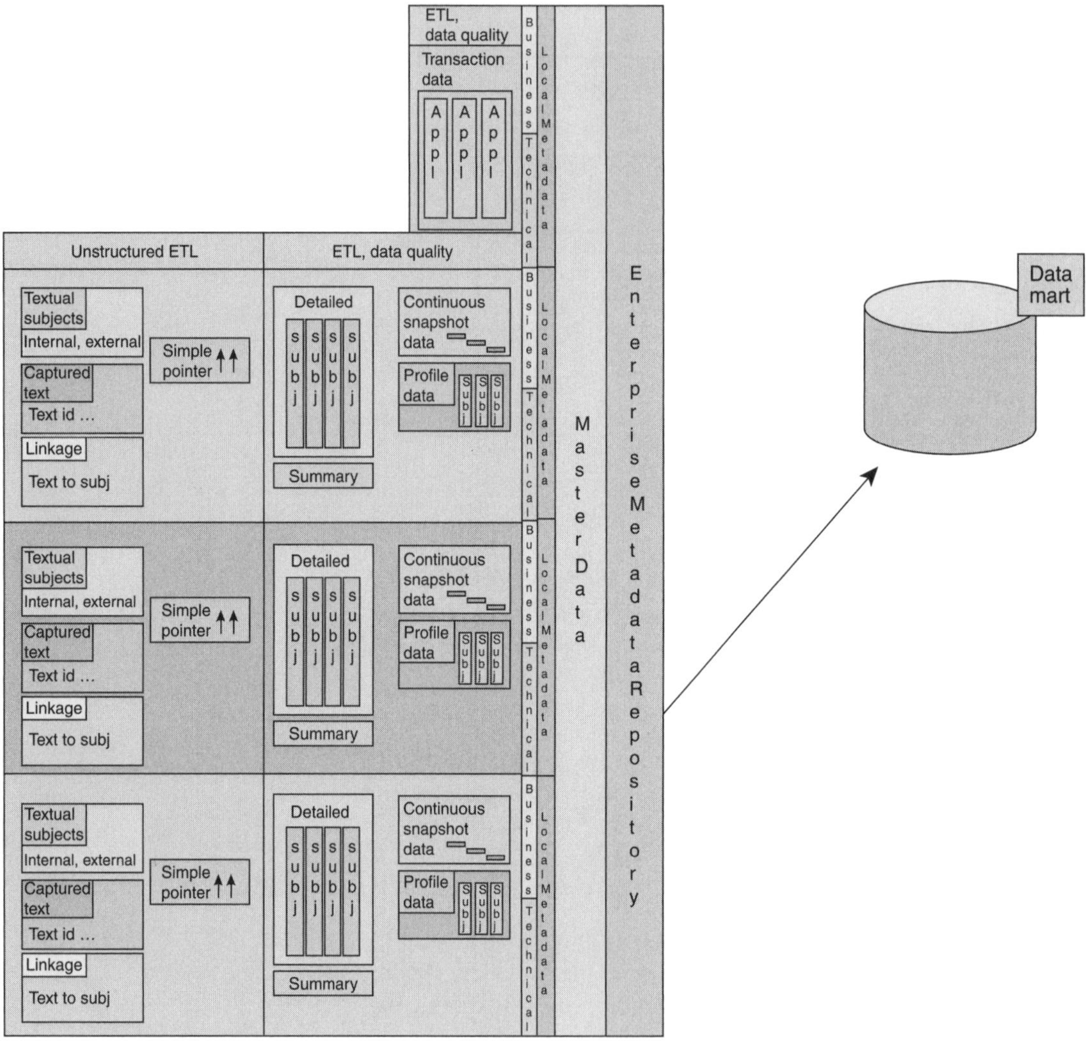

■ **FIGURE 15.14** Moving data to a data mart is another way to enhance performance.

EXPLORATION FACILITIES

The creation of exploration facilities also enhances DW 2.0 performance in much the same ways as data marts. Figure 15.15 depicts the creation of exploration facilities to enhance the performance of the DW 2.0 enterprise data warehouse environment.

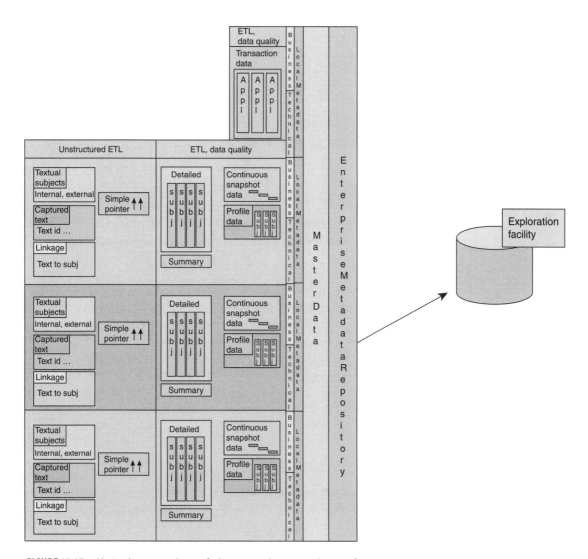

■ **FIGURE 15.15** Moving data to an exploration facility is yet another way to enhance performance.

SEPARATION OF TRANSACTIONS INTO CLASSES

The separation of transactions into different classes is another good way to enhance data warehouse performance. Figure 15.16 illustrates the separation of transactions into two different classes.

One of the interesting questions about the technique of the separation of transactions into different classes is, How does an organization

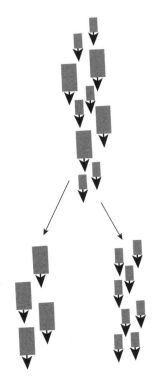

■ **FIGURE 15.16** Dividing the work stream into processes that are going to take a lot of resources and processes that will not take a lot of resources is a very good thing to do.

determine if a transaction is going to be fast or slow? As a general rule, the more data a transaction accesses the slower it is going to be. If a transaction is going to access a whole data base, then the transaction is likely to be slow. If a transaction accesses only a small amount of data, then the transaction is likely to run in a short amount of time.

SERVICE LEVEL AGREEMENTS

One way to govern the execution of transactions once the speed of the transaction has been determined is to create what are called "service level agreements," or SLAs.

An SLA is a statement of the expected levels of service. Normally the SLA is for transaction response time and system availability.

Figure 15.17 shows a service level agreement.

It is noteworthy that there are different service level agreements for the different sectors of the DW 2.0 environment. For example, there is an OLTP response-time SLA for the Interactive Sector. There is a class of transaction response-time SLA for the Integrated Sector. There is a transfer of data SLA for the Near Line Sector, and so forth. As such there is a measurable set of operating parameters that outline the end-user expectation for performance and availability. The service level agreement defines the operating boundaries between the IT organization and the end user.

PROTECTING THE INTERACTIVE SECTOR

Another way to protect the DW 2.0 environment performance is by protecting the Interactive Sector. Data in the Interactive Sector should not be removed to the Integrated Sector until it is sure that the probability

Service level agreement
- 8:00 AM–5:00 PM, Mon–Fri
  - max 5-second response time
- 5:00 PM–12:00 AM, Mon–Fri
  - 30-second response time
- 12:00 AM–8:00 AM, Mon–Fri
  - undetermined response time
Sat, Sun
  - undetermined response time

■ **FIGURE 15.17** A service level agreement is a good way to measure service in the transaction and the analytical environments.

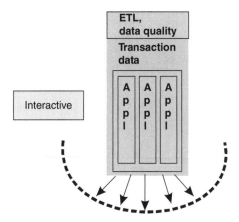

■ FIGURE 15.18   Make sure data does not leave the Interactive Sector until it is ready.

of access has abated. Consider what happens when data is removed prematurely from the Interactive Sector. The request for the data is routed to the Integrated Sector, where online response time is *not* guaranteed. It may take a while to find the data in the Integrated Sector. Therefore, if there is any doubt about the probability of data needing to be accessed in the Interactive Sector, then the data should remain in the Interactive Sector of DW 2.0.

Figure 15.18 illustrates that data needs to remain in the Interactive Sector while the probability of accessing it is still high.

PARTITIONING DATA

Partitioning data requires that data be divided up into physically distinct sectors when stored. Partitioning of data ensures that different sets of data can be handled separately, which greatly increases the flexibility of data.

To illustrate the benefits of physically partitioning data, consider a data base that is 10 terabytes in size. One day some data needs to be added or recalculated for some small part of the data base. The entire data base may be made unavailable while this activity occurs. Now consider what happens if the data base is partitioned into 1-terabyte chunks. Only a fraction of the data is paralyzed while repair work goes on. The impact is that major amounts of data remain free to fulfill processing demands that otherwise would have been unavailable.

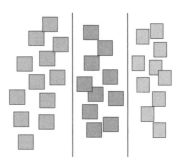

■ **FIGURE 15.19**   Partition data in storage.

Partitioning applies to anywhere in the DW 2.0 environment there are large stores of data. Figure 15.19 depicts partitioning.

CHOOSING THE PROPER HARDWARE

Choosing the proper hardware and software for the DW 2.0 environment also has a big impact on performance (Figure 15.20).

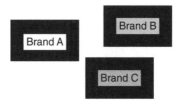

■ **FIGURE 15.20**   Choose the technology with performance capabilities that are suited to the performance needs.

SEPARATING FARMERS AND EXPLORERS

Another way to optimize performance is to separate the processing workload based on the different ways that data can be used. To this end, users can be roughly divided into two classes—farmers and explorers.

Farmers are end users who do analytical activities with regularity and predictability. Farmers know what they want before they set out to look for it. Explorers are people who are hard to predict. Explorers may go 6 months without doing any analytical activity and then suddenly need to do a lot of analytical processing in the same week.

Explorers do not know exactly what they want before they embark on a search.

Both farmers and explorers are legitimate users of the DW 2.0 environment. Both deserve resources, and both make valuable contributions to the decision-making process of the corporation. But, farmers and explorers need to be separated for a very good reason. The analytical activities performed by these two different types of data warehouse users are radically different, like oil and water. Performance of the entire data warehouse environment is enhanced when the analytical activities of these two different user communities are not mixed together. Figure 15.21 reinforces the message that farmers and explorers do not mix well in the same environment and need to be separated.

■ **FIGURE 15.21**   Separate farmers from explorers.

PHYSICALLY GROUP DATA TOGETHER

Another very fundamental activity that should be done to enhance data warehouse performance is to group data together physically when it is used in groups by a vast majority of the users of that data.

Figure 15.22 depicts five different kinds of data by color coding. If the analyst determines that 95% of the time the elements of data are accessed together, it makes sense for the data base designer to group the data together physically by the way it is most often accessed. By grouping the data together in this manner, the system can very efficiently retrieve the data.

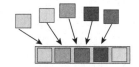

■ **FIGURE 15.22**   When data is used together, it should be physically grouped together, even though it is denormalized.

Grouping data according to access and usage patterns like this is recognized as data "denormalization." As a rule denormalization of data is not a good data architecture practice for an enterprise data warehouse and is discouraged. The data in the company's primary enterprise data warehouse should not be denormalized in this manner unless an extremely compelling, consistent, and enduring pattern of data subset access is identified.

CHECK AUTOMATICALLY GENERATED CODE

Checking the actual code created by an analytical tool is always a good data warehouse performance-enhancing practice. It is often assumed that analytical tools such as business intelligence products automatically and always produce efficient and effective code. This is not a safe assumption to make, because analytical tools often

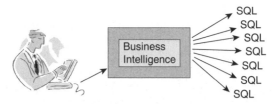

■ **FIGURE 15.23** Do not assume that the code produced by your analytical tool is efficient, or even proper.

produce very inefficient code. Therefore, it behooves the analyst to make sure that the efficiency of the code that is being produced is at least satisfactory. Figure 15.23 depicts the practice of checking to be sure that automatically generated BI query logic is as efficient as it needs to be.

There are many facets to achieving good data warehouse performance. Nearly all of the practices discussed above should be followed all of the time and all at once.

FROM THE PERSPECTIVE OF THE BUSINESS USER

The business user is keenly aware of performance throughout all activity passing through DW 2.0. He/she is aware of performance by the delivery or lack of delivery of performance.

It is incumbent upon the business user to let systems administration know when performance is flagging. Usually there are service level agreements that either strengthen or weaken the case for the conversation the business user has with systems administration.

Rarely is the business user involved in the remedy of poor performance. It is the job of systems administration to care for problems that arise inside the DW 2.0 environment.

On occasion the business user will ask for new levels of performance. For example, it is possible to ask for online response time in the archival environment. As long as the business user is willing to pay for performance, the level of performance indeed can be increased. Unfortunately most business users are not used to having to pay for system resources and services. However, if the business user is willing to pay for upgrades in technology, then there can always be an improvement in system performance.

It is at this point that the value of a service level agreement becomes obvious. With an SLA and with the measurement that goes along ith an SLA, the business user and the systems administrator can have a productive discussion. Real problems can be isolated. But without a service level agreement it is very difficult to have an intelligent conversation between the business user and the DW 2.0 administrator.

SUMMARY

Performance throughout the DW 2.0 environment is an essential characteristic.

There are two types of performance—transaction and analytical. When transaction performance suffers, the operational activities of the corporation suffer. When analytical performance suffers, the analytical capabilities of the corporation suffer.

Good performance is a result of many factors, including but not limited to the following:

- Choosing proper indexes
- Removing dormant data as soon as possible
- Educating the end user in how to distinguish between good and bad code
- Monitoring the transaction and the data warehouse environment so that when performance goes bad, there is a starting point to determine what has gone wrong
- Capacity planning, so that the organization can be in a proactive state when it comes to running out of resources
- Upgrades, making sure the latest releases of hardware and software are being used
- Metadata, so reusability minimizes the work that needs to be done
- Batch parallelization, to decrease elapsed time
- Transaction parallelization, to handle a large workload efficiently
- Workload management, to ensure that jobs do not conflict with each other because of size
- Data marts, to offload whole bodies of analytical processing from the central data warehouse
- Exploration facilities, which move statistical processing to another location
- Separation of transactions into classes based on the resources that a transaction will consume
- Service level agreements, which establish quantified goals for the measurement of performance

- Protection of the Interactive Sector to minimize resource contention
- Partitioning of data into different classes for separate management
- Choosing the right hardware and software for the achievement of performance
- Separating the work done by farmers and explorers
- Denormalizing data and placing data that is commonly accessed together in the same physical location
- Examining the code that is automatically created by tools, such as business intelligence tools

This is just a sample of the techniques and approaches that can be used to enhance performance in the DW 2.0 environment.

16

Migration

The DW 2.0 environment is a large complex environment. It requires many resources over a long period of time to build the DW 2.0 environment. Figure 16.1 indicates that the DW 2.0 environment is more like a city than a house.

HOUSES AND CITIES

A house is built over a relatively short amount of time. There is a finite starting point and a finite ending point in the building of a house. A house reaches a single point of usefulness—at one point it is not useful and at another point it is useful.

A city has a very different path of construction. A city is built over a very long period of time. A city is useful as soon as the first building is constructed. The city may or may not be planned. And, cities take on their own character. Even though they have common characteristics, there is a distinctiveness to each city. For example, Athens, Rome, New York, and Tokyo all have airports, a municipal building, residential areas, and high-rent districts, but no one mistakes these

A house

A city

■ **FIGURE 16.1**   When you are building DW 2.0, you are building a city, not a house.

cities for one another. Athens has the Parthenon, Paris has the Eiffel Tower, New York has its financial district, and Tokyo has corkscrew traffic bridges over Yokohama Bay.

The same is true for DW 2.0 data warehouses. The implementation of DW 2.0 will look very different for Coca Cola, Citicorp, CIBC, and Chrysler; yet all of their DW 2.0 data warehouses will still recognizably share the same architecture.

If corporations almost never set out to build a DW 2.0 environment, how do they end up with one? The answer is that they evolve to one. Corporations migrate to the DW 2.0 architecture over time.

MIGRATION IN A PERFECT WORLD

In a perfect world, the order of the building of a DW 2.0 data warehouse mimics the flow of data into and through the DW 2.0 environment.

Figure 16.2 depicts a "perfect world" implementation of the DW 2.0 architecture.

This figure depicts the order in which the DW 2.0 data warehouse would be built if there were no other existing data warehouse infrastructure. As each level of processing is built, the foundation is set for the next level.

THE PERFECT WORLD ALMOST NEVER HAPPENS

But the sequence shown in Figure 16.2 is a theoretical sequence. A DW 2.0 data warehouse is almost never built in top-down sequential steps as depicted. The primary reason a DW 2.0 data warehouse is not built in this "natural order" is that almost everyone who builds a DW 2.0 data warehouse already has an existing data warehouse environment in place.

Figure 16.3 depicts the infrastructure that almost everyone starts with, including a legacy applications environment, ETL processing, and a data base or data warehouse. These are the bare-bone components in the infrastructure that are found in most corporations.

ADDING COMPONENTS INCREMENTALLY

One of the really good pieces of news about the DW 2.0 architecture is that most of its components can be added incrementally and

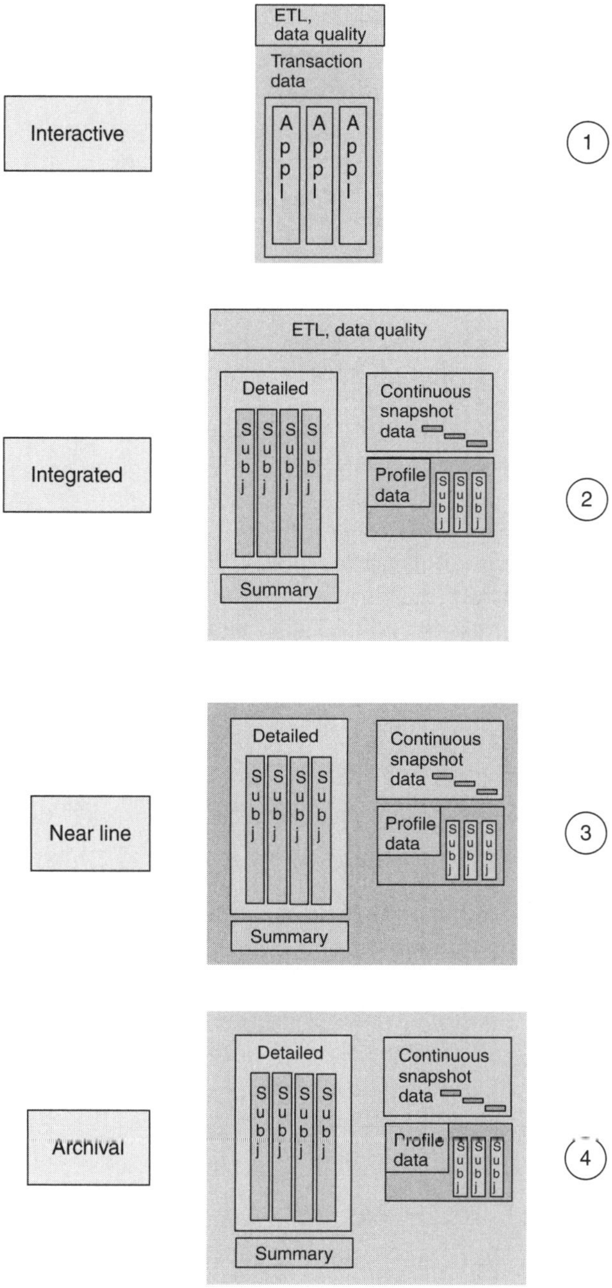

■ **FIGURE 16.2** The "natural" order in which DW 2.0 is built.

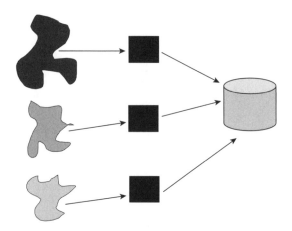

■ FIGURE 16.3   Where most organizations begin.

independently, on an as-needed basis. This ability to add components independently and incrementally means that companies can migrate and evolve to the DW 2.0 environment in an orderly manner. Nowhere in the migration to the DW 2.0 architecture is there a call to uproot and discard existing systems. Instead, the path to DW 2.0 is one by which the DW 2.0 infrastructure components can be built on top of an already-existing data warehouse.

Adding a near-line storage component to an existing data warehouse infrastructure is a good example of incremental migration to the DW 2.0 architecture. Although near-line storage is optional and is not for every corporation, when it is needed, there is nothing else like it. Adding near-line storage to a first-generation data warehouse environment is an architecturally easy thing to do. No special work or preparation is needed to attach new near-line storage facilities to a first-generation data warehouse.

Figure 16.4 depicts the addition of near-line storage to an existing data warehouse environment.

ADDING THE ARCHIVAL SECTOR

Next consider the Archival Sector. The Archival Sector can also be built with no advance preparation. One day the archival facility is not there, the next day it is, and nothing special had to be done to the first-generation data warehouse in the process.

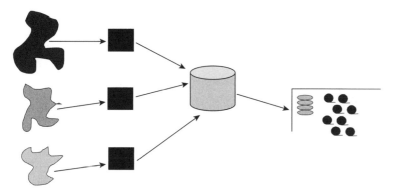

■ **FIGURE 16.4**   Adding near-line storage is incremental.

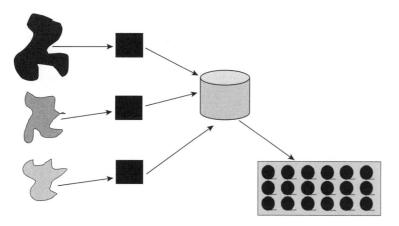

■ **FIGURE 16.5**   Adding archives is relatively easy to do.

Figure 16.5 depicts the addition of an Archival Sector to an existing first-generation data warehouse environment.

CREATING ENTERPRISE METADATA

The same considerations are true for the DW 2.0 metadata facility. As a rule, local metadata is already in place. Whether it is being used or not, the vendors that supply technology often provide a facility for the local storage and management of metadata, such as ETL metadata, business intelligence metadata, and DBMS metadata. So the local foundation of metadata is usually already in place. What needs

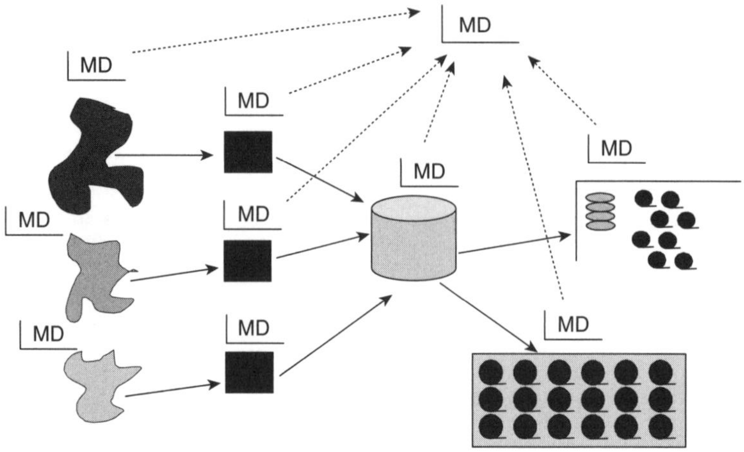

■ **FIGURE 16.6** Metadata has to be gathered from many sources to form the enterprise metadata repository.

to be added is enterprise metadata. Building enterprise metadata usually consists of three steps:

- Building the enterprise metadata repository
- Moving local metadata into the enterprise metadata repository
- Reconciling the local metadata with an enterprise metadata format

The last of these steps is always the hardest. Revising local metadata to conform to a corporate, enterprise format and structure is a difficult task to do.

BUILDING THE METADATA INFRASTRUCTURE

At no point does building an enterprise-level metadata repository require tearing down or discarding the existing environment. Instead the DW 2.0 metadata infrastructure is built over any already existing data warehouse infrastructure.

Figure 16.6 depicts the building of the enterprise metadata infrastructure over an existing first-generation data warehouse.

"SWALLOWING" SOURCE SYSTEMS

If there is any place where there is likely to be some amount of decommissioning of systems in the existing operational application environment, it is legacy applications that need to be consumed by

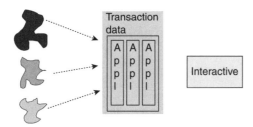

■ **FIGURE 16.7**   The applications morph into the Interactive Sector.

the Interactive Sector of the DW 2.0 environment. In many cases the Interactive Sector will "swallow up" the old source applications. In other cases, the source applications will be left "as is" and simply continue to contribute data to the Interactive Sector.

In the cases in which a source application is swallowed up by the Interactive Sector, it is a good bet that the application was an old out-of-date legacy system. The legacy application that is swallowed up was designed to satisfy business requirements from a long time ago—requirements that have long since changed. If the Interactive Sector had not come along, then the legacy application would have needed to be refurbished in any case.

Figure 16.7 depicts the absorption of some legacy applications into the Interactive Sector.

ETL AS A SHOCK ABSORBER

ETL processing acts like a shock absorber for the entire data warehouse evolution and migration process. A drastic change can occur in the operational source application world, and through ETL transformation the effect on the Interactive Sector is minimized. Likewise, a major change may occur in the Interactive Sector, and through ETL transformation the effect on the Integrated Sector is nonexistent or at worst minimal.

Figure 16.8 shows ETL acting as a shock absorber between the different sectors.

MIGRATION TO THE UNSTRUCTURED ENVIRONMENT

The unstructured data domain is one of the newest and most important features of the DW 2.0 data warehouse environment. In many

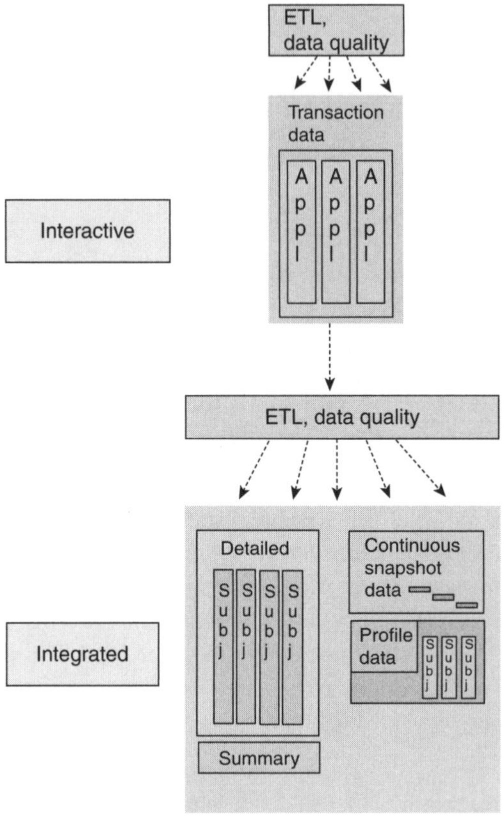

■ **FIGURE 16.8**   ETL processing acts like a shock absorber.

DW 2.0 environments, unstructured data is the added component that unlocks the door to many new kinds of analytical and decision-support processing.

The migration to the DW 2.0 environment for unstructured data is quite different from the migration for structured data. Whereas the structured environment almost always exists in the form of a first-generation data warehouse, the same cannot be said for the unstructured component. There almost never is preexisting unstructured data that can be added to a DW 2.0 data warehouse environment.

Figure 16.9 shows that unstructured data is almost always captured in its entirety from its textual sources and is passed through a new unstructured data ETL routine into the unstructured side of the DW 2.0 data warehouse.

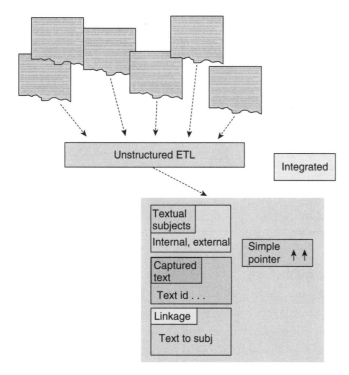

■ FIGURE 16.9   Unstructured data is entered from text and other forms of unstructured data.

After unstructured data has been processed into the DW 2.0 data warehouse, linkages are formed between structured data and unstructured data. Figure 16.10 depicts the formation of linkages between the unstructured and the structured data domains within a DW 2.0 sector.

Over time, as unstructured data ceases to be used, the unstructured data migrates to the DW 2.0 Archival Sector's unstructured data domain. There is more information in Chapter 19 about unstructured data.

FROM THE PERSPECTIVE OF THE BUSINESS USER

Migration is something the business user is indirectly involved in. The business user determines what new subject areas are to be included in DW 2.0. He/she determines when data should be placed in archives and near-line storage. He/she also determines the transformations that occur as data passes from one sector to another.

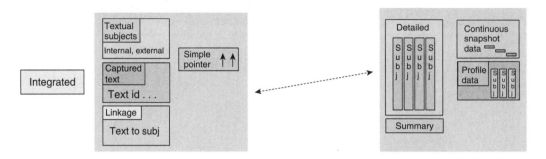

■ FIGURE 16.10 The unstructured environment is linked to the structured environment.

But at the end of the day, the business user is only tangentially involved in the migration of data that occurs as the DW 2.0 environment is being built.

SUMMARY

There is a natural migration order to a DW 2.0 data warehouse architecture. The natural migration order follows the same path on which data flows—first to the Interactive Sector, next to the Integrated Sector, then to the Near Line Sector, and finally to the Archival Sector. Although the natural order is well defined, it is only theoretical.

In reality, the DW 2.0 environment evolves from the first-generation data warehouse one component at a time. The archival environment can be added independently. The near-line environment can be added independently. So can the enterprise metadata infrastructure and the unstructured data domain.

The different components of the DW 2.0 environment are added in response to business needs.

The only preexisting systems components that are sometimes destroyed and replaced during migration to the DW 2.0 architecture are legacy application systems. On occasion, a legacy systems environment is so out of date and so fragile that it is easier to rewrite the system than it is to integrate data from the old system.

17

Cost justification and DW 2.0

There is no question that the infrastructure for DW 2.0 costs a lot. It costs to build it. It costs to operate it. And the equipment that it is built on costs as well.

And most corporations are adverse to large expenditures.

IS DW 2.0 WORTH IT?

So it is natural that the conversation about the worth of DW 2.0 inevitably arises. The conversation goes something like this:

"This new stuff is going to cost a lot. Are you sure it is worth it? Why should I make this big investment?"

It is absolutely normal for top management to question the worth of the DW 2.0 environment. And it simply is inadequate for you to sit there and say—"My intuition tells me that it is the right thing to do."

So how do you answer top management when they question the value of a DW 2.0 infrastructure?

MACRO-LEVEL JUSTIFICATION

One way to respond to management is at the macro level. The macro level says that you look at very large factors and attach the worth of DW 2.0 to those factors. You might say, "The ABC Corporation brought in DW 2.0 and their stock went up." Or you might say, "The XYZ Corporation brought in DW 2.0 and their profits soared."

Although it may well be true that DW 2.0 had a salubrious effect on the stock price or profitability, making such an appeal lacks credibility.

271

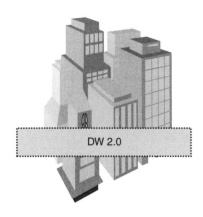

■ **FIGURE 17.1** Cost justification at the macro level for DW 2.0 is difficult to do.

There are many, many factors that affect a corporation's stock price. In the best of circumstances, a DW 2.0 facility is only one of many factors. The same is true of profitability.

The effect of a DW 2.0 environment on such large macro factors is so specious that the credibility of the person making the claim is at stake.

Looking to macro factors is a very difficult way to convince management of the value of DW 2.0.

Figure 17.1 shows a DW 2.0 justification at the macro level.

A MICRO-LEVEL COST JUSTIFICATION

A much more credible way to address the issue of cost justification of the DW 2.0 environment lies at the micro level. At the micro level, there is a very convincing argument that can be made for the creation and operation of the DW 2.0 environment.

Consider two companies—company A and company B—as seen in Figure 17.2.

■ **FIGURE 17.2** Consider two companies.

The information infrastructures of these two companies are very similar. Both company A and company B have a host of older legacy systems. The day-to-day business of the companies is conducted in older transaction-oriented technology and has been for a long time.

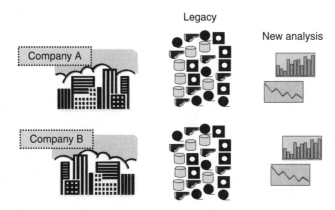

■ FIGURE 17.3   Both A and B have old legacy systems and a need for fresh new analysis.

Figure 17.3 shows that company A and company B both have legacy data and a need for new, fresh analysis.

COMPANY B HAS DW 2.0

In all basic architectural components company A and company B are almost identical. There is one major difference, however. Company A does not have a DW 2.0 facility, whereas company B does. Figure 17.4 shows this basic difference between the two companies.

CREATING NEW ANALYSIS

In any case there is a need for new analysis. How exactly does company A go about creating new information from its foundation of legacy data? Figure 17.5 shows that company A has to go back to its base of legacy applications to create new and fresh analysis.

The legacy data is really the only data that company A has to operate on. There just isn't any other data.

So what does company A have to do to create new analysis? Company A has to go to the legacy environment and

- find the data that is being sought;
- gather the data;
- integrate the data;
- stage the data; and
- create a report or new analysis.

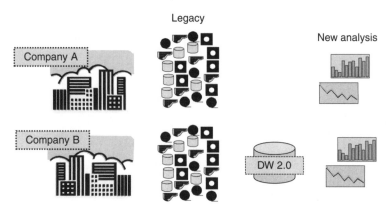

■ FIGURE 17.4 The only difference between the two companies is that company B has a DW 2.0 environment.

■ FIGURE 17.5 So how does company A produce new analysis?

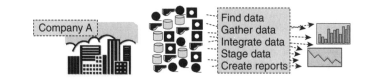

■ FIGURE 17.6 So what needs to be done to produce new analysis?

Figure 17.6 shows the steps that company A must go through.

EXECUTING THE STEPS

These are normal and natural steps. But let's consider exactly what is required to execute these steps.

To find the data, the old legacy data must be documented. A lot of older legacy systems have no documentation whatsoever. And when documentation is found, the documentation has not been kept up to date. And there is much confusion when the older legacy systems are examined. There are no naming standards. There is a different calculation wherever you look. There are all sorts of coding standards.

Exacerbating the fact that there is no documentation, the technology that the old legacy environment is locked up in is ancient. There are no more programmers or analysts that even understand the technology of yesterday. There is old IMS code, old Model 204 code, old Adabas code, old System 2000 code. And there just are not any workers who understand that code anymore.

So finding and understanding the data that populates the old legacy systems environment are no trivial tasks.

Assuming that the old legacy code can be found and deciphered, the next step is to gather the data from the legacy environment. This requires locating skills that have long disappeared. Once those skills have been found, then the data is pulled from the legacy environment.

Next comes integrating the data. If the data comes from only one system, then there is no problem. But if the data comes from multiple systems, then there is a problem with integration. Key structures are not the same. Date formats are different. Some data is missing and default values have to be applied. Attributes have different names. The definitions of data are different, and so forth.

The person dealing with the old legacy data is asked to merge data from systems that were never designed for such a merger. Given that there is inadequate documentation and that the systems are written in technology that is arcane, making a proper job of integration is dicey, at best.

After the data is found, gathered, and integrated, then the data needs to be staged. In this case many sources of data are collected together in a single physical location.

Now, and only now, can the process of writing the report begin.

Given these challenges, how much does it cost for the creation of a new analysis? It depends entirely on the legacy environment and the analysis that is required. Some legacy environments are really a mess. Other legacy environments are fairly tame. Some reports and analyses are simple. Other reports and analyses are very difficult.

SO HOW MUCH DOES ALL OF THIS COST?

A range of costs for the building of an analysis is shown in Figure 17.7.

Depending on the particulars, it may cost $100,000 to $10,000,000 to build a new analysis. And it may take 3 months to 3 years to build such an analysis. The costs vary widely because of many factors, such as:

- Number of legacy programs
- Complexity of legacy systems
- Documentation of legacy applications
- Technologies housing the legacy environment
- Complexity of the request for new data
- Volume of underlying data that is required to be analyzed
- Number of data elements underlying the request for new information
- Degree to which data bases have been kept up with current releases
- Operating systems of older legacy environments

CONSIDER COMPANY B

Now consider company B. Company B also needs a new analysis. How much money does it cost to build a new analysis from the DW 2.0 facility? The answer is shown in Figure 17.8.

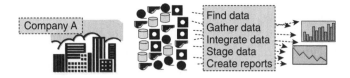

■ **FIGURE 17.7** And how much does this cost and how long does it take? From $100,000 to $10,000,000; from 3 months to 3 years.

■ **FIGURE 17.8** Once the DW 2.0 environment is built, how much does it cost to make a new analysis and how long does it take? From $1000 to $10,000; from 1 hour to 5 days.

In Figure 17.8 it is seen that it takes from $1000 to $10,000 and an hour to maybe 5 days to build an analysis. From these figures it is seen that company B has a much, much easier time with the information facility than company A. And the only difference between company A and company B is the existence of a DW 2.0 facility.

From these observations it is seen that DW 2.0 greatly lowers the cost of information for a corporation. Stated differently, DW 2.0 opens the door to information that has always been there but has been essentially inaccessible.

FACTORING THE COST OF DW 2.0

But the comparison of the figures for information is somewhat biased. The bias comes in the cost of the DW 2.0 facility that has not been factored in to the equation.

What happens when the cost of the DW 2.0 facility is factored in?

Figure 17.9 shows that the equation needs more work.

Building and operating the DW 2.0 facility is not cheap. Of course a lot depends on the volume of data, the number of users, the number of old legacy systems, the length of time data will be kept, the types of analysis, and so forth.

But for the purpose of this analysis, it is assumed that a DW 2.0 facility has cost $5,000,000.

Now, how much does it cost for company A to build a report? Let us assume that it costs $700,000 to build a report. And how much does it cost for the same report from company B? The answer is $10,000.

Now that these report costs are factored in along with the cost of the DW 2.0 environment, what does the cost equation look like?

■ **FIGURE 17.9** But what about the cost of building the DW 2.0 environment?

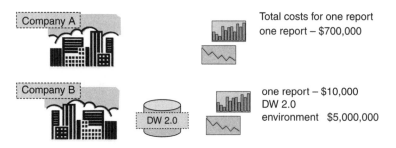

■ **FIGURE 17.10**   So what if all we want is one report?

Figure 17.10 shows us the figures.

Using this analysis, it seems that building a DW 2.0 environment is quite expensive. The figures in Figure 17.10 show that a report costs $700,000, whereas the same report with a DW 2.0 facility costs $5,010,000. In this analysis the cost of a DW 2.0 is prohibitive.

REALITY OF INFORMATION

But there is something very unrealistic about Figure 17.10. This figure makes the assumption that the corporation will want only one report. And there is no corporation of any size and sophistication that operates all of its business on one report. For even a midsize corporation, at least 100 reports are necessary. The finance department needs its reports one way. The marketing department needs its reports another way. The sales department needs its reports yet another way.

And for a large corporation, there are not hundreds of reports. There are thousands of reports.

But for the purpose of our analysis, let us assume that 100 reports are needed. How does the reality of the number of reports needed change the economics?

Figure 17.11 shows the consequences of considering how many reports are really needed by the corporation.

In the case of company A, the cost of the reports is multiplied by 100 to $70,000,000. In the case of company B, the cost of the reports is multiplied by 100 to $1,000,000. But there is only one DW 2.0 facility that is needed. So the cost of the DW 2.0 environment remains static.

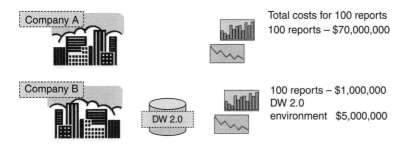

Total costs for 100 reports
100 reports – $70,000,000

100 reports – $1,000,000
DW 2.0
environment $5,000,000

■ FIGURE 17.11   But what if we want 100 reports?

THE REAL ECONOMICS OF DW 2.0

Now the real economic analysis of the cost justification of a DW 2.0 environment becomes apparent. DW 2.0 drops the cost of a new analysis by an order of magnitude or more. It is simply true that DW 2.0 allows a corporation to access and analyze its data as it never has before.

But the raw economics of DW 2.0 do not tell the full story.

THE TIME VALUE OF INFORMATION

There is a very real case to be made for the time value of information. DW 2.0 greatly facilitates the speed with which information can be retrieved.

Consider this. Your boss walks into your office and asks for a report. You get to work, traipse through a bunch of old legacy systems, and get the analysis to your boss 6 months later. When you walk into your boss's office with your report, your boss has forgotten what he/she asked you to do months ago.

Compare that scenario with the following.

Your boss walks into your office and asks for an analysis. You get to work and you have the analysis ready for your boss the next day. You walk into your boss's office at 8:00 AM the next morning with the report. How useful is that information to your boss?

The point is that information that is 6 months late is usually not useful at all. The fresher and the more current the information, the better the chance that the information will be useful in the business equation.

■ **FIGURE 17.12**   But what about the time value of information?

There is a real time value of information, and it is the DW 2.0 environment that greatly accelerates the speed with which information is accessible.

Figure 17.12 depicts the time value of information.

THE VALUE OF INTEGRATION

But there are other major benefits which are not measured by the raw economic calculation that has been presented. There is the value of integration as well.

To many corporations, integration itself is worth the cost of the DW 2.0 environment. With integration, information from one place and one use can be connected to and related to information from another place and another use.

The result of this connectivity is integration. And with integration such valuable things as being able to create a true 360° view of the customer can be accomplished.

Figure 17.13 shows that integration is an intangible benefit of the DW 2.0 environment.

HISTORICAL INFORMATION

There is yet one more intangible benefit of the DW 2.0 environment and that benefit is the ability to look across information from the perspective of time.

Prior to DW 2.0 there were legacy systems. Many of those legacy systems were transaction oriented. And where there are transactions, there is a need for high performance. Where there is a need for high performance, there is a need to rid the system of any unnecessary

■ **FIGURE 17.13**   And what about the value of integrated information?

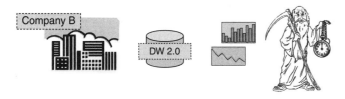

■ **FIGURE 17.14**   And then there is the issue of the value of historical data.

data. Unnecessary data inside a system acts like cholesterol inside the human body.

Therefore, in the legacy environment, the tendency is to jettison historical data as fast as possible. The more historical data found in a legacy system, the slower the system runs. The net result is that there is only a minimum of history in the legacy systems environment.

The problem is that there is real value in historical data.

If the legacy, transaction-processing environment is not the place to store historical data, the DW 2.0 environment *is* the place to store historical data.

Figure 17.14 shows that the DW 2.0 environment is the place for historical data to reside.

FIRST-GENERATION DW AND DW 2.0—THE ECONOMICS

There is yet another perspective on the economics of data warehousing. First-generation data warehousing had the habit of collecting lots of data on disk storage. In fact many first-generation data warehouses stored data on nothing but disk storage.

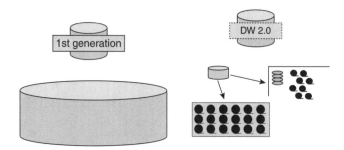

■ **FIGURE 17.15** The cost of a DW 2.0 data warehouse is significantly less than the cost of a first-generation data warehouse.

But DW 2.0 recognizes that there are at least two places where data should be stored on other than disk storage. DW 2.0 recognizes that data should be stored in near-line storage when it still needs to be accessed but has a low probability of access. And DW 2.0 recognizes that archival data is not normally stored on disk storage.

Because of the usage of different storage devices, the cost of DW 2.0 is significantly less than the cost of traditional first-generation data warehouses.

Figure 17.15 compares the storage media for the different generations of data warehousing.

FROM THE PERSPECTIVE OF THE BUSINESS USER

Cost justification is an activity that is usually done once in the life of DW 2.0. Under all normal circumstances there is no need to do repeated justifications.

The business user is very heavily involved with the process of cost justification of DW 2.0. Indeed, in many ways the exercise of cost justification is done for the business user.

It is understood that the business user pays—either directly or indirectly—for the DW 2.0 infrastructure. Therefore it is the business users and their management that have to be satisfied with the results of cost justification.

SUMMARY

Trying to cost-justify DW 2.0 at the macro level is a difficult thing to do because the benefits of the DW 2.0 environment get lost among many other macro factors. Instead the best way to cost-justify a DW 2.0 environment is to look at cost justification in a micro fashion.

Look at two companies—one with a DW 2.0 environment and one without a DW 2.0 environment. Then look at the costs of

- finding data;
- gathering data;
- integrating data;
- staging data;
- reporting and analyzing the data; plus
- the cost of the warehouse.

Look at these factors for many reports and many analyses, and the cost of the DW 2.0 environment comes out as much lower than that of an environment without DW 2.0.

But there are other noneconomic factors to be considered. There is the time value of data. There is the integration of data. And there is the historical data, which is now available (for the first time).

DW 2.0 unlocks data for analytical purposes and enables the organization to look at and do analyses that they have never been able to do before.

18

Data quality in DW 2.0

The DW 2.0 environment departs from the "code, load, and explode" world that was the norm for first-generation data warehouses. In the latter case, no attention was paid to data quality until the very last moment—the 11th hour of the project. That was the point in time when the project team was loading the data warehouse with data extracted from source systems and only then discovering the "gremlins" that were lurking in the source data. This led to enormous frustration and inevitably to major delays in implementation schedules. Data quality problems discovered during the testing or loading stage can be a major cause of projects going over time and budget, both of which are leading indicators of project failure.

The DW 2.0 next-generation approach to data warehousing ensures that the data quality team is "riding" way out ahead of the data warehouse "wagon train" as it heads into new territories. Just as in the days of old, the pioneers in their wagon trains had scouts that went ahead to scout out the territory the train was about to pass through, so also the data quality team are the scouts for the data warehouse development team. They should be profiling the data sources in the Interactive Sector to uncover the problems and anomalies in the data and give early warning to the development team. The data profiling team should consist of both business and information technology professionals.

The data discovery tasks should be built into the methodology and performed even before iteration planning starts. (Data profiling is only one of the activities needed to analyze the quality of data; another task is checking that the data adheres to business rules.) By using this approach the project team will discover ahead of time many of the data pitfalls and will therefore be able to plan for them.

When data quality problems are found, they should be escalated to the business community, which should decide which of these data quality problems it cares about and wants fixed. It is important to note that not all data quality problems are important to the business. When the business has indicated which of the data quality problems are important, it needs to identify the business rules that should be applied to cleanse the data. These cleansing rules drive the specifications for transformation of source data, obviating the code, load, and explode scenario.

In the DW 2.0 next-generation data warehouse, the data quality team is also expected to be able to select from a series of strategies to address data quality problems that are found. Some of these strategies include the following:

- Fix the source data: Actually go into the data store and physically repair the data.

- Fix the source program: Apply the correct edits to validate the data.

- Fix the business process: A broken business process is very often the main cause of poor-quality data.

- Adjust for changes: Recognize and resolve situations in which data attributes are being used for a purpose other than their original intent, e.g., a gender code that has more than two distinct values.

- Transform the data: Transform the data on the way into the data warehouse—the most common strategy, but not the only strategy that should be employed.

In an ideal world one wants to fix the cause of the problem rather than the effect. Fixing the data and the program at the source and fixing the business process constitute fixing the cause.

It is important to note that there are two alternative approaches for transforming data on the way into the Integrated Sector. The first approach is simply to change the data and load it into the data warehouse. The second approach does that and more by actually loading the unchanged data alongside the changed data. There are many times when this may be a preferable strategy: the business community can see what has been done to the data and therefore it is more inclined to trust it.

THE DW 2.0 DATA QUALITY TOOL SET

There are of course many tool types to consider. The data profiling tools find the problems in the data. There is another whole set of tools that fix data anomalies. There are tools that monitor data quality and yet others that report on data quality. ETL tools that are responsible for extracting, transforming, and loading data often also have data quality capabilities.

There are essentially four domains in the DW 2.0 data quality tool set, as follows (Figure 18.1):

- Find it—in which data profiling and discovery are performed to find the data anomalies and rules

- Fix it—in which data is cleansed according to specific rules

- Move it—in which ETL or ELT tools transform the data on the way to the data warehouse

- Monitor it and report it—in which data quality is monitored and reported

During first-generation warehousing, these four domains manifested themselves as distinct specialized tool categories. Although many of these tools still have their own very specific capability domains

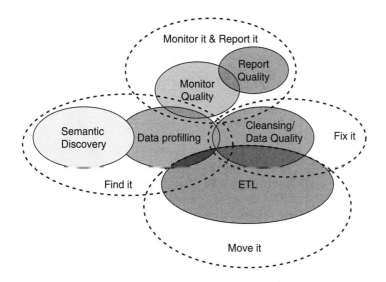

■ **FIGURE 18.1** Data quality tool functionality categories. After Bonnie O'Neill and Derek Strauss.

in DW 2.0 data warehousing, they have been undergoing enhancement and today have overlapping functionality with other tools in adjacent domains. New tool functionality categories have emerged, e.g., semantic discovery tools, which use fuzzy logic to discover rules in the data. Some tools are even able to analyze semistructured data. Mergers and acquisitions among data quality tool vendors have led to further bundling and enhancement of data quality tool set offerings. Against this backdrop, DW 2.0 architects need to anticipate a tool set that can find data quality anomalies, fix data quality problems, move data, and monitor/report on data quality.

DATA PROFILING TOOLS AND THE REVERSE-ENGINEERED DATA MODEL

Is it possible to perform data profiling manually? Yes it is possible. Here are some of the options:

- An organization could hire some additional staff to comb the data bases and find duplicate records and deduplicate them. Unfortunately this would not identify relationships within files or across files/systems and would be very expensive as the new recruits would have to be trained and supervised to ensure that they follow business rules.

- Another way of doing this would be to write programs to find data anomalies. This option will typically address only known problems. It may also take a very long time and there is no guarantee that the exercise will be effective. The reason for this is that "we don't know what we don't know."

- The best option to uncover data quality issues is to use a data quality profiling tool.

There are many data profiling tools to assist today's data quality team (Figure 18.2). The tools facilitate analysis of the data values held in a column, sometimes looking simultaneously at multiple columns in a table, sometimes looking across tables or even across systems to see if there are any patterns in the values held in the selected columns. These patterns can uncover hidden business rules, e.g., every time the value in column 1 is "a," the value in column 5 can be "x" or "y."

The best of these data profiling tools go one step further. After analyzing the actual data values in the columns of a system, the tools can suggest a normalized schema. What in effect happens is the

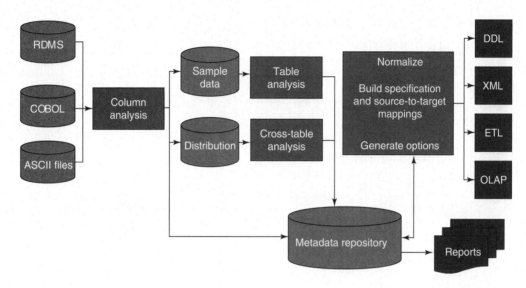

■ **FIGURE 18.2** Data profiling process components.

tool develops a third normal form data model, based on bottom-up analysis, abstracted from the actual data values in the physical data base. This abstracted data model is very useful input into the top-down data modeling process, which should happen in parallel with the development of the warehouse. In fact, ensuring that high-quality data model architecture is developed for the DW 2.0 data warehouse greatly assists in improving the data quality of the enterprise data warehouse.

DATA MODEL TYPES

So what types of data models belong in a good DW 2.0 architecture? Before answering this question, it is necessary to do some level-setting. The diagram in Figure 18.3 depicts the six rows of the data column of the Zachman framework introduced in Chapter 6.

The top three rows represent a technology-independent view, and the bottom three rows are technology-dependent representations. The top row typically consists of a list of data subjects that comprise the planner's view or the scope and context of the enterprise. Each of the data subjects in the top row could be broken down further into major data entities. The second row depicts the owner's view; the major concepts of the enterprise are represented in a data model, often referred to

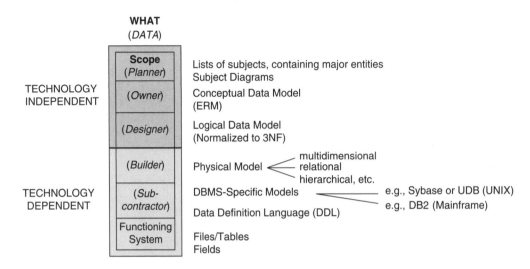

FIGURE 18.3 Types of data models: a slice of the Zachman framework.

as the entity relationship model or entity relationship diagram. The third row, the designer's view, contains the logical data model. This is typically a fully attributed third normal form data model.

Technology-dependent data representations are below the line separating Row 3 and Row 4 in the data column of the Zachman framework. The fourth row represents the physical data model. There may be many physical data models in a data warehouse. There could be physical data models for the primary warehouse, other physical data models for the marts, and still other physical data models for the other components of the warehouse environment. Models represented at this level could therefore include a mix of relational models, dimensional models, and denormalized physical data models. It is important to note that star schemas and snowflake schemas are, in fact, physical data models.

Data definition language or DDL is found next down the data column in Row 5. These instructions, when followed, result in the creation of the actual files and tables, which are represented in Row 6.

The diagram in Figure 18.4 represents the various components that make up the DW 2.0 landscape. They are shown superimposed on the four major sectors of DW 2.0—the Interactive Sector, the Integrated Sector, the Near Line Sector, and the Archival Sector. Each of the data stores should be traceable back to a context level, a concept level,

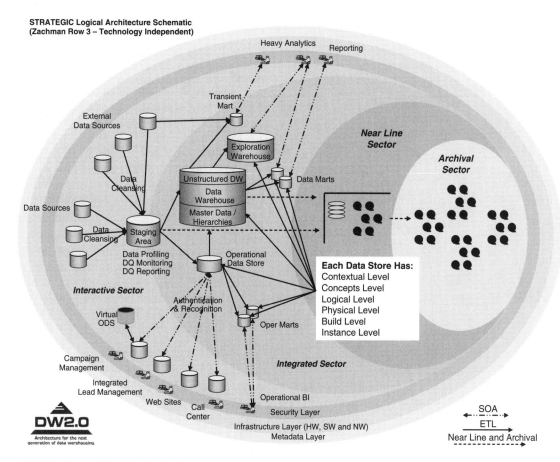

STRATEGIC Logical Architecture Schematic
(Zachman Row 3 – Technology Independent)

Each Data Store Has:
Contextual Level
Concepts Level
Logical Level
Physical Level
Build Level
Instance Level

■ **FIGURE 18.4** The DW 2.0 data base landscape.

a logical level, a physical level, a build level, and an instance level artifact.

A good concepts data model illuminates the major concepts in the business and how they interrelate. A good third normal form logical data model contains and presents all the attributes pertaining to the business entities and also the cardinality and optionality of the relationships between those entities. The logical data model gives a great logical view of the business and its data and should be the starting point for the third model type—the physical data model.

Physical data models for DW 2.0's Integrated Sector can differ widely in their structure. They will range from normalized and near-normalized models for the data warehouse hub through to star schema and snowflake schema models for the data marts. Still other data model structures are best suited to exploration warehouses, data mining warehouses, operational data stores, and "oper marts" (operational data marts). Data moving to the Near Line Sector should be kept as close to third normal form structure as possible. It is normal for data to be restructured as it enters the Archival Sector.

Multidirectional traceability between data models is important to the DW 2.0 data environment. It should be possible to navigate from a physical model back up through the logical model and up still further to the concepts model. Likewise, it should be possible to move from the top down, from the concepts model to the logical data model and on to the physical data models. A rigorous set of interlocking models will go a long way toward improving the quality of the data in the enterprise, linking business meaning and structural business rules to physical instantiations of data entities and attributes.

So once again, What are the critical models in a DW 2.0 data architecture? The diagram in Figure 18.5 answers this question and depicts all of the critical data models used in DW 2.0 next-generation data warehousing.

Each of the source systems is reverse engineered to create a logical model. A corporate logical data model derived from the concepts model is used as the basis for the data warehouse logical data model and the data mart logical data models. Physical data models for both the data warehouse and the data marts are derived from the respective logical data models.

The relationship between the corporate logical data model and the other logical data models deserves further examination. For example, the relationship between the data warehouse logical data model and the corporate logical data model is illustrated in Figure 18.6.

The large rectangle in the diagram represents the cell in Row 3, Column 1 of the Zachman framework, i.e., the logical data model (LDM) cell. Every cell of the Zachman framework has a "scope dimension," represented by the thin horizontal rectangle across the top of the LDM cell, and a "detail dimension," represented by the thin vertical rectangle, placed down the side of the LDM cell. It is always good practice to have an enterprise-wide view of the data expressed in a corporate logical data model. A corporate LDM covers the entire scope of the enterprise, but it is not very detailed.

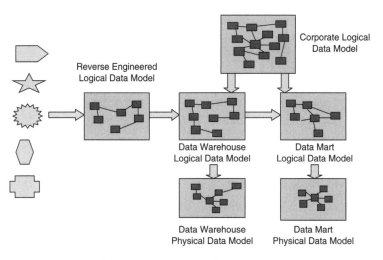

■ **FIGURE 18.5** Types of data models used in DW 2.0 next-generation data warehouses.

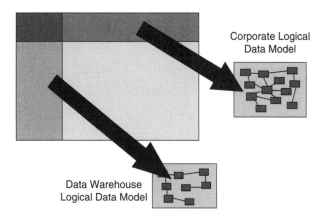

■ **FIGURE 18.6** Corporate versus data warehouse logical data models.

Full attribution of a model such as this would take too much time and cost too much money. Only the corporation's major entities and the relationships between those entities are depicted in the corporate logical data model.

Each successive iteration of the data warehouse is driven by a logical data model, which is fully attributed for the entities required by the iteration. The beauty of having a corporate logical data model is that it allows this type of incremental development to take place without compromising the logical data blueprint. Many data quality problems can trace their genesis back to inadequate or uncoordinated logical data modeling. Without a corporate logical data model, there is no way to put the pieces of the puzzle together; each successive increment would have been developed in complete isolation, resulting in data redundancy and a lack of data integration.

DATA PROFILING INCONSISTENCIES CHALLENGE TOP-DOWN MODELING

In Figure 18.7, Example 1, various inconsistencies have been uncovered in a file by data profiling. During top-down data modeling sessions, an entity called "Party" was identified as being an individual or organization. The "Individual" subtype was identified as having the attribute "Gender," with valid values for male and female. Simultaneously, the team was using a data profiling tool to look at the actual data in the source systems. The data profiling tool revealed that seven values had been actually used in the Gender attribute field. It quickly became evident that the field had been used for purposes other than simply to reflect the gender of the individual. This revelation of the multiple purposes for which the Gender attribute

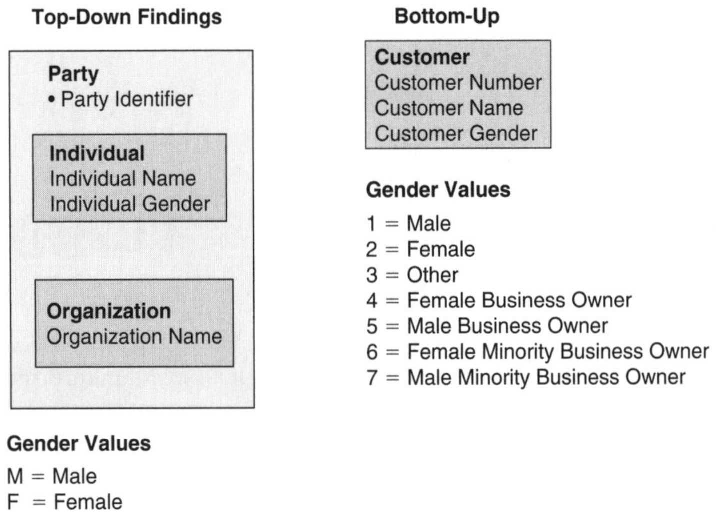

Top-Down Findings

> **Party**
> • Party Identifier
>
> > **Individual**
> > Individual Name
> > Individual Gender
> >
> > **Organization**
> > Organization Name

Gender Values

M = Male
F = Female

Bottom-Up

> **Customer**
> Customer Number
> Customer Name
> Customer Gender

Gender Values

1 = Male
2 = Female
3 = Other
4 = Female Business Owner
5 = Male Business Owner
6 = Female Minority Business Owner
7 = Male Minority Business Owner

■ **FIGURE 18.7** Example 1: Finding data inconsistencies within a file.

had been used, and their implied entities, could become the basis for adding corresponding entities and attributes to the logical data model.

Example 2 in Figure 18.8 shows how inconsistencies across two or more files can also change the way the logical data model is built. In the top-down modeling session, it was identified that a "Product" entity should be created. The Product Identifier was given as a numeric 10 attribute. A number of source systems were then profiled, and it became evident that only the checking account numbers were numeric 10, whereas credit card account numbers were typically numeric 16. The logical model could now be corrected to reflect a numeric 16 attribute for Product Identifier.

Best practice therefore suggests that a healthy combination of bottom-up data modeling, driven by data profiling tools, in conjunction with a rigorous top-down data modeling initiative will produce the best data architecture for next-generation data warehousing. A solid data architecture like the one depicted in Figure 18.9 is one of the critical success factors for achieving data quality improvement.

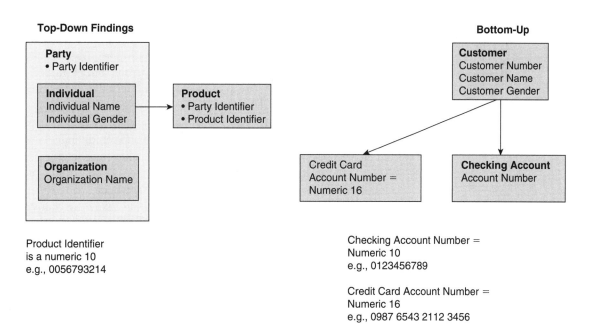

FIGURE 18.8 Example 2: Finding data inconsistencies across files.

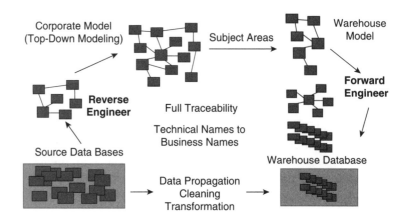

■ FIGURE 18.9   Source to DW 2.0 warehouse—components of a solid data architecture.

SUMMARY

Reusability is a critical success factor for second-generation data warehousing and there is a much-needed focus on the quality of the data models that underpin the program. The models must accurately reflect the business and they must be reusable in all future releases of the program.

The foundational model is the corporate data model. Traditionally, this model was derived using a top-down approach and by utilizing joint requirements planning and joint application design techniques. These techniques can deliver a good model relatively quickly. The problem with models derived in this way is that they are based purely on business rules as perceived by management and senior analysts. In reality, the systems that use the data may have a different set of rules. This is due to the fact that the systems are often 20 years old (and sometimes older). Undocumented changes have been made to the data and in the majority of cases the people that made the changes are no longer with the organization.

The only way to uncover what the data actually looks like is to reverse engineer the data into an abstracted logical data model. First-generation data warehouse initiatives attempted this in the past but the tools available to help were limited. Today a new set of tools has evolved—data profiling tools. These tools are an ideal aid to reverse engineer data and build a data model from the bottom up. When a model is built in this way, it is based on actual data content, and the chance of errors and omissions in the data modeling process is reduced. This bottom-up model is used as an input into the creation of the model that results from the top-down approach; in effect the former is used to challenge the latter model being drawn up by the business.

The corporate data model is not the only data model required in a successful business intelligence implementation. The recommendation is that all the models defined in the data column of the Zachman framework be created.

19

DW 2.0 and unstructured data

It is estimated that more than 80% of the data that exists in corporations is unstructured text. Unfortunately the technology that runs on computers today is dedicated to handling structured, repeatable data. The result is that there is valuable information that is not being used for decision making in the corporation. The useful information found in text is not a big part of the decision-making process.

DW 2.0 AND UNSTRUCTURED DATA

The DW 2.0 architecture for the next generation of data warehousing recognizes that there is valuable information in unstructured textual information. DW 2.0 recognizes that quite a bit of work must be done to the text to make it fit for analytical processing.

The starting point is the document itself. Figure 19.1 shows that text comes in all sorts of forms, such as emails, documents, medical records, contracts, spreadsheets, and voice transcriptions.

READING TEXT

The first step in the process of preparing unstructured data for analytical processing is to read the text. The text resides in a wide variety of formats. The formats may need to be read in as input.

Figure 19.2 depicts the reading of unstructured source texts.

After the original source text has been read, the next step is to prepare the data for entry into a data base. This textual preparation is an involved process. There are several good reasons text must be processed:

- Unstructured data needs to be fit into a relational format.

299

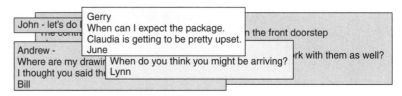
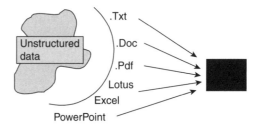

■ **FIGURE 19.1**   Documents, spreadsheets, emails—some common types of unstructured data.

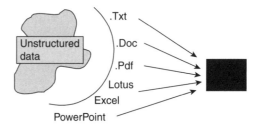

■ **FIGURE 19.2**   The first task is reading the unstructured data.

- Unstructured data must be "integrated" so that the analytical processing can be done in a meaningful manner. If raw text is simply shoved into a data base, the result is text that cannot be efficiently or even meaningfully analyzed.

WHERE TO DO TEXTUAL ANALYTICAL PROCESSING

At this point an important strategic decision is about to be made. That decision is where to do textual analytical processing. There are essentially two alternatives. One alternative is to do it at the place where unstructured text resides—in the unstructured environment. The other alternative is to do it in the structured environment. To do textual analytics in the structured environment requires that the unstructured text be read, integrated, and processed and then placed in the structured environment.

There is no question that reading, integrating, and processing textual unstructured data is an arduous task. But once the unstructured text has been processed, and once it is placed inside the structured environment, an entire world of opportunity opens up. Once unstructured data has been integrated and placed in the structured environment, there is the possibility of using standard analytical technology.

Organizations have already spent millions of dollars on the training of staff and users for the purpose of creating an analytical environment inside the world of structured technology. In the structured environment there already is data base technology, business intelligence, ETL, statistical processing, and so forth. It simply makes sense that the existing analytical environment be used—as is. All that is required is the ability to read and integrate textual information. And for that purpose there is textual ETL.

So choosing the environment in which to do textual analytical processing is easy. The structured environment is the place where analytical processing is best done.

INTEGRATING TEXT

The process of "integrating" text prior to placing it in a data base has many different facets. A number of steps are involved in preparing text for incorporation into a data base and subsequent analytical use as part of a DW 2.0 data warehouse. The key tasks that must be performed to groom unstructured data for the data warehouse are:

- Simple editing
- Stop-word removal
- Synonym replacement or concatenation
- Homographic resolution
- Thematic clustering
- External glossary/taxonomy overlay
- Stemming
- Alternate spelling resolution
- Foreign language accommodation
- Direct and indirect search support

A description of each of these different facets of unstructured data grooming follows.

SIMPLE EDITING

The first step in the preparation of unstructured text for analytical processing is to do simple editing on case, punctuation, and font. The reason this simple type of editing is important is that future analytical searches do not need to be impeded by discrepancies in typography. For example, if a search is done for "bill inmon," the search needs to find "Bill Inmon," even though the first letters of the two words in the text are in uppercase. Figure 19.3 illustrates the elimination of case, font, and punctuation from unstructured text as it is prepared for analytical processing.

STOP WORDS

The next step is to eliminate stop words. A stop word is a word that is useful for the lubrication or flow of language, but is not a useful or meaningful part of the message. Some typical stop words are

- a;
- and;
- the;
- was;
- that;
- which;
- to;
- from.

Figure 19.4 depicts the elimination of stop words.

Before
Lincoln stood and said - "Four score and seven years ago, our forefathers . . ."
After
lincoln stood and said four score and seven years ago our forefathers . . .

■ **FIGURE 19.3**   Basic punctuation, capitalization, case, font, and other aspects are removed as obstacles to searching.

Before
Lincoln stood and said - "Four score and seven years ago, our forefathers . . ."
After
Lincoln Four score seven years forefathers . . .

■ **FIGURE 19.4**   Stop words are removed.

SYNONYM REPLACEMENT

Another optional step in the process of textual integration is the creation of synonym substitutes. Synonym replacements are used to rationalize text from different terminologies into a single terminology. Synonym replacement involves substituting one standard word for all words with the same meaning. Consistent use of a single terminology can be a major step in the direction of ensuring reliable, repeatable queries against unstructured data after it is incorporated into the data warehouse. Figure 19.5 illustrates synonym replacement.

SYNONYM CONCATENATION

Synonym concatenation is an alternative to synonym replacement. In synonym concatenation, instead of replacing synonyms with a chosen standard word, the standard word is inserted next to, or concatenated with, all occurrences of other words that have the same meaning, its synonyms. Figure 19.6 illustrates synonym concatenation.

HOMOGRAPHIC RESOLUTION

Homographic resolution is the reverse of synonym concatenation and synonym replacement. Homographic resolution is used to clarify words or phrases that can mean more than one thing. The actual thing that the word means replaces or overlays the word or

Before
Lincoln stood and said - "Four score and seven years ago, our forefathers . . ."
After
Lincoln arose and said - "Eighty seven years ago, our ancestors . . ."

■ **FIGURE 19.5** Synonyms are replaced.

Before
Lincoln stood and said - "Four score and seven years ago, our forefathers . . ."
After
Lincoln stood arose and said - "Four score and eighty seven years ago, our forefathers ancestors . . ."

■ **FIGURE 19.6** Synonyms are concatenated.

Before

"The heart doctor recognized a ha immediately. He sat down . . ."

"The endocrinologist saw the first patient with ha and prescribed a therapy. . ."

"The small town doctor saw she had a terrific ha after the horse kicked her . . ."

After

"The heart doctor recognized a heart attack immediately. He sat down . . ."

"The endocrinologist saw the first patient with Hepatitis A and prescribed a therapy. . ."

"The small town doctor saw she had a terrific head ache after the horse kicked her . . ."

■ **FIGURE 19.7**   Homographic resolution.

phrase appearing in the text. Figure 19.7 illustrates homographic resolution.

Bond
- coupon
- maturity date
- yield
- face value
- issued on
- yield type
....

Diamond
- clarity
- flaw
- weight
- color

Postage stamp
- selvage
- glue
- face value
- country
- cancelled
- mint
- 1900
- 2000
- ....

■ **FIGURE 19.8**   Some themes and their descriptors.

CREATING THEMES

One of the interesting and useful things that is done with the text after it has been integrated is to produce a "cluster" of the text. Clustering text produces "themes." In the clustering of text, words and phrases are logically grouped together based on the number of occurrences of the words and their proximity to each other.

Clustering can also lead to the creation of a glossary or taxonomy. The glossary or taxonomy is called an "internal glossary" or an "internal taxonomy," because it is created from the text that has been entered into the system. Figure 19.8 shows the clustering of text and the themes that are produced.

EXTERNAL GLOSSARIES/TAXONOMIES

Whereas internal glossaries or taxonomies are useful, external glossaries and taxonomies are also useful. External glossaries and taxonomies can come from anywhere—books, indexes, the Internet, and so forth. External glossaries and taxonomies can represent anything. External glossaries and taxonomies can be used to superimpose a structure over text. Text can be read into the system, and a comparison can be made to determine whether the text belongs to or is otherwise related to an external glossary or taxonomy.

Figure 19.9 illustrates some external glossaries/taxonomies.

```
Sarbanes Oxley
   – revenue recognition
   – contingency sale
   – promise to deliver
   – delayed shipment       Accounting
   – deferred payment          – account
   ............................    – balance
                                   – interest
Anhydrous ammonia              – payoff amount
   – storage tank              – date opened
   – pressure                  – owner
   – crop                      ....................
   – reserve
   – percent ammonia
   ............................
```

■ **FIGURE 19.9**   Some external taxonomies.

STEMMING

Stemming is another step in the integration of text and the preparation of text for textual analytics. Text is stemmed when it is reduced to its Greek or Latin root. Stemming is important if the foundations of words are to be recognized. Stated differently, if words are compared literally, related words will not be clustered together as they should be. Figure 19.10 shows some words and their stems.

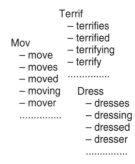

```
                          Terrif
                             – terrifies
                             – terrified
               Mov           – terrifying
                  – move     – terrify
                  – moves     ..............
                  – moved
                  – moving   Dress
                  – mover        – dresses
                   ..............  – dressing
                                 – dressed
                                 – dresser
                                  ..............
```

■ **FIGURE 19.10**   Stemming words.

ALTERNATE SPELLINGS

If searches are to be done effectively, the need for and practice of alternative spellings must be accommodated. Some words have alternative spellings and many names have alternative spellings. As an example of the utility of accommodating alternative spellings, suppose the name "Osama Bin Laden" is being searched. It would be a shame to miss a reference to "Usama Bin Laden" because the name is spelled differently. Figure 19.11 illustrates why different spellings of the same thing must be recognized.

```
osama bin laden
usama bin laden
osama ben laden
usama ben laden
osama bin ladeen
usama bin ladeen
osama ben ladeen
usama ben ladeen
............................
```

■ **FIGURE 19.11**   Alternate spellings of the same name or word.

TEXT ACROSS LANGUAGES

Another useful feature of textual analytics is that of the ability to operate in multiple languages. Figure 19.12 shows different languages.

```
Este es un pobrecito
     The girl ran inside her house
J'ai un chat, seulemente. . . .
```

■ **FIGURE 19.12**   Operating in different languages.

DIRECT SEARCHES

Yet another important feature of textual analytics is that of the ability to support different types of searches. The integration of text needs to set the stage for this feature. One type of search that needs to be supported is the direct search. A direct search is typified by Yahoo or Google. An argument is passed to the search engine and the search engine looks for any occurrence of the search argument. Figure 19.13 depicts a direct search.

INDIRECT SEARCHES

Another kind of search is the indirect search. Whereas search arguments are also passed to the search engine, in an indirect search,

Query –
find all references to Sarbanes Oxley

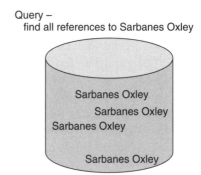

■ **FIGURE 19.13**   A direct search.

Query –
find all indirect references to Sarbanes Oxley

■ **FIGURE 19.14**   An indirect search.

there is no search made on the argument itself. Instead, the search is based on whatever relates to the argument. For example, Figure 19.14 depicts an indirect search on "Sarbanes Oxley." The search does not look for "Sarbanes Oxley." Instead the search looks for text relating to Sarbanes Oxley.

TERMINOLOGY

There is a major problem in the handling of text for the purpose of analytical processing. That problem is the handling of terminology. Terminology exists as a problem because language is spoken in terminology. Consider the human body. For any part of the human body there may be as many as 20 different ways of referring to that part. One doctor uses one set of terminology. Another doctor uses another set of terminology. A nurse uses another set of terminology. These professionals are all talking about the same thing. However, these people are speaking different languages.

If analytical processing is ever to be done on text, there must be a resolution of terminology. The final data base of textual words and phrases must be stored at both the specific and the generic level. The final textual data base on which textual analytics is done must contain the original specific word that the doctor or nurse used, and the textual data base must also contain the generic term that will be understood across the entire community of analysts.

If an organization does not solve the issues of terminology, it simply is impossible to do effective textual analytic processing.

SEMISTRUCTURED DATA/VALUE = NAME DATA

Unstructured data comes in all sorts of flavors. The simplest form unstructured data comes in is that of text in a document. Where there is text in a document, the words and phrases have no order or structure. An unstructured document is just that—an unstructured document.

But there are other forms of textual documents. In some cases the author of the document has given an inferred structure to the document. A simple example of an inferred structure inside a document is that of a recipe book. Inside a recipe book are many recipes. There is one document. But inside the document there are implied beginnings and endings. One recipe ends and another begins.

There often is a need to map the implied structure of the book onto the textual analytical data base. In some cases this is a very easy and obvious thing to do. In other cases it is not obvious at all as to how to do the mapping.

Another form of unstructured data that needs to be treated specially in a DW 2.0 environment is a form that can be called a VALUE = NAME form of data. To understand this form of unstructured data, consider a handful of resumes. On each resume is found common information, such as name, address, education, salary, and so forth. It is quite useful to be able to understand what kind of data in the unstructured data is being considered. In other words, for "name— Bill Inmon," it is convenient for the system to recognize that "name" is an important field and that "Bill Inmon" is the person being named. This capability means that text can be read and words can be picked up symbolically, not literally. The ability to sense symbolic words is very important in the building of a textual analytics data base.

THE TECHNOLOGY NEEDED TO PREPARE THE DATA

The technology that accomplishes the integration of unstructured text is commonly called textual ETL technology and is depicted at a high level in Figure 19.15.

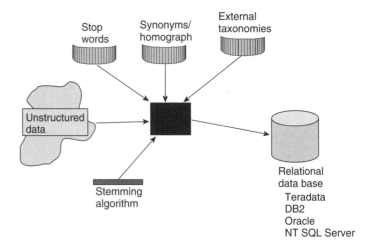

■ **FIGURE 19.15**   How unstructured data is turned into a relational data base.

THE RELATIONAL DATA BASE

When the unstructured text is ready for analytical processing, the text is placed in a relational data base. The relational data base may then be accessed and analyzed by many different tools, such as business intelligence tools.

Figure 19.16 shows the usage of business intelligence against unstructured data.

STRUCTURED/UNSTRUCTURED LINKAGE

After the unstructured relational data base is created, it is then linked to the structured data bases, forming a DW 2.0 foundation for the organization.

Figure 19.17 depicts the creation of the linkage between the two types of data bases.

Business Objects
Cognos
Micro Strategy
Crystal Reports

■ **FIGURE 19.16**   Once the data is in a relational format, it can be accessed and analyzed by practically any business intelligence tool.

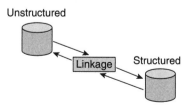

■ **FIGURE 19.17**   Linkage between unstructured data and structured data is created.

FROM THE PERSPECTIVE OF THE BUSINESS USER

If there is any data the business user is close to it is unstructured textual data. Unstructured textual data makes up the daily commerce of the life of the end user. Therefore the end user is highly involved when it comes to the inclusion of unstructured textual data in the DW 2.0 environment.

The business user is involved with specification of stop words. He/she is involved with terminology and with what languages are to be used in DW 2.0. The end user is involved with stemming—whether it is useful or not. The end user is involved with the sources of unstructured textual data—email, reports, contracts, and so forth.

In short the business user is heavily involved in all aspects of the capture, preparation, and entry of unstructured textual data into the DW 2.0 environment.

In general the business user has only a passive involvement in the design of the structured aspects of DW 2.0. But the reverse is true for the unstructured textual aspects of DW 2.0. For example, the business user is heavily involved in the specifications for the textual ETL transformations.

SUMMARY

Unstructured data is an important component of the DW 2.0 data warehouse.

Unstructured data must be read in and integrated into the DW 2.0 environment. The process of unstructured data integration includes but is not limited to the following:

- Removing punctuation, font, etc., as obstacles to data access and analysis
- Managing alternate spellings
- Stemming
- Stop-word management
- Creation of internal themes and taxonomies
- Synonym replacement
- Synonym concatenation
- Homographic resolution
- External taxonomy/glossary classification

After the gathering and integration of textual data have occurred, the stage is set for the creation of a relational data base for the purpose of supporting analytical processing. After integration the textual data is placed in a relational format and a relational data base is created. Then the relational data base is ready for business intelligence processing. Finally, the unstructured relational data base is linked with the structured data base in the DW 2.0 data warehouse.

20

DW 2.0 and the system of record

The foundation for most of the data population of the DW 2.0 data warehouse environment is the operational or legacy application systems environment. Figure 20.1 represents this type of data source.

Written many years ago and undocumented in many cases, operational application systems are where data first enters the corporate environment. The data often enters into the Interactive Sector in the form of a by-product of the execution of a transaction.

The typical elements of the operational legacy environment are shown by Figure 20.2.

■ **FIGURE 20.1** The operational/legacy systems environment.

The kinds of elements found in the operational legacy environment include programs, reports, processors, files, and data bases.

Because most of the data that enters the data warehouse environment originates in the operational environment, great care needs to be taken with it. The data that eventually finds its way in needs to be as accurate, up to date, and complete as possible. The data's system "source of record" needs to be defined. The identified source system of record is the best available source of the data.

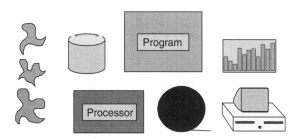

■ **FIGURE 20.2** The elements of the operational environment.

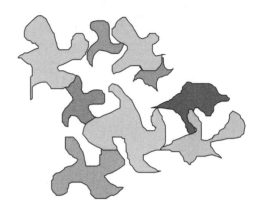

■ **FIGURE 20.3**   The legacy environment is a bunch of unintegrated applications.

There is an important relationship between finding the best source of the data for DW 2.0 and the data quality. The most important step a person makes toward good data quality is to choose the system of record carefully. Stated differently, if the system of record is not chosen at all or is chosen poorly, then the suffering shows up in the form of poor data quality.

The place to start the search for the best source of data is the applications that inhabit the legacy operational environment. Figure 20.3 depicts those applications.

The operational application systems environment in many companies is constrained by the transaction processing that occurs inside of it. While the business's operational transaction processing is occurring, especially when there is a large amount of transaction processing, the operational environment cannot be disturbed. The operational environment can be thought of as being very delicate when in this state. No large batch processes can be executed during these peak business periods. The challenge is that in many environments the operational transaction processing window is quite large, often lasting much longer than from 8:00 AM to 5:00 PM.

Figure 20.4 shows that there are moments when transaction processing in the legacy environment causes the operational environment to be unable to service any other kind of request.

There are other limitations associated with the legacy operational environment. One of those limitations is that in many places the legacy operational environment was built, and there is no documentation

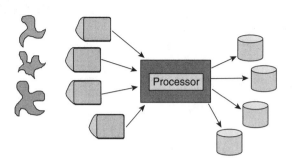

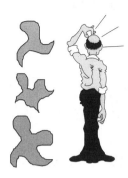

■ **FIGURE 20.4**   The operational environment is often constrained by the discipline required for online transaction processing (OLTP).

■ **FIGURE 20.5**   Often there is no documentation.

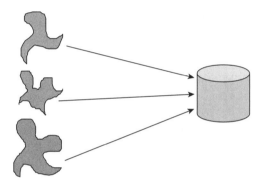

■ **FIGURE 20.6**   Preparing for the movement of data to DW 2.0.

or no up-to-date documentation for it. Trying to go back and find out what the operational application does is not an easy thing to do. Figure 20.5 shows that there are many undocumented legacy operational applications.

Despite these limitations (and more!) the architect must prepare for the movement of data from the legacy operational environment to the Interactive and Integrated Sectors of DW 2.0, as shown in Figure 20.6.

The job of the data warehouse architect is to find out what data in the legacy operational environment is the best source of data for the data warehouse. Figure 20.7 shows this task.

Not all of the data found in the operational environment is likely to find its way into the Interactive Sector of DW 2.0. Different parts of the operational environment will serve as a source for data.

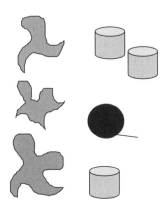

■ **FIGURE 20.7**   Finding what data is the best source.

The data that is chosen from the operational environment is the best source data that is available. The best source data is

- the most accurate;
- the most complete;
- the most up to date;
- the most trusted;
- the most accessible.

This definition of the best data for the Interactive Sector is called the source data system of record. Where data passes from the Integrated Sector to the Archival Sector, there is an extension of the system of record.

In some cases two or three files will serve as the source for the same unit of data inside the Interactive Sector of DW 2.0. In other cases there will be only a single source of data in the operational application systems environment.

After the definition of the best source data from the operational environment has been formulated, a mapping of the source data to the target data needs to be constructed. This activity is called data mapping (Figure 20.8). In some cases the mapping is as simple as saying that data starts in one place and ends in another. Figure 20.9 depicts a simple mapping.

But in other cases the mapping is more complex. Figure 20.10 suggests that calculations may also be required as data is moved. Not only is calculation required, but the date and rate of the calculation are required as well.

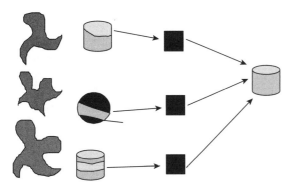

■ **FIGURE 20.8**   Now a formal mapping from the legacy environment to the data warehouse is created.

■ **FIGURE 20.9**   A simple mapping.

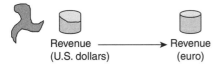

■ **FIGURE 20.10**   A more complex mapping.

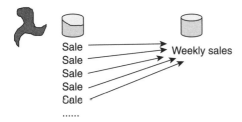

■ **FIGURE 20.11**   Another mapping.

Simple calculations may not be the only type of calculations necessary. Figure 20.11 suggests a different calculation, in which different records are used in a single calculation. The calculation is not so difficult, but the arrangement of data can be challenging.

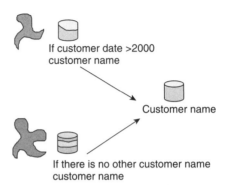

■ **FIGURE 20.12** When there are multiple sources, logic is used to determine which sources are best.

■ **FIGURE 20.13** On occasion it is necessary to supply a default value.

■ **FIGURE 20.14** Mapping includes rectifying encoded values.

Another form of mapping occurs when there is more than one source of data, and logic for determining which source is best under which condition is required. Figure 20.12 illustrates this kind of logic.

On some occasions it is necessary to supply a default value when no source of data can be found (Figure 20.13).

Another consideration of data mapping is that of reconciling different encoded values. In some cases, the source data has data encoded one way, and the target data needs to have the data encoded differently. Figure 20.14 depicts the reconciliation of encoded values.

After the mapping is done, the population of the Interactive Sector can begin. Figure 20.15 shows the entire data mapping from source to target.

The data mapping is the input needed to feed the ETL process (Figure 20.16).

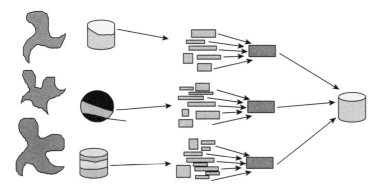

■ **FIGURE 20.15**   Once the mapping is done, population of DW 2.0 is ready to begin.

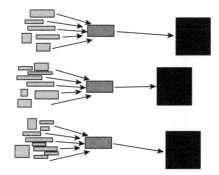

■ **FIGURE 20.16**   The mapping specifications turn into ETL specifications.

OTHER SYSTEMS OF RECORD

Another place the system of record is useful is in the creation of a data mart. A data mart can draw from many different sources in the enterprise data warehouse environment. Data marts can draw from the Interactive, Integrated, Near Line, and Archival Sectors of a DW 2.0 data warehouse. All of the many different places from which a data mart draws its data are considered to be the systems of record for the data mart.

Figure 20.17 depicts the different sectors of the DW 2.0 enterprise data warehouse serving as the system of record for the data in a data mart.

FROM THE PERSPECTIVE OF THE BUSINESS USER

In terms of importance, the single most important thing the business user can contribute to the building of DW 2.0 is the specification of

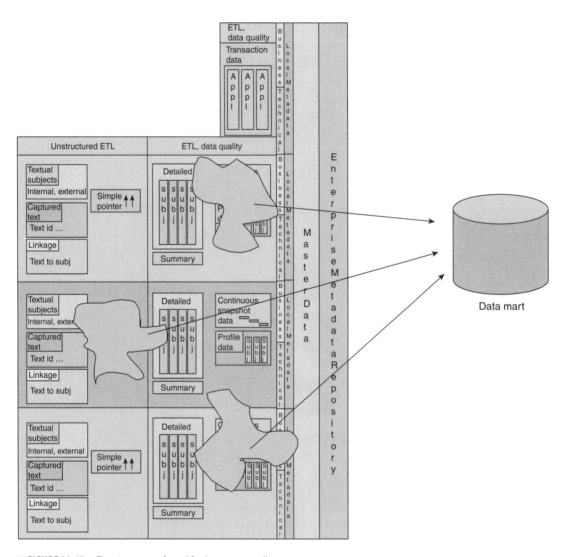

■ **FIGURE 20.17** There is a system of record for data marts as well.

the system of record. The final authority for the system of record is business. If the system of record does not reflect business, then it is worthless.

The final arbiter of whether transformation and the system of record have been done properly is the business user.

SUMMARY

The data warehouse environment contains the source of data and the target of data. The source of data—from the Interactive Sector or from external legacy applications—is called the system of record. The system of record is the definition of the best source of data.

The best source of data is data that is complete, accurate, and up to date. Data of the highest quality makes the system of record even better.

There are many reasons the system of record is important. It is important to the developer who will use the mapping from the system of record as a specification for populating the target data. Most importantly, the end-user analyst will need to understand the system of record as part of the analytical process.

The system of record is a major contributor to the integrity of the data in the environment.

21

Miscellaneous topics

This chapter is for topics that are important enough to write about but are not large enough by themselves to warrant their own chapter. The following miscellaneous topics are addressed in this chapter:

- Data marts
- Monitoring the DW 2.0 environment
- Moving data from one data mart to another
- What to do about bad data
- The speed of the movement of data within DW 2.0
- Data warehouse utilities

DW 2.0 has been presented as a representation of the base data that resides at the core of the DW 2.0 enterprise data warehouse. However, there are independent structures that use that data for analytical purposes. The exploration facility is one such structure. Another structure that takes data from DW 2.0 is the data mart.

DATA MARTS

Figure 21.1 depicts a data mart being fed data from the DW 2.0 enterprise data warehouse.

A data mart is built for the convenience of people who look at the data in the same way. Typically data marts are built for departments. Examples of corporate departments that typically have their own data marts include finance, sales, marketing, and accounting.

Any part of the DW 2.0 environment can be used to source a data mart. The normal DW 2.0 source of data mart data is the Integrated Sector. However, it is possible to populate data marts with data from other places in the DW 2.0 environment.

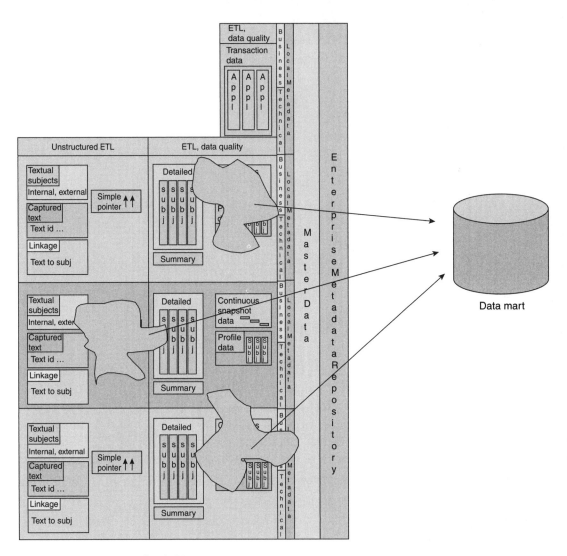

■ **FIGURE 21.1** Data marts emanate from the DW 2.0 environment.

THE CONVENIENCE OF A DATA MART

The convenience of the data mart is that data in DW 2.0 is detailed and data in a data mart is usually not so detailed. When people have a common way of looking at data, it is more efficient and more convenient to take the detailed data, structure it once the way the group wants to look at it, and make it available. That way, when someone wants to see their data, it is always structured and formatted the way that individual wants to see it. He/she does not have to worry about the work of taking detailed data and restructuring it.

There are some other important reasons data marts are so popular. Data marts are appealing because the cost of processing normally goes way down when data is taken out of the organization's enterprise data warehouse. The cost of processing on the machine(s) that houses DW 2.0 is usually as high as computing cycles ever get to be. When data is taken offline and onto another much smaller, departmental machine, the cost of data mart processing goes down.

Another reason data marts are popular is that by taking the data mart to another machine, the machine cycles for the DW 2.0 enterprise data warehouse environment are preserved. Moving machine cycles from the DW 2.0 environment to another environment greatly enhances the performance in the main DW 2.0 environment.

Yet another reason taking a data mart to another machine is a good idea is that different departments like the idea of ownership of their own data and their own processing.

There are many good reasons data marts are popular and separating data from the main DW 2.0 environment makes a lot of sense. Figure 21.2 shows that different groups of people have similar ways of looking at data.

TRANSFORMING DATA MART DATA

The kinds of processing that occur as data is moved from the DW 2.0 environment to the data mart environment include summarization of data, aggregation of data, selection and filtering of data, and restructuring of fields and other data attributes.

Figure 21.3 depicts the types of activities that occur as the detailed data found in the DW 2.0 environment is reformed into the data mart structure.

Determining at what point it makes sense to move analytical processing from the enterprise data warehouse to a data mart is one of the most interesting questions faced by the data warehouse architect. The answer is that when a lot of people look at the data in the same way and are doing a lot of queries, then it makes sense to create a data mart.

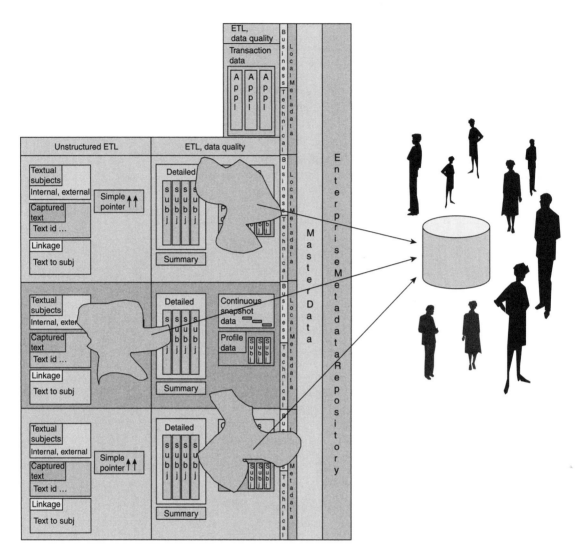

■ **FIGURE 21.2** Data marts serve groups of people who look at and use data in approximately the same way.

MONITORING DW 2.0

A data warehouse monitor is one of the best ways to know when the time has come to add one or more data marts. Figure 21.4 depicts a data warehouse monitor examining the activities going on inside a data warehouse. When a consistently high usage pattern is detected, it is probably time to build a data mart.

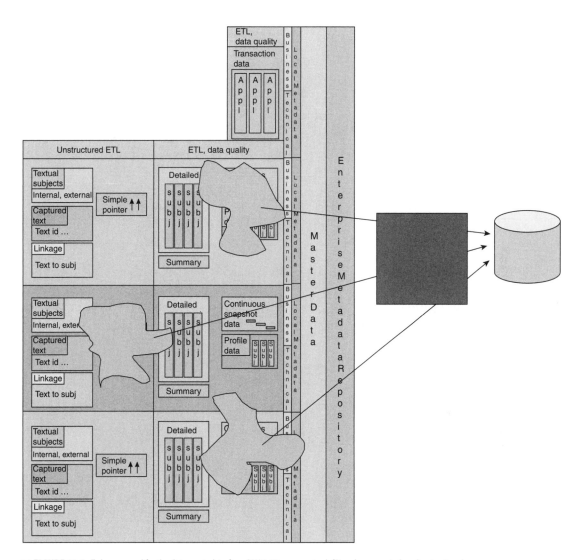

■ **FIGURE 21.3** To be prepared for the data mart, data from DW 2.0 is summarized, filtered, aggregated, and restructured.

Data marts are generally autonomous after they have been created. End users pretty much do whatever they want to do with their data mart(s).

MOVING DATA FROM ONE DATA MART TO ANOTHER

The practice of moving data directly from one data mart to another is architecturally unsound. Figure 21.5 indicates that in nearly every

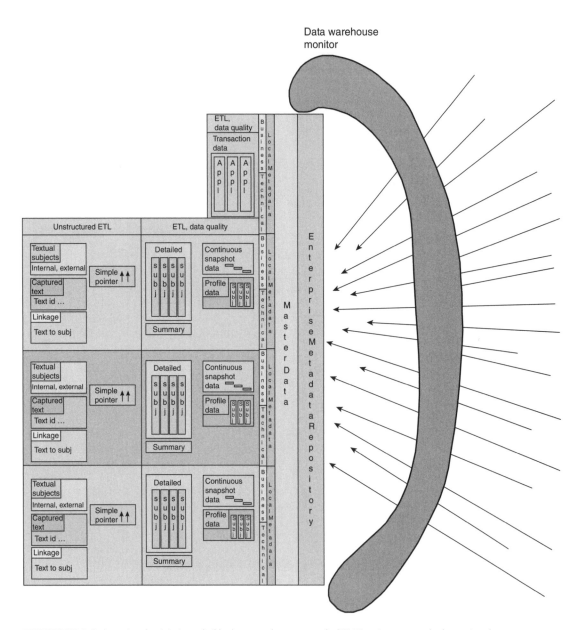

■ **FIGURE 21.4** To determine when it is time to build a data mart, the accesses to the DW 2.0 environment need to be monitored.

circumstance, data should not be moved directly from one data mart to another.

If there is a need for data to be shared between two or more data marts, the data in question should be placed in the DW 2.0 enterprise data warehouse environment.

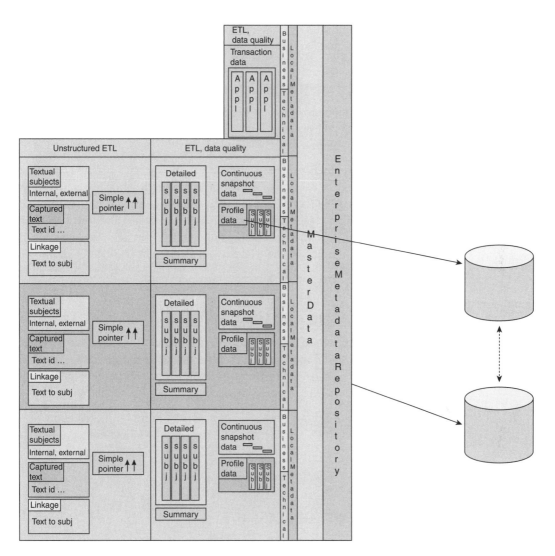

■ **FIGURE 21.5** In nearly every circumstance, data sharing between data marts is a very poor practice.

BAD DATA

It is not reasonable to expect that all data will always be entered perfectly into a large, complex enterprise data warehouse environment. Figure 21.6 depicts the question—What should be done about bad data in the DW 2.0 environment?

The first thing that should be done is to try to identify the source of bad data. If the source can be found, the next step is to correct the

■ **FIGURE 21.6** What to do about bad data?

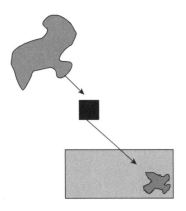

■ FIGURE 21.7 Find out how the bad data got into the DW 2.0 environment and make corrections in ETL or elsewhere.

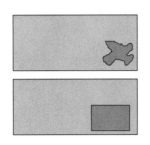

■ FIGURE 21.8 Add a "balancing" record, if possible.

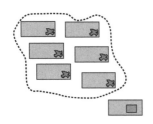

■ FIGURE 21.9 Make an arbitrary adjustment for a group of records.

data at the source. Figure 21.7 shows that the first step is to try to find out how bad data got into DW 2.0.

A BALANCING ENTRY

Correcting a process that is sending bad data to the data warehouse does not address the problem of what to do about bad data that has already gotten into the data warehouse.

One approach to correcting data in DW 2.0 is to find the bad data and make a "balancing" entry. If it is found that there is an erroneous entry of $23.61 in the system, then another entry equal to –$23.61 will correct it. This approach keeps the books balanced and leaves an audit trail. But this approach works only where there is a finite amount of data to be adjusted and where erroneous data can be identified.

Figure 21.8 depicts a balancing entry.

RESETTING A VALUE

Unfortunately there are many circumstances in which there is not a finite number of incorrect records that can be found and for which a balancing entry can be created. In this case an arbitrary entry is made that "resets" the values for an account.

When an arbitrary resetting of values is done by the creation of a new entry, the audit trail should carefully show how the resetting was done.

Figure 21.9 depicts the resetting of values.

MAKING CORRECTIONS

A third approach to correcting values in a DW 2.0 environment is the practice of finding bad records and then changing the values in those records. Unfortunately there are many drawbacks to this approach. The first problem is that there is no clear and obvious audit trail. A second disadvantage is that the integrity of data has been destroyed.

For example, a report is run at 9:31 AM and a summary value of $5918.91 is calculated. Then at 10:14 AM a lot of direct adjustments are made. Now at 11:57 AM the values are recalculated, and a sum of $4817.73 is calculated. The problem is that there is no way to relate the different summarizations or reconcile why the values are different.

■ **FIGURE 21.10** Go in and change values in the incorrect record.

Figure 21.10 shows the actual replacement of values in records in the DW 2.0 environment.

THE SPEED OF MOVEMENT OF DATA

The speed with which data moves into and through the DW 2.0 data warehouse environment raises an interesting philosophical issue. One school of thought says that data ought to move as quickly as possible throughout the DW 2.0. In other words, if a transaction occurs at 7:13 PM, then the transaction should have its data entered into and reflected in the Interactive Sector at 7:14 PM. There are many advocates of this "as soon as possible" speed of data throughout the DW 2.0 environment, as suggested by Figure 21.11.

The alternative approach is to move data in a slower, more deliberate manner throughout the DW 2.0 environment. For example, a transaction might be executed on January 14th and the data may not find its way into the DW 2.0 environment until January 21st. This means that a week will pass before the data enters the DW 2.0 environment. The data is allowed to "settle" while it is awaiting movement into the DW 2.0 environment.

Data settles when it has been allowed enough time for an activity to be adjusted if made incorrectly. For example, suppose a transaction executes on Monday. On Tuesday, it is discovered that an adjustment needs to be made to the transaction. On Wednesday another adjustment that needs to be made is found. Finally, on Friday the transaction is sent to the DW 2.0 environment. Not being in a hurry to enter the transaction data into DW 2.0 has allowed time for the transaction data to settle into a finalized state. The result is much more accurate data and much simpler processing for the DW 2.0 environment.

Figure 21.12 illustrates allowing data to settle before being transmitted to the DW 2.0 environment.

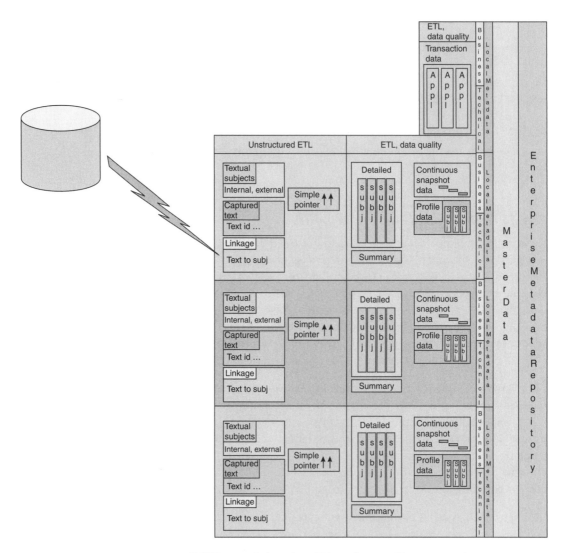

■ **FIGURE 21.11** Updating data in DW 2.0 as fast as possible—one approach.

DATA WAREHOUSE UTILITIES

A data warehouse utility (DWU) is a facility that takes some or all data warehouse processing and transparently supplants some or all of the existing data warehouse infrastructure. There are many good reasons for deploying a data warehouse utility, including performance, cost, and extending the license of a DBMS. "Dataupia" is a good example of a data warehouse utility.

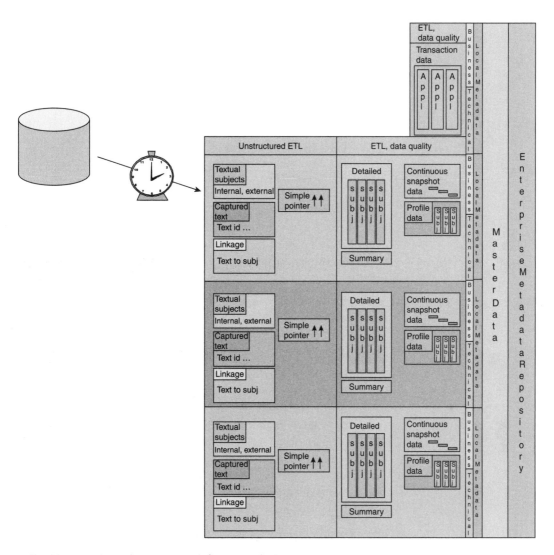

■ FIGURE 21.12 Allowing data time to "settle" before it is moved to DW 2.0.

The following example illustrates why a data warehouse utility offers significant advantages. Consider a "standard" data warehouse processing environment as depicted in Figure 21.13.

This figure depicts an end user communicating directly with technology such as SAP. SAP in turn communicates directly with a DBMS such as Oracle. Oracle communicates directly with traditional SAN technology, such as EMC, IBM, or Hitachi.

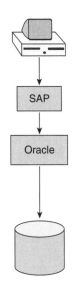

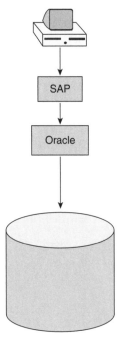

■ **FIGURE 21.14** What happens when DW 2.0 ages.

Over time the amount of data in the traditional environment depicted in Figure 21.13 starts to grow and can become very large. Figure 21.14 depicts what happens to the traditional data base environment over time.

There are three basic reasons data grows so steadfastly in this environment:

- Data is collected at the granular level.
- Data is collected historically.
- Data is collected and integrated from a wide variety of sources.

There are many consequences of the growth of data. One of the biggest consequences is that the cost of the data and the infrastructure to support it grows dramatically as well. Figure 21.15 illustrates that the cost of the infrastructure rises as a function of the volume of data that is managed.

And the cost does not just increase incrementally—it increases dramatically.

The cost of storage is an interesting factor in data warehouse processing. In the first 2 or 3 years of building and developing a data warehouse, the cost of storage is almost incidental. But as a data warehouse matures, the costs of other data warehouse features diminish, while the costs of storage increase. And it is not just the cost of storage, it is the cost of storage infrastructure that increases as well. There are the processor costs, the software license costs, and the channel costs. In addition, after the storage has been acquired and implemented, there is the ongoing operations cost. When the actual cost of storage is considered in light of these other factors, it is seen that the cost of actual storage is only a fraction of the total costs of storage.

Unfortunately, the increase in storage and storage infrastructure costs is inevitable. Once an organization gets to be locked into a way of processing, the organization continues down that path for a long, long time.

But organizations have a way of needing to manage their budget. A major increase in expenditures each year cannot continue indefinitely. It is only natural that organizations desire to find ways to manage their budget. Therefore, it is normal for them to turn to the data warehouse utility to help them manage their budget and their data warehouse environment.

The data warehouse utility is a means of storing and managing data for a fraction of the cost of traditional SAN storage.

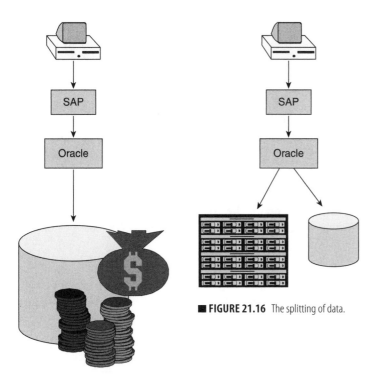

■ FIGURE 21.16 The splitting of data.

■ FIGURE 21.15 The cost of the infrastructure.

Figure 21.16 depicts a data warehouse managed under a combination of traditional storage and a DWU.

This figure shows that part of the data is managed under traditional storage and another part is managed under a DWU. The net effect of such a split is that it significantly drives down the cost of operating a data warehouse on a day-to-day basis.

Depending on the particulars, the cost of operating a data warehouse may drop as much as an order of magnitude with the addition of a DWU. For example, suppose an organization has a 10-terabyte data warehouse and the operating budget is $10,000,000 annually. Now suppose the organization reduces its data warehouse storage requirements by half by adding a DWU. The annual operating costs look like:

Five terabytes traditional storage—$5,000,000
Five terabytes DWU storage—$500,000
Total operating costs—$5,500,000
Total savings—$4,500,000

The movement to DWU has cut the ongoing operating cost of storage significantly. Implementing a DWU is not as simple as plugging an electric cord into a wall socket. There are multiple strategies for the deployment of DWU technology. Each style of deployment has its advantages and disadvantages.

One approach to DWU deployment is to replace the traditional technology completely—the DWU is rolled in and the traditional technology is rolled out. The advantage of the replacement strategy is the immediate reduction in the cost of storage. There are also some disadvantages, including:

- License disruption: The existing traditional environment cannot be simply discarded without consideration of existing contracts and licenses.

- Software disruption: In some cases (not the case for Dataupia), some DWUs are not transparent to the controls needed to manage the storage processing. In this case the DWU cannot supplant the traditional storage without an upheaval.

- Storage optimization: The DWU storage is not optimized for OLTP processing. In some cases, the DWU is optimized for data warehouse processing only.

Another approach is to supplant some traditional data warehouse storage incrementally.

The disadvantage of the incremental approach to supplanting traditional data warehouse data storage is that there must be transparency of the data. The DWU must be compatible with the operating system and DBMS that controls the traditional storage. If the DWU is not transparent to the operating system and DBMS of the traditional storage environment, then it must access and manage slices of the traditional environment that can be easily separated from the traditional environment. Unfortunately this incremental, separated approach is somewhat limited in its application.

The third approach to the implementation of DWU technology is the deployment of DWU technology with transparency. In this case, the transparency means that the user of the DBMS does not know where the data resides. The data can reside on the DWU or on traditional storage. The system simply does not care. The actual physical location and management of the data are transparent to the user and the DBMS. For the transparency approach to work, the software that controls the DWU

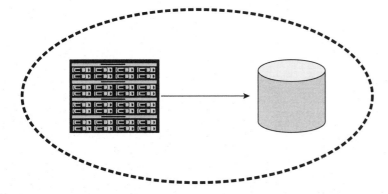

■ FIGURE 21.17 Data base transparency.

must be compatible with both the operating systems and the DBMS that is used to manage traditional storage.

Figure 21.17 depicts the transparent approach.

SUMMARY

Data marts contain departmental data for the purpose of decision making. There are lots of reasons for the creation of a data mart, including

- the cost of machine cycles is low;
- the end user has control;
- the performance of the DW 2.0 environment is enhanced.

When bad data enters the DW 2.0 environment

- the source of the bad data should be identified and corrected;
- a balancing entry can be created;
- a value may be reset;
- actual corrections can be made to the data.

Chapter 22

Processing in the DW 2.0 environment

The distinguishing characteristics of the DW 2.0 environment are the types of data found in the various sectors. In many ways the data and the sectors define DW 2.0. But from an architectural standpoint there is more to DW 2.0 than a data architecture. Another way to perceive DW 2.0 is through the processes found in the various environments or sectors.

There are various types of transactions and processes that run through the DW 2.0 environment. Perhaps the simplest of these transactions is the simple request for data. Figure 22.1 shows a simple request for data.

In a simple request for data there is a desire to find one or two rows of data and then to display them interactively. This simple kind of transaction uses very few system resources and is very simple in terms of its logic. This type of transaction is found in the online environment because it is very easy to get good performance when the system is executing this kind of transaction.

■ **FIGURE 22.1** A simple access transaction.

The transaction depicted here is predetermined. It and its logic are preprogrammed so that the end user merely sets the transaction in motion for it to execute.

A variation of the simple transaction is the complex transaction. The complex transaction usually looks at more rows of data than the simple transaction. And the complex transaction entails quite a bit of logic, something not found in the simple transaction. As long as the complex transaction does not require too many rows of data to execute, it can be freely mixed in the interactive workload with no serious degradation of performance.

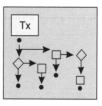

■ **FIGURE 22.2** A complex transaction.

Figure 22.2 shows a complex transaction.

■ **FIGURE 22.3** An ad hoc transaction.

Complex transactions are almost always preprogrammed. They are merely set in motion by the end user for the program to be executed.

Another variation of the simple transaction is the transaction that is created on an ad hoc basis. Figure 22.3 depicts an ad hoc transaction.

An ad hoc transaction is usually fairly simple. It is not often that there is complex logic found in the ad hoc transaction. As a rule the ad hoc transaction does not look at too many rows of data. But occasionally an end user will submit an ad hoc query that looks at a very large amount of data. When an ad hoc transaction that looks at very large amounts of data is set in motion, performance suffers.

For this reason there usually are not too many ad hoc transactions that are found in the interactive environment. Instead it is much more normal for the ad hoc query to be found in the integrated environment.

In many cases the ad hoc query is found in the data mart environment. The ad hoc queries are often produced by business intelligence software. The end user actually does not enter anything but parameters into the business intelligence software. Once the parameters are written, the software actually shapes the query.

Another kind of query is the access query. The access query differs from the simple access query in that the access query often accesses many rows of data.

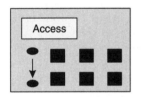

■ **FIGURE 22.4** An access transaction.

Figure 22.4 shows an access query.

The logic behind an access query is usually fairly simple. However, the volume of data touched by the access query can be considerable.

Access queries are used by analysts to scan entire vistas of data. There are times when looking at one or two rows of data simply does not supply the needed information. Because they access lots of data, access transactions are not normally run in the Interactive Sector. If they are run there, they are run at odd times of the day when there is no deleterious effect on the overall performance of the system. Instead it is much more common to see access transactions run in the Integrated and Archival Sectors. Once in a great while an access query is run in the near-line environment.

Another common type of process found in the DW 2.0 environment is the transformation process. The transformation process is one in which whole vistas of data are accessed, altered, and written out as another file. Transformation processes are almost never run in the interactive environment during peak-period processing.

Figure 22.5 illustrates a transformation process.

Transformation processes usually entail complex algorithms. In some cases the transformation process entails seriously complex processes. For this reason it is unusual for a transformation process to be written in any other than a preprogrammed basis. Stated differently, ad hoc transformation processes are almost never ad hoc in nature.

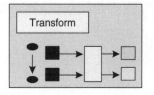

■ **FIGURE 22.5**   A transformation process.

One of the by-products of the transformation process is metadata. The transformations that the transformation process executes are formed by metadata. Therefore, as documentation of the processing, the metadata is written out and is useful for many people in the DW 2.0 environment.

Transformation processing applies to both structured and unstructured data.

Yet another type of process is statistical processing. Statistical processing is useful for a mathematical analysis of large amounts of data. In almost every case statistical processing entails the access of many rows of data. For this reason statistical processes are not run when online response time is an issue.

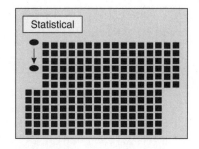

■ **FIGURE 22.6**   A statistical transaction process.

Figure 22.6 shows a statistical process.

Statistical processes often entail complex processing logic. They are often a part of a stream of analysis known as heuristic processing. In heuristic processing one step of analysis is not obvious until the immediately preceding step is complete.

As such, heuristic processing mandates a sort of ad hoc processing.

The various sectors of the DW 2.0 environment typically run different kinds of processes.

Figure 22.7 shows the kinds of processes found in the Interactive Sector.

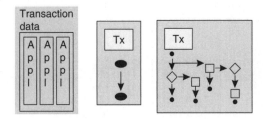

■ **FIGURE 22.7**   What the workload of the interactive environment looks like, for the most part.

In the Interactive Sector are found simple transactions and complex transactions. There are no statistical processes. There are no access processes. There are only transactions that can be run in a disciplined manner and that are run when there is no conflict for resources. In other words, the job stream of the interactive environment is for small, fast-running, well-disciplined transactions.

Anything other than small, fast-running, well-disciplined transactions disrupts the flow of transactions and has a negative impact on performance.

The integrated environment runs a wide variety of transactions. Figure 22.8 shows the transaction types that are run in the integrated environment.

In Figure 22.8 it is seen that transformation processing is run as data enters the integrated environment. Once the environment has been created, the environment has ad hoc transactions run, access transactions run, and complex transactions run.

The net result of the transactions run in the integrated environment is a mixed workload. Because the workload is mixed, the overall system performance is spotty.

The near-line processing is shown in Figure 22.9.

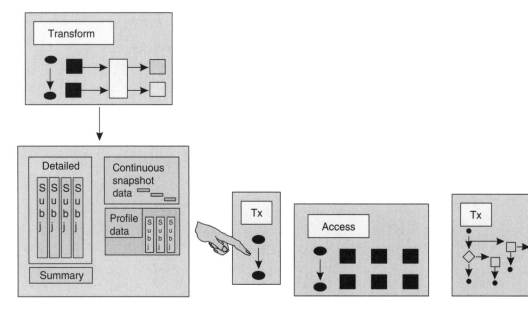

■ **FIGURE 22.8**   What processing in the integrated structured environment looks like.

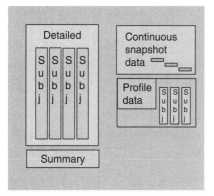 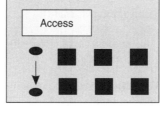

■ **FIGURE 22.9**   There is little or no end-user transaction processing in the near-line environment.

There are actually very few transactions run in the near-line environment. About the only two types of transactions run in the near-line environment are access transactions and replacement transactions. A replacement transaction is a specialized transaction in which small amounts of data are taken from the near-line environment and placed in the Integrated Sector.

There are actually very few transactions that are run in the archival environment. However, the transactions that are run there are usually very resource intensive transactions.

Figure 22.10 shows the transaction types that run in the archival environment.

The types of transactions that are common to the archival environment are the statistical process and the access transactions. If passive

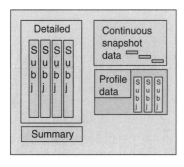 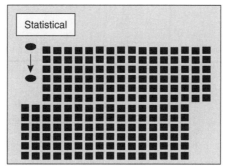 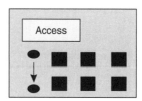

■ **FIGURE 22.10**   Only access and statistical processing is found in the archival environment.

indexes have been built, then oftentimes processing in the archival environment is reasonably efficient. But if passive indexes have not been built, then it is normal to have to do full data base scans in the archival environment.

Online and high performance is not an issue in the archival environment.

The only environment in which processing occurs for unstructured data is the integrated environment.

Figure 22.11 illustrates the unstructured integrated environment and the types of transactions that are typically found there.

There is a polyglot of transactions found in the unstructured integrated environment. Simple transactions, simple ad hoc transactions, complex transactions, and access transactions are found in the unstructured Integrated Sector. In addition, data that is placed in the unstructured integrated environment is passed through the transformation process for unstructured data.

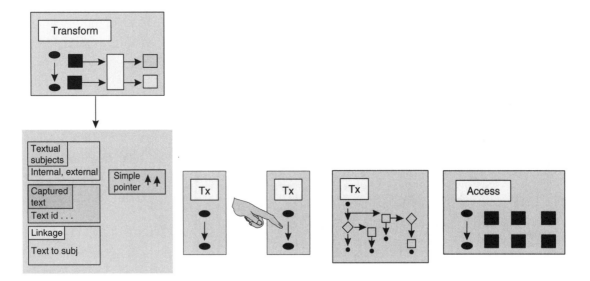

■ **FIGURE 22.11** All sorts of analytical processing are found in the unstructured integrated environment.

SUMMARY

A part of the DW 2.0 environment is processing. Some of the various kinds of processes found in the DW 2.0 environment include

- simple transactions;
- complex transactions;
- transformations;
- access transactions;
- statistical transactions.

Because of the data found there and the performance characteristics of the various sectors, different kinds of processes have an affinity for different places in the DW 2.0 environment.

23

Administering the DW 2.0 environment

The DW 2.0 environment is a complex environment that is built over a long period of time. The DW 2.0 environment touches many parts of the corporation—day-to-day operations, management, tactical decisions, strategic decisions, and even the boardroom. There are many facets to the DW 2.0 environment—technical, business, legal, engineering, human resources, and so forth. As such, the DW 2.0 environment is one that is a long-term management issue and requires careful management and administration.

This chapter will touch on some of the many issues of management and administration of the DW 2.0 environment.

THE DATA MODEL

At the intellectual heart of the DW 2.0 environment is the data model. The data model is the description of how technology meets business. The data model is used to direct the efforts of many different developers over a long period of time. When the data model is used properly, one piece of development fits with another piece of development like a giant jigsaw puzzle that is built over a period of years. Stated differently, without a data model, coordinating the long term development of many projects within the DW 2.0 environment with many different people is an almost impossible task.

The data model is built at different levels—high, middle, and low. The first step (and one of the most difficult) is the definition of the scope of integration for the data model. The reason the scope of integration is so difficult to define is that it never stays still. The scope is constantly changing. And each change affects the data model.

When the scope changes too often and too fast, the organization is afflicted with "scope creep."

Over time, the high-level data model needs the least amount of maintenance. The long-term changes that the organization experiences have the most effect on the midlevel model and the low-level model. At the middle level of the data model, over time the keys change, relationships of data change, domains of data change, definitions of data change, attributes change, and occasionally even the grouping of attributes changes. And as each of these changes occurs, the underlying related physical data base design also changes.

Part of the job of the administration of the data model is to ensure that it is being followed with each new development and with each new modification of the data warehouse. The biggest challenges here are to ensure that

- no new primitive attributes are being developed that are not in the data model, or if new primitive data elements are introduced, they find their way into the data model;
- new developers view the data model as an accelerant to progress, not a barrier to progress;
- new modifications to DW 2.0 follow the data model.

It is important to note that groupings of attributes and keys/foreign keys are very important for compliance, but other aspects of the data model may be less important.

In addition, it is not necessary for the derivatives of primitive data to be in compliance with the data model.

ARCHITECTURAL ADMINISTRATION

In addition to an administrative organization tending to the data model for compliance with the data model, it is necessary to have a general architectural organization that administers the DW 2.0 architecture. The architectural administration is one that tends to the long-term oversight of the architecture. Some of the concerns of the architectural administration are the following.

Defining the moment when an Archival Sector will be needed

In most environments it is not necessary to build the archival environment immediately. Usually some period of time passes before it is necessary to build the archival environment. The architectural administration provides the guidance for when and how the archival environment is to be built. The architectural administration determines many aspects of the archival environment, such as

- when data will be passed into the archival environment;
- how long data will stay in the archival environment;
- the criteria for moving data out of the archival environment;
- the platform the archival environment will reside on;
- the data base design for the archival environment;
- whether passive indexes will be created;
- how passive indexes will be created;
- the level(s) of granularity for archival data;
- and so forth.

Determining whether the Near Line Sector is needed

If the Near Line Sector is needed, the architectural administration determines such important parameters as when data will be moved into the Near Line Sector, when it will be moved back into the Integrated Sector, and when it will be moved to the Archival Sector; what metadata will be stored; what platform the Near Line Sector will reside on; and so forth. Over time the need for a Near Line Sector can change. At the point of initial design it may be apparent that there is no need for a Near Line Sector. But over time the factors that shape the need may change. Therefore, there may come a day when the Near Line Sector is needed. It is the job of the architectural administration to make that decision. Some of the decisions made by the architectural administrator include

- whether near-line storage is needed;
- the criteria under which data is passed into near-line storage;
- the platform that is needed for near-line storage;
- the metadata that will be stored;
- the criteria under which data passes out of near-line storage.

Another sector of the DW 2.0 environment that is of concern to the architectural administrator is the Interactive Sector. In some organizations, there is no interactive environment. In other organizations there is an interactive environment. The architectural administrator addresses such issues as the following:

- Is an interactive environment needed?

- If there is an interactive environment, is response time adequate, meeting all SLA requirements? Is availability adequate, meeting all SLA requirements? Is the interactive environment available for any reporting that needs to be done? Are the capacity requirements being met?

■ Is data being properly integrated as it leaves the interactive environment?

■ If legacy data is being read into the Interactive Sector, is that data being integrated properly into applications?

■ What platform is the Interactive Sector being run on?

Another task of the architectural administrator is that of making sure there is never a flow of data from one data mart to another. Should the administrator find that such a flow occurs, he/she redirects the flow from a data mart to the DW 2.0 environment and then back to the data mart receiving the data.

Yet another ongoing task of the architectural administrator is to ensure that monitoring is occurring properly and that the results of the monitoring are properly interpreted. Various kinds of monitoring activity need to occur in the DW 2.0 environment. There is the monitoring of transactions and response time in the interactive environment and there is the monitoring of data and its usage in the other parts of the DW 2.0 environment.

Some of the questions that should be considered in monitoring the DW 2.0 environment follow:

■ Are transactions being monitored in the Interactive Sector?
■ Is availability being monitored in the Interactive Sector?
■ Is data usage being monitored in the Integrated Sector?
■ Is dormant data identified?
■ Are the monitors consuming too many system resources?
■ When are the results of monitoring being examined?

One of the most important determinations made as a result of monitoring the usage of the Integrated Sector is whether it is time to build a new data mart. The administrator looks for repeated patterns of usage of the Integrated Sector. When enough requests for data structured in the same way appear, it is a clue that a data mart is needed.

These then are some of the activities of the architectural administration of the DW 2.0 environment. But there are other aspects of the DW 2.0 environment that need administration as well.

It should go without saying that one of the skills the architectural administrator needs to have is that of understanding architecture. It is futile for an individual to try to act as an architectural administrator without understanding what is meant by architecture and what the considerations of architecture are.

Another important part of architectural administration is that of managing the ETL processes found in DW 2.0. The first kind of ETL process found in DW 2.0 is that of classical integration of data from application sources. The issues that need to be monitored here include the traffic of data that flows through the ETL process, the accuracy of the transformations, the availability of those transformations to the analytical community, the speed and ease with which the transformations are made, and so forth. The second type of ETL tool is that of textual transformation by which unstructured data is transformed into the data warehouses contained in DW 2.0. The issues of administration here include the volume of data that arrives in the DW 2.0 environment, the integration algorithms that are used, the type of data that is placed in the DW 2.0 environment, and so forth. It is noted that the two forms of ETL transformation are entirely different from each other.

METADATA ADMINISTRATION

One of the most important aspects of the DW 2.0 environment is that of metadata. For a variety of reasons the administration of metadata is its own separate subject. Some of those reasons are:

- The tools for metadata capture and management have lagged behind the rest of the industry considerably.
- The history of metadata management has not been good. There have been far more failures than successes.
- The business case for metadata requires much more attention than the business case for other aspects of the DW 2.0 environment.

And there probably are more reasons metadata management is a sensitive issue.

The problem is that it is metadata that is needed for the many different parts of the DW 2.0 environment to be meaningfully held together. Stated differently, without a cohesive metadata infrastructure, the many different parts of DW 2.0 have no way of coordinating efforts and work.

There are many aspects to metadata administration. Some of these aspects include

- the original capture of metadata;
- the editing of metadata;
- the making of metadata available at the appropriate time and place in the DW 2.0 environment;
- the ongoing maintenance of metadata;
- the distribution of metadata to different locations in the DW 2.0 environment;
- the further extension of metadata;
- the archiving of metadata.

In addition to these considerations, the metadata administrator makes such important decisions as

- what platform(s) metadata will reside on;
- what technologies will be used to capture and store metadata;
- what technologies will be used to display and otherwise make available metadata.

One of the issues of metadata is its ephemeral nature. Unlike structured data, metadata comes in many forms and structures. It simply is not as stable or as malleable as other forms of data.

Another major issue relating to metadata is that of the different forms of metadata. There are two basic forms of metadata. Those forms are

- business metadata and
- technical metadata.

As a rule technical metadata is much easier to recognize and capture than business metadata. The reason technical metadata is easier to find and capture is that it has long been understood. The truth is that business metadata has long been a part of the information landscape, but business metadata has not been formally addressed—by vendors, by products, by technology. Therefore, it is much easier to find and address technical metadata than it is to find and address business metadata.

DATA BASE ADMINISTRATION

Another essential aspect of the DW 2.0 environment is that of data base administration. In data base administration the day-to-day care and tending of data bases is done. Data base administration is a technical job. The data base administrator needs to know such things as how to restore a data base, how to recover lost transactions, how to determine when a transaction has been lost, how to bring a data base back up when the data base goes down, and so forth.

In short, when something malfunctions with a data base, it is the data base administrator who is charged with getting the data base back up and running.

One of the challenges of data base administration is the sheer number of data base administration activities that are required in the DW 2.0 environment. There are so many data bases and tables that the data base administrator cannot possibly devote huge amounts of time to any one data base. There simply are too many, all of which are too important to focus on any one data base. Therefore, the administrator needs tools that can look over the many aspects of the many data bases and tables that comprise the DW 2.0 environment.

Some of the considerations of data base administration in the DW 2.0 environment are

- selecting tools for monitoring the data base administration aspects of the DW 2.0 environment;
- selecting tools for the cure of data and prevention of its travails in the DW 2.0 environment;
- making sure that the tools are applied when needed.

As a rule the data base administration job is a 24/7 job. Someone from data base administration is on call all the time to be able to advise computer operations as to what to do when a problem arises. Especially in the case of the interactive environment, when a data base problem occurs, the data base administrator needs to be as proactive as possible, because malfunctions and down time equal dissatisfaction with the environment. But being proactive is difficult because the vast majority of the tasks facing the data base administrator are reactive.

STEWARDSHIP

In recent years, with governance and compliance becoming large issues, the role of stewardship has become an important topic. In years past it was sufficient simply to get data into and through the system. In today's world, the quality and accuracy of the data have become important.

It is in this framework that stewardship has been elevated into a position of recognized responsibility.

Stewardship entails the following:

- The identification of what data elements make up the system of record.
- The specification of the criteria of data quality for those data elements.
- The specification of algorithms and formulas pertinent to those data elements.

To differentiate between the role of data base administrator and that of data steward, consider the following. When a data base has "gone down" and is unavailable to the system, the data base administrator is called. When performance suffers and there is a general system slowdown, the data base administrator is called. When there is an incorrect value in a record that the end user has encountered, the data steward is called. And when it comes time to create a new data base design, and the sources of data and their transformation are considered, the data steward is called.

There are, then, related yet different sets of activities that the data base administrator and the data steward have.

As a rule the data base administrator is a technician and the data steward is a business person. Trying to make the job of the data steward technical is usually a mistake.

Some of the aspects of the data steward's working life include

- being available for data base design, especially where transformation and mapping are a part of the design;
- being available to answer questions with regard to the contents of a given data element;
- teaching business analysts what data there is and how it is best interpreted;
- ensuring that mapping and transformation are done accurately;
- describing how algorithms and program logic should be done to reflect the true business meaning of data.

As a rule a large corporation will have more than one data steward. There are usually many business people that act as data stewards. Each primitive data element will have exactly one and only one data steward at any moment in time. If a data element has no data steward or if a data element has more than one data steward at any point in time, then there is an issue.

SYSTEMS AND TECHNOLOGY ADMINISTRATION

An integral part of the DW 2.0 environment is systems and technology. In its final format the world of DW 2.0 resides on one or more platforms. Because of the diverse nature of the data, processes, and requirements that are served by the different parts of the DW 2.0 environment, it is very unusual to have a single platform serve the entire DW 2.0 environment. Instead, many different technologies and many different platforms need to be blended together to satisfy the needs of DW 2.0 processing.

In one place DW 2.0 requires high performance. In another place DW 2.0 focuses on integration of data. In other places DW 2.0 mandates the storage of data for a long period of time. And in yet other places DW 2.0 caters to the needs of the analytical end user. In brief, there are many different kinds of measurement that determine the success of the DW 2.0 environment in different places.

These needs are very different and it is not surprising that no single platform or no single technology meets all of these needs at once.

Therefore, the technical and systems administrator of the DW 2.0 environment wears a lot of hats. Some of the aspects of the job of the technical administrator are

- ensuring compatibility of technology, such as ensuring that data can be passed from one environment to the next, that the performance needs of one system are not impaired by another system, and that data can be integrated throughout all systems, and ensuring availability throughout the environment;
- ensuring that there is a long-term growth plan for all the components of DW 2.0;
- ensuring that metadata can be meaningfully exchanged between the components of the DW 2.0 environment;

- making sure that it is clear to the end user which component of DW 2.0 is appropriate to be used for different kinds of processing;
- network management—making sure that communications are possible and efficient throughout the DW 2.0 environment;
- timing—making sure that data that must interface with other data is flowing in a smooth and unimpeded manner;
- performance—making sure that performance is acceptable throughout the DW 2.0 environment;
- availability—making sure that the components of DW 2.0 that are needed are up and running when needed;
- making sure that metadata flows where needed and is available to the end user when needed.

An important aspect of the technical administrator's job is capacity planning. In many ways the job of the technical administrator is like that of the data base administrator. The technician operates in many cases in a reactive mode. And no person likes to be constantly bombarded with the need to have everything done yesterday. And yet that is exactly the world in which the technician and the data base administrator often find themselves.

One of the most important ways that the technician can get out of being in a reactive mode is to do proper capacity planning. Not all errors and problems in the DW 2.0 environment are related to capacity, but many are. When there is adequate capacity, the system flows normally. But when a system starts to reach the end of its capacity, it starts to fall apart, in many different manifestations.

The sorts of capacity and related measurements that the technician pays attention to in the DW 2.0 environment include

- memory, for all types of processing but especially for online transaction processing that occurs in the interactive environment;
- queue length and capacity (queue length is usually an indicator of a bottleneck in the system);
- caching capacity and cache hits;
- hard disk space;
- near-line space;
- archival space;

- archival processors;
- networking capacity;
- and so forth.

By looking at these various measurements, the technician can pre-empt many problems before they occur.

Other important measurements include the growth of dormant data in the Integrated Sector, the growth of near-line storage, the growth of archival storage, the measurement of the probability of access of data throughout the environment, network bottlenecks, and so forth. In short, any place the technician can preempt a critical shortage, the better.

One of the most important jobs of management of the DW 2.0 environment is that of managing end-user relationships and expectations. If management ignores this aspect of the DW 2.0 environment, then management is at risk. Some of the ways in which the end-user expectations are managed include

- the creation and staffing of a help desk;
- the publication of a periodic newsletter containing success stories and helpful hints as to how to use the DW 2.0 environment;
- occasional in-house classes describing the contents and usage of aspects of the DW 2.0 environment;
- the conduct of steering committees in which the end user gets to decide on or at least give input on priorities and schedules;
- involvement of the end user in the entire development and design life cycle for the DW 2.0 environment;
- corporate "show and tell" sessions during which in-house sessions are conducted;
- the occasional day-long seminar by outside professionals that complements the experience or information found in the DW 2.0 environment.

Another important element of the management of end-user relationships is the establishment of an SLA, or service level agreement. The SLA is measured throughout the day-to-day processing that occurs in the DW 2.0 environment. The SLA provides a quantifiable and open record of system performance. The establishment of the SLA benefits both the end user and the technician. As a rule the SLA addresses both online performance and availability. In addition, the SLA for the analytical environment is very different from the SLA for the transactional environment.

In the case in which there is statistical processing to be done in the DW 2.0 environment, the technician must carefully monitor the full impact of the statistical processing on resource utilization. There is a point at which a separate facility must be built for research statistical analysis.

MANAGEMENT ADMINISTRATION OF THE DW 2.0 ENVIRONMENT

Sitting over all of these administrative activities is management. It is management's job to make sure that the goals and objectives of the DW 2.0 environment are being met. And there are many aspects to the management of the DW 2.0 environment. Some of the more important aspects are the following.

Prioritization and prioritization conflicts

The buck stops at the manager's office when it comes to prioritization. It is almost mandatory that certain parts of the organization want changes and additions to DW 2.0 at the same time that other parts also want changes and additions. It is the job of the manager to resolve (or at least ameliorate) the conflicts. Typical considerations include

- which additions to the DW 2.0 environment will achieve the biggest financial payback;
- which additions to the DW 2.0 environment are the easiest and fastest to make;
- which additions to the DW 2.0 environment can be made in a time frame that is acceptable to the organization;
- which additions to the DW 2.0 environment have the greatest strategic payback.

The manager must juggle all of these considerations when determining the order of additions and adjustments to the organization. But there are other considerations when managing the DW 2.0 environment.

Budget

The primary way in which management influences the organization is through budget. The projects that receive funding continue and flourish;

the projects that do not receive funding do not. Some budgetary decisions are long term and some are short term. Nearly everything that is done in the DW 2.0 environment is done iteratively. This means that management has the opportunity to make mid-term and short-term corrections as a normal part of the budgeting process.

Scheduling and determination of milestones

One of the most important parts of management is the setting of milestones and schedules. Usually management does not create the original schedules and milestones. Instead management has the projects that are being managed propose the schedules and milestones. Then management approves those milestones that are acceptable. Because nearly all aspects of DW 2.0 are constructed in an iterative manner, management has ample opportunity to influence the corporate schedule.

Allocation of resources

The manager chooses who gets to lead projects. There is an art to selecting leadership. One school of thought says that when a project is in trouble more resources need to be added. Unfortunately this sends the wrong message to the organization. One sure way to get more resources is to get a project in trouble. Another approach is to remove the project leader of any project that gets in trouble. Unfortunately there often are legitimate circumstances that cause a project to become mired down. The art of management needs to be able to determine which of these circumstances is at hand and to make the proper decision. Another way of saying this is that management needs to be able to tell the difference between running over a speed bump and running off a cliff.

Managing consultants

Because the development skills for DW 2.0 are in short supply, it is very normal for an organization to turn to outside consultants for help. Management needs to be able to select a consulting firm objectively and not necessarily select the consulting firm that has always been the preferred supplier. The reason is that the preferred supplier may not have any legitimate experience. In addition management needs to be wary of consulting firms that sell a corporation on their capabilities and then staff the project with newly hired people who are "learning the ropes" at the expense of the client. There are several ways to ensure that a consulting firm does not "sell the goods" to an unsuspecting firm.

- Never sign off on a contract over 12 months. If a consulting firm is worth its salt, it knows that at the end of 12 months, if the work has been done satisfactorily, the contract will be continued. Conversely if the contract has not been done well, then a new consulting firm can be engaged.

- Make sure there are tangible short-term deliverables. This is a good measure of whether progress is really being made.

- Make sure the consulting firm tells you specifically who will be staffing the project. The key positions are in design and management.

- Place two or three corporate employees in key positions in the project working hand-in-hand with the consultants so that if there is a problem, the corporate employees can judge for themselves whether management should be alerted.

- Place key design decisions in writing and make that documentation available to management at any time.

- Check the credentials of the consulting firm. Do not take it on faith that the consulting firm can build a DW 2.0 environment just because they are a large and well-known firm.

- Be wary of a consulting firm that will not allow the work to be occasionally reviewed by an outside expert. A confident and competent consulting firm will be happy to have its work reviewed by outside experts, especially if there is a problem with design, development, or implementation.

- Be wary of consulting firms that are attached to a hardware and/ or a software vendor. At the bottom line of the consulting firm's proposal is often a subtle sales pitch for that vendor's products.

- Be open to sharing experiences with the management of other organizations. You can learn a lot if other managers are open to discussing their experiences.

- Be wary of vendors who "showcase" a manager from another company. Oftentimes these managers have agendas you are not aware of. In some circles, managers of consumer companies are de facto employees of the vendor, or at least agents of the vendor.

- Be wary of vendors who readily bring forth an independent consulting firm to bolster their position. Many software vendors have favorite consulting firms who have hidden arrangements with the vendor. The work or the evaluation you get will not be unbiased.

- Be wary of publicly available consultants who purport to do market evaluations of suites of products. Oftentimes these consultants have "under the table" arrangements with vendors in which their goal is to influence you to buy the vendor's products rather than to give you an honest evaluation of products in the marketplace.

- Be wary of firms that purport to do marketplace research and evaluations of products. You should know that many of these research firms sell services to the vendors that they are supposedly evaluating and that the sale of those services to the vendors has a way of influencing the evaluation made of the vendor's products. If a market evaluation company includes how much money is being spent with the marketing research firm along with its evaluations of the vendor's products, then the evaluations of the vendor's products may be valid. But if a marketing research firm will not disclose how much money is being spent by the vendor companies that are being evaluated, then the advice and rankings made by the marketing research firm must be discredited.

SUMMARY

In summary, there are many aspects to the management and administration of the DW 2.0 environment. Some of the aspects include the administration of

- the data model;
- the ETL environment;
- data bases;
- stewardship;
- technology and systems;
- network management;
- archival processing;
- near-line storage;
- interactive processing;
- metadata management.

Index

4GL technology, 3–4

A

access. *See* data access
access query, 340
active data warehouse, 14–16
active metadata repository, 99–100
ad hoc transactions, 340
Address data, 196
administration
  architectural, 348–351
  Archival Sector, 348–349
  budget, 334, 358–359
  data base, 352–353
  data models, 347–348
  management, of DW 2.0
   environment, 358–361
  managing consultants, 359–361
  metadata, 41, 351–352
  Near Line Sector, 349–351
  prioritization/conflicts, 358
  resource allocation, 359
  scheduling and milestones, 359
  stewardship, 353–355
  systems/technology, 355–358
aggregate data
  data models, 159
  granularity managers, 235
airline metadata example, 106–109
analysis
  creating new, 273–277
  creating new, from DW 2.0 data,
   276–277
analytical productivity and response
  time, 243–244
analytical response time, 241
applications
  active data warehouse, 14–16
  from application to corporate data,
   216, 219–221
  evolution of data warehousing, 2–3,
   5–6, 9–10
  Interactive Sector, 29
  monitoring, 172
  OLAP, 20
  transaction monitor and response
   time, 171–172

transaction processing. *See* OLTP
  useful, 51–52
architecture
  architectural administration, 348–351
  building "real" data warehouse, 21–22
  creating new analysis, 273–277
  flow of data through, 203
  new paradigm of DW 2., 0, 24, *25*
Archival Sector, 76–86
  adding, 264–265
  architectural administration, 348–349
  data access, 33–34, 80–81, 84–85
  flow of data, 48–49, 209
  life cycle of data, 27–30
  metadata, 31–33, 105–106
  passive indexes, 81–83, 344
  performance, 80–81
  processes, 343–344
  reasons for, 30–31
  searching, 80–85
  time-variant data, 192–193, 199–200
  volumes of data, 50–51, 80, 85
  workload, 80
archiving data. *See also* Archival Sector
  business perspective, 26
  with metadata, 32
ASCII/EBCDIC conversions, 223
assets and ROI, 128
ATM transactions, 28
attacks on data, sensing, 185–187
audience and star schemas, 18–19
audit trail
  correcting/resetting data, 330–331
  ETL processing, 223–224

B

backflow of data
  from exploration facilities, 152–154
  from Integrated Sector, 212–213
bad data
  balancing entry for, 330
  introduction, 329–330
  making corrections, 330–331
  resetting values, 330
balancing entry for bad data, 330
bank account information, 116
banking transactions, 193, 217

barrier security, 172
Basel II taxonomy, 104, 109
batch mode
  ETL processing, 217–218
  exception-based flow of data, 212
beverage sales data, 143–144
BI (business intelligence) universe,
  97–98
big bang approach, 8–9
blather, 38
brittleness and star schemas, 18
Brooks, Fred, 115
budget, 334, 358–359
business
  BI universe, 97–98
  changing requirements, 47–48,
   114–115
  corporate data and Integrated
   Sector, 62
  corporate data model, 162–163
  corporate information factory, 12,
   13, 134
  enterprise knowledge coordination
   stream, 129–133
  impact of data warehousing, 11
  metadata, 44, 102–103, 352
  representation and data models,
   157–158
"Business Intelligence Road Map"
  (Moss), 125–126
business perspective
  cost justification, 282
  data models, 166
  DW 2.0 environment, 24, 26, 90–92
  ETL processing, 227–228
  evolution of data warehousing, 5–6, 14
  flow of data, 213–214
  granularity managers, 238
  metadata, 109–110
  migration, 269–270
  monitoring DW 2.0 environment, 178
  performance, 258–259
  security, 187–188
  statistical processing, 155–156
  system of record, 319–320
  technology infrastructure, 121–122
  time-variant data, 200
  unstructured data, 310

C

caching data, 54, 71, 356
calculations and data mapping, 317
capacity/disk storage
  active data warehouse, 15
  costs, 335–336
  DBMS activities, 2
  evolution to DW 2.0 environment, 10
  history of data warehousing, 1
  Near Line Sector, 73
  optimization, 336
  planning and performance, 247–248,
    356–357
captured text, 87
CDC (changed data capture), 226
changes
  in business requirements, 47–48,
    114–115
  CDC, 226
  growth of data, 334
  infrastructure. *See* technology
    infrastructure
  mitigating business change, 119
  propagation of, 20
  rapid business changes, 114
  states of data, 215, 219–221
  treadmill of change, 114–115
click-stream data, 232
CMSM (cross-media storage manager),
  74–75, 211–212
Coca Cola sales data, 143–144
code
  checking automatically generated,
    257–258
  ETL, 225
concepts data models, 291
consultants, managing, 359–361
continuity of data, 198
continuous time span data
  beginning/ending sequence of
    records, 197–198
  features of, 194–196
  nonoverlapping records, 197
  overview, 63
  sequence of records, 196
conversions, data, 62, 221–223
corporate data
  from application data to, 216,
    219–221
  enterprise knowledge coordination
    stream, 129–133

Integrated Sector, 62
  model, 162–163
corporate information factory, 12, 13,
  134
correcting/resetting data, 330–331
costs/cost justification
  active data warehouse, 16
  business perspective, 24
  creating new analysis, 273–277
  creating new analysis from DW 2.0
    data, 276–277
  DW 2.0 implementation, 271, 273
  economics and evolution of data
    warehousing, 10–11
  factoring cost of DW 2.0, 277–278
  factors affecting, for new analysis, 276
  first-generation vs. DW 2.0, 281–282
  historical information, 280–281
  macro-level justification, 271–272
  micro-level justification, 272–273
  Near Line Sector, 72–73
  perspective of business users, 282
  real economics of DW 2.0, 279
  reality of information, 278
  storage, 335–336
  time value of information, 279–280
  value of integration, 280
credit card data, 11, 295
cross-media storage manager (CMSM),
  74–75, 211–212
currency conversions, 62, 221–223
customer metadata, 101–102
customer profiles, 11

D

data access
  Archival Sector, 33–34, 80–81, 84–85
  business perspective, 26
  in DW 2.0 environment, 33–34
  Integrated Sector, 66–67, 69–70
  Interactive Sector, 59
  Near Line Sector, 74
  probability of, 30–31, 209–210
  security, 181
  unstructured data, 89–90
  volumes. *See* volumes of data
data base
  administration, 352–353
  DBMS, 1–2, 223, 332–337
  relational, 309
data correction stream, 133

data flow. *See* flow of data
data integration
  Integrated Sector, 58
  introduction, 7–8
data item set (dis) level, 159–160
data mapping, 219, 223, 316–319
data marts
  convenience of, 324–325
  as data warehouse, 15, 20–21
  described, 13
  vs. exploration facilities, 152
  moving data, 327–328
  performance, 251
  source data, 323
  system of record, 319
  transforming data from, 325
data models
  business representation, 157–158
  concepts, 291
  corporate, 162–163
  corporate, and seven streams
    approach, 131
  data item set level, 159–160
  ERD level, 159–160
  granular vs. summarized data, 159
  intellectual road map, 157
  Interactive Sector, 161–162
  levels of, 159–161
  logical, 291–294
  perspective of business users, 166
  physical model, 159–160, 290–292
  scope of integration, 158–159
  top-down modeling, 294–296
  transformation, 163–164
  types used in DW 2.0, 289–294
  unstructured data, 164–166
data profiling
  enterprise knowledge coordination
    stream, 129–133
  inconsistencies, 294–296
  and mapping stream, 133
  tools and reverse-engineered data
    model, 288–289
data quality
  checking, 170–171, 174–175, 224
  data model types, 289–294
  data profiling inconsistencies,
    294–296
  data profiling tools, 288–289
  DW 2.0 environment, 285–286
  reverse-engineered data model,
    288–289

TIQM, 134–137
tool set, 287–288
TQdM, 134
data quality editor, 63
data quality monitor, 170–171,
174–175, 224
data warehouse
active approach, 14–16
bad data, 329–330
building "real" vs. variations, 21–22
business appeal of DW 2.0, 24
business impact, 11
business perspective, 26, 90–92
changing business requirements,
47–48, 114–115
compared to data mart, 21
data mart. See data marts
defined, 7
different development approach, 8–9
diversity of, 40–41
DW 2.0 technology foundation, 45–46
environment. See environment,
DW 2.0
exploration warehouse, 13
federated approach, 14–15, 16–18
first-generation. See history of data
warehousing
house/city analogy, 261–262
integrating data, 7–8
new paradigm of DW 2.0, 24, 25
shaping factors of DW 2.0, 23–24
speed of data movement into/
through, 331
star schema approach, 15, 18–19
suboptimal, 19
useful applications, 51–52
variations, 14–15
volumes of data, 8, 50–51
data warehouse monitor
falling probability of data access,
209–210
features of, 176–177, 326–327
overview, 171
security, 185
data warehouse utility (DWU), 332–337
Dataupia, 332, 336
date formats, 62, 222
Date of Birth data, 196
DBMS (data base management systems)
conversions, 223
data warehouse utilities, 332–337
purpose of, 1–2

DDL (data definition language), 290
Decision Support Systems (DSS)
processing, 41, 70–71
default values and ETL processing, 223
demographics, 51
development
data warehouse approach, 8–9
ETL programs, 224–225
PCs and 4GL technology, 3–4
devolution, 19
dis (data item set) level, 159–160
discontinuity of data, 197
discrete data
continuity, 198
time-variant data, 194
disk storage. See capacity/disk storage
diversity and metadata, 41
dividing data and technology
infrastructure, 121
domain checking, 63, 174, 224
domains in data quality tool set, 287
dormant data
monitoring, 176–177
removing, 245–246
Dow Jones Industrial average, 194
DSS (Decision Support Systems)
processing, 41, 70–71
dump, data, 184–185
DW 2.0. See data warehouse;
environment, DW 2.0
DWU (data warehouse utility),
332–337

E

EBCDIC/ASCII conversions, 223
edited text, 87, 302
ELT (extract/load/transform) processing
described, 226–227
Interactive Sector, 58
managing, 351
perspective of business users,
227–228
email
blather, 38
as unstructured data, 299
view of customer, 51
encryption
features of, 181–182
limiting, 184
end-user perspective. See business
perspective

English, Larry, 134, 137
enterprise knowledge coordination
stream, 129–133
enterprise reference model stream, 130
enterprise-wide metadata
features of, 101–102
local metadata, 43–45, 97–98, 103
metadata in DW 2.0 environment,
97–98
environment, DW 2.0
access of data, 33–34
components of, 11–13
cost justification, 271
data access, 33–34
data flow, 48–49
data warehouse, 6
data warehouse monitor, 171
DW 2.0 landscape, 290
ETL processing, 215–216
evolution, 9–11
management administration, 358–361
metadata, 31–33, 40–44, 96–99
migration to unstructured, 267–269
monitoring, 169, 246–247
performance, 239
preparing unstructured data, 38–40
referential integrity, 52
reporting, 53, 206
responding to business changes,
47–48
spider web, 4–5, 6
structured/unstructured data, 34–35,
86–90
technology foundation, 45–46
textual data, 34–35
transaction monitor, 169–170
transaction monitor and response
time, 171–172
volumes of data, 50–51
ERD (entity relationship level),
159–160
ETL (extract/transform/load) processing
from application to corporate data,
216, 219–221
audit trail, 223–224
batch mode, 217–218
CDC, 226
changing states of data, 215, 219–221
code creation/parametrically driven,
225
compared to ELT, 226–227
complex transformations, 221

ETL (*Contd.*)
  creating programs, 224–225
  data flow in DW 2.0, 48, 205
  data quality monitor, 170–171,
    174–175, 224
  default values, 223
  domain checking, 174, 224
  in DW 2.0 environment, 215–216
  Integrated Sector, 29, 63, 67–68
  Interactive Sector, 27–29, 58–59
  introduction, 12
  mapping, 219
  metadata, 223
  migration shock absorber, 267
  online mode, 216–217
  real-time processing, 218
  rejected data, 225–226
  source/target, 218–219
  system of record, 218
  technology to prepare data, 308
  throughput, 222–223
  unstructured processing, 87–88
evolution of data warehousing. *See*
    history of data warehousing
exception-based flow of data, 210–213
exploration facilities
  backflow of data, 152–154
  data marts compared to, 152
  features of, 147
  frequency of analysis, 147
  project-based data, 13, 150–151
  refreshing exploration data, 149
  sources for exploration processing,
    149
  using data internally, 155
exploration processing, 146
exploration warehouse, 13, 24
extensibility
  nonextensibility and data marts, 20
  star schemas, 18
external taxonomies, 104–105, 304–305
extract/load/transform (ELT)
    processing, 226–227
extracts
  ETL. *See* ETL (extract/transform/load)
    processing
  proliferation and data marts, 20

F

federated data warehouse
  described, 16–18
  variations of data warehouses, 14–15

filtering data, 232–234
Find it domain, 287
firewalls, 182
first-generation data warehousing. *See*
    history of data warehousing
Fix it domain, 287
flow of data
  Archival Sector, 48–49, 209
  bulk batch mode, 212
  in DW 2.0 environment, 48–49
  exception-based, 210–213
  falling probability of data access,
    209–210
  Integrated Sector, 48–49, 205–207
  Interactive Sector, 48–49, 203–205
  Near Line Sector, 48–49, 207–209
  performance, 241–242
  perspective of business users,
    213–214
  role of ETL, 205
  staging request, 213–214
  throughout architecture, 203
  triggers, 206–207
foreign keys, 174–175
freezing data, 145–146
frequency of analysis, 147
frequent flyer programs, 11

G

gender data, 63, 174, 196, 223
general/specific text, 39–40
glossaries, 304
granularity
  in data warehouse, 7
  devolution, 19
  in federated data warehouse,
    17–18
  granular vs. summarized data, 159
  Integrated Sector, 65, 70–71
  Interactive Sector, 60
  in star schemas, 19
granularity managers
  aggregate data, 235
  compared to ELT, 231–232
  eliminating data, 234
  filtering data, 232–234
  functions of, 234–236
  home-grown vs. third-party, 236
  metadata as by-product, 237–238
  parallelizing, 237
  perspective of business users, 238
  raising level of granularity, 232

recast data, 235
  summarizing data, 234
growth of data, 334

H

hardware/software selection, 256
heuristics
  analysis and statistical processing,
    145–146
  freezing data, 145–146
  processing, 243, 341
highway analogy for workload, 64, 66
historical data
  data warehouse, 7
  federated data warehouse, 17
  Integrated Sector, 65, 67, 70
  Interactive Sector, 60
  value of information, 280–281
historical record, 120
history of data warehousing
  from business perspective, 5–6, 14
  capacity/disk storage, 1
  data warehouse environment, 6
  DBMS, 1–2
  DW 2.0 compared to first-generation,
    23–24
  early progression of systems, 2
  forces shaping, 9–11
  master files, 5
  online applications, 2–3
  PCs and 4GL technology, 3–4
  spider web environment, 4–5, 6
homographs
  resolution, 303–304
  taxonomies, 105
house/city analogy, 261–262

I

*Improving Data Warehouse and Business
    Information Quality* (English), 137
indexing
  passive indexes for archival data,
    81–83, 344
  performance, 245
information factory development
    stream, 133
infrastructure
  stream, 133
  technology. *See* technology
    infrastructure
integrated data

in data warehouse, 7–8
evolution of data warehousing, 10
federated data warehouse, 17
integrating text, 301–307
scope of, and data models, 158–159
value of integration, 280
Integrated Sector, 62–71
    changes to data, 67
    continuous time span data, 63
    corporate data, 62
    data access, 66–67, 69–70
    data key reconciliation, 62
    data quality editor, 63
    DSS processing, 70–71
    ETL processing, 29, 63, 67–68
    flow of data, 48–49, 205–207
    granularity, 65, 70–71
    historical data, 65, 67, 70
    life cycle of data, 27–30
    performance, 65–66
    processes, 341–342
    profile data, 63
    queries/searches, 65–67
    reasons for, 30–31
    referential integrity, 68–69
    subject-oriented detailed data, 62–63
    summary data, 63
    time relativity, 192–193
    transactions, and time-variant data, 193–194
    volumes of data, 50–51, 65
    workload, 64
integrity of data
    active data warehouse, 15
    comparisons, 144–145
    referential, 52
    star schemas, 19
    statistical comparison, 144–145
Interactive Sector, 55–61
    access of data, 33–34
    data access, 59
    data models, 161–162
    ETL processing, 58
    flow of data, 48–49, 203–205
    granularity, 60
    historical data, 60
    life cycle of data, 27–30
    metadata, 31–33
    performance, 57, 254–255
    protecting, 254–255
    reasons for, 30–31
    referential integrity, 58
    searches, 58

time relativity, 192
volumes of data, 50–51, 57
workload, 56
internal taxonomies, 104–105
intersector/intrasector referential
    integrity, 52
inventory management, 11, 127–128
IT (information technology)
    reducing IT response time, 115
    technology infrastructure, 112–113

K

Kalido, 121
keys
    reconciliation, 62
    restructure/creation, 223

L

LDM (logical data model), 291–294
legacy data. *See also* ETL (extract/
    transform/load) processing
    creating new analysis, 273–275
    as data source, 315
    federated data warehouse approach,
    16–18
    life cycle of data, 27–30
    operational/legacy systems
    environment, 313
licenses and DWU, 336
life cycle of data
    reasons for sectors, 30–31
    sectors, described, 27–30
linkages, 87, 309
local metadata, 43–45, 97–98, 103
logic
    data mapping, 318
    LDM, 291–294
    transactions, 339–341
logical data model (LDM), 291–294

M

macro-level cost justification, 271–272
maintaining metadata, 106
management administration of DW 2.0
    environment, 358–361
mangled characters, monitoring, 175
mapping, data, 219, 223, 316–319
maps, level of detail, 159–160
master files, 5
meltdowns, 173

metadata
    active/passive repositories, 99–100
    administration, 41, 351–352
    in Archival Sector, 31–33, 105–106
    building infrastructure, 266
    business, 44, 102–103, 352
    business perspective, 26
    as by-product of granularity manager,
    237–238
    card catalog analogy, 95
    creating enterprise, 265–266
    in DW 2.0 environment, 31–33,
    40–44, 96–99
    end-user perspective, 109–110
    enterprise-wide, 101–102
    ETL processing, 223
    infrastructure and performance, 248
    in Interactive Sector, 31–33
    local, 43–45, 97–98, 103
    maintaining, 106
    repositories, 98–99
    reusability of data and analysis, 96,
    249
    stop words, 105, 302
    structure of, 96–97
    system of record, 102–103
    taxonomies, 104–105
    technical, 44, 102–103, 352
    transformation process, 341
    unstructured data, 41, 103, 104–105
    using, airline example, 106–109
methodology
    seven streams approach, 129–139
    spiral, 123–129, 137–139
    waterfall, 123–126
micro-level cost justification, 272–273
migration
    adding Archival Sector, 264–265
    adding components incrementally,
    262–264
    building metadata infrastructure, 266
    creating enterprise metadata,
    265–266
    ETL as shock absorber, 267
    in perfect world, 262
    perspective of business users,
    269–270
    swallowing source systems, 266–267
    to unstructured environment,
    267–269
milestones and scheduling, 359
money data, 17, 162, 220–221
Monitor it and report it domain, 287

monitoring DW 2.0 environment
    application monitoring, 172
    by architectural administrator, 350
    data quality, 170–171, 174–175, 224
    data warehouse monitor, 171,
      176–177, 185, 326–327
    domain checking, 174, 224
    dormant data, 176–177, 245–246
    mangled characters, 175
    meltdowns, 173
    null values, 175
    outlying range, 175
    overview, 169
    peak-period processing, 172–174
    performance, 246–247
    perspective of business users, 178
    queue monitoring, 171
    sniffing, 176
    transaction monitor, 169–170
    transaction monitor and response
      time, 171–172
    transaction queue monitoring, 171
    transaction record monitoring, 172
    unmatched foreign keys, 174–175
Moss, Larissa, and spiral methodology,
    125–128
Move it domain, 287
Mythical Man Month, The (Brooks), 115

N

Name data, 196
NAME data, 308
Near Line Sector, 71–76
    architectural administration, 349–351
    CMSM, 74–75, 211–212
    cost and performance, 72–73
    data access, 74
    data storage, 73
    flow of data, 48–49, 207–209
    life cycle of data, 27–30
    processes, 342–343
    reasons for, 30–31
    security, 187
    time relativity, 192–193
    volumes of data, 50–51, 76
    workload, 73–74
nonextensibility and data marts, 20
nonoverlapping records, 197
normalization of textual data, 38–40
normalized data, 38
null values, monitoring, 175

O

ODS (operational data store), 13
offline data and security, 182–184
OLAP (online application processing), 20
OLTP (online transaction processing)
    DWU, 336
    federated data warehouse, 16–17
    long queue time, 243
    ODS, 13
    performance, 239
    SLA, 254
O'Neill, Bonnie, 287
online applications/processing
    active data warehouse, 14–16
    evolution of data warehousing, 9–10
    history of data warehousing, 2–3, 5–6
    OLAP, 20
    transaction processing. *See* OLTP
online mode for ETL, 216–217
online response performance, 239–241
operational application systems
    environment, 218, 313–314, 316
operational/legacy systems
    environment, 313
organizational charts, 116–117, 120
outlying range, 175

P

paradigm of DW 2.0, 24, *25*
parallelization
    batch, and performance, 249
    granularity managers, 237
    transaction processing, 249–250
partitioning data, 255–256
passive indexes for archival data, 81–83,
    344
passive metadata repository, 99–100
password flooding attacks, 186
patient's records, 51, *52*
PCs and 4GL technology, 3–4
peak-period processing, 172–174
performance
    analytical productivity and response
      time, 243–244
    analytical response time, 241
    Archival Sector, 80–81
    batch parallelization, 249
    capacity planning, 247–248
    checking automatically generated
      code, 257–258

data marts, 251
data models and Interactive Sector,
    161–162
in DW 2.0 environment, 239
end-user education, 246
exploration facilities, 252
facets to, 244–245
federated data warehouse, 16–17
flow of data, 241–242
hardware/software selection, 256
heuristic processing, 243
indexing, 245
Integrated Sector, 65–66
Interactive Sector, 57, 254–255
metadata infrastructure, 248–249
monitoring environment, 246–247
Near Line Sector, 72–73
OLTP, 239
online response time, 240–241
parallelization for transaction
    processing, 249–250
partitioning data, 255–256
perspective of business users,
    258–259
physically grouping data, 257
protecting Interactive Sector, 254–255
queues, 242–243
reducing IT response time, 115
removing dormant data, 245–246
separating farmers/explorers,
    256–257
separation of transactions into
    classes, 253–254
service level agreements, 254
transaction monitor and response
    time, 171–172
unstructured data, 88–89
workload management, 250–251
physical model, 159–160
physically grouping data, 257
pointers and unstructured processing,
    87
preprogrammed complex transactions,
    340
prioritization/conflicts and
    administration, 358
probability of data access
    for different sectors, 30–31
    elevated, 210
    falling probability, 209–210
processing in DW 2.0 environment,
    339–344

in DW 2.0 sectors, 341–344
transaction types, 339–341
profile data, 63, 131
project-based data, 13, 150–151
proliferation and star schemas, 19
protecting Interactive Sector, 254–255

Q

quality monitor, 170–171, 174–175,
    224. *See also* data quality
queries. *See also* data access; searches
    access, 340
    ad hoc, 340
    Interactive Sector, 58
    nonreplicable, in federated data
        warehouse, 17
    statistical processing, 141–143
queue monitoring, 171
queues, 242–243

R

random data access, 33–34
range checking, 63, 175, 224
rationalization of textual data, 39–40
reading text for analytical processing,
    299–300
reality of information, 278
real-time ETL processing, 218
reasonability checking, 224
recast data, 235
reconciliation
    data marts, 20
    encoded values for data mapping,
        318
    keys, 62
referential integrity
    described, 52
    Integrated Sector, 68–69
    Interactive Sector, 58
refreshing exploration data, 149
rejected data, 225–226
relational data base, 309
reports, 53, 206, 278
repositories for metadata, 98–100
resetting data values, 330
resource allocation, 359
response time
    analytical productivity, 243–244
    IT, reducing, 115
    online response time, 240–241

transaction monitor, 171–172
transaction monitoring, 171–172
return on investment (ROI), 128
reusability
    data and analysis, 96
    metadata, 249
    spiral methodology, 127–128
revenue metadata, 101–103
reverse-engineered data model,
    288–289
road maps
    "Business Intelligence Road Map"
        (Moss), 125–126
    DW/BI project road map, 137–138
    intellectual road map, 157

S

sales data
    in Integrated Sector, 62–63
    semantically stable data, 117
sales territories, 116–117
SAN technology, 333, 334
SAP technology, 333
Sarbanes Oxley taxonomy, 109,
    306–307
scheduling and milestones, 359
scope creep, 348
screening data, 38
SDLC (systems development life cycle),
    123
searches. *See also* data access; queries
    Archival Sector, 80–85
    direct/indirect, 306–307
    indexing, 81–83, 245, 344
    Integrated Sector, 65–67
    Interactive Sector, 58
sectors. *See also* Archival Sector;
        Integrated Sector; Interactive
        Sector; Near Line Sector
    data access, 33–34
    metadata, 31–33
    reasons for different sectors, 30–31
    types of sectors, 27–30, 55
security
    barrier security, 172
    data access, 172
    data warehouse monitor, 185
    direct dump of data, 184–185
    drawbacks, 182
    encryption, 181–182, 184
    firewall, 182

moving data offline, 182–184
Near Line Sector, 187
password flooding attacks, 186
perspective of business users, 187–188
protected unstructured data, 187
sensing attacks, 185–187
Self Organizing Map (SOM), 165
semantic relationships
    enterprise metadata, 101
    mitigating business change, 119
    mixing stable/unstable data, 118
    separating stable/unstable data, 118
    stable data, 117
    temporal data, 116–117
    temporal/static data, 115–116
semantically temporal/static data,
    116–117
semistructured data/value, 307–308
sequence of records, 196
sequential data access, 33–34
service level agreements (SLAs), 254,
    259, 349–350
settling data, 331
seven streams approach
    data correction stream, 133
    data profiling and mapping stream,
        133
    DW/BI project road map, 137–138
    enterprise knowledge coordination
        stream, 129–133
    enterprise reference model stream,
        129
    information factory development
        stream, 133
    infrastructure stream, 133
    overview, 129
    summary, 137–139
    total information quality
        management stream, 134–137
shared data mart data, 327–328
SLAs (service level agreements), 254,
    259, 349–350
slivers and spiral methodology, 127
snapshots of data, 119–120
sniffing and data warehouse monitor,
    176
software
    creating ETL, 224–225
    disruption and DWU, 336
    performance, 256
SOM (Self Organizing Map), 165
source data system of records, 316

sources
  best source data from operational
    environment, 316
  data mapping, 219, 223, 316–319
  data marts, 323
  ETL processing, 218–219
  exploration processing, 149
  swallowing source systems, 266–267
  system of record, 313–319
specific/general text, 39–40
speed of data movement, 331
spellings, alternate, 105, 305
spider web environment
  history of data warehousing, 4–5
  transition to data warehouse
    environment, 6
spiral methodology, 123–129, 137–139
stable/unstable data, semantically
  features of, 117
  mixing/separating, 118
staging request, 213–214
star schemas, 15, 18–19
states of data, changing, 215, 219–221
static/temporal data, 115–117
statistical analysis, 141–143
statistical comparison, 144–145
statistical processing
  active data warehouse, 16, 141
  backflow of data, 152–154
  data marts and exploration facilities,
    152
  in DW 2.0 environment, 141–142, 341
  exploration facilities, 147
  exploration processing, 146
  freezing data, 145–146
  frequency of analysis, 147
  heuristic analysis, 145–146, 341
  integrity of comparisons, 144–145
  perspective of business analyst,
    155–156
  project-based data, 150–151
  queries, 141–143
  refreshing exploration data, 149
  sources for exploration processing,
    149
  using exploration data internally, 155
  using statistical analysis, 143
stemming, 301, 305
stewardship, 353–355
stop words, 105, 302
storage. *See* capacity/disk storage
Strauss, Derek, 287

structured data
  data flow, 48–49
  linkages, 87, 309
  metadata, 41
  vs. unstructured data, 34–35
  volumes of data, 50–51
subject-oriented detailed data, 62–63
subjects
  subject area definitions, 101–102
  system of record, 102–103
summary data
  granular vs. summarized data, 159
  granularity manager, 234
  in Integrated Sector, 63
synonyms
  replacement/concatenation, 303
  taxonomies, 105
system of record
  best source data from operational
    environment, 316
  data mapping, 316–319
  data marts, 319
  ETL processing, 218
  metadata, 102–103
  operational/legacy systems
    environment, 313
  perspective of business users, 319–320
systems development life cycle (SDLC),
  123
systems/technology administration,
  355–358

T

targets
  data mapping, 219, 223, 316–319
  ETL processing, 218–219
taxonomies
  external, 104–105, 304–305
  features of, 104–105
  stop words, 105, 302
  synonyms, 105
  unstructured processing, 87
technical metadata, 44, 102–103, 352
technology
  administration, 355–358
  for different sectors, 34
  evolution of data warehousing, 9
  federated data warehouse, 17
  responding to business changes,
    47–48
  seven streams approach, 129–139

spiral methodology, 123–129,
  137–139
technology infrastructure
  creating snapshots of data, 119–120
  dividing data, 121
  end-user perspective, 121–122
  features of, 112–113
  getting off treadmill, 115
  historical record, 120
  mitigating business change, 119
  mixing semantically stable/unstable
    data, 118
  overview, 111–112
  rapid business changes, 114
  reducing IT response time, 115
  semantically stable data, 117
  semantically temporal data,
    116–117
  semantically temporal/static data,
    115–116
  separating semantically stable/
    unstable data, 118
  treadmill of change, 114–115
temporal/static data, 115–117
terminology
  handling text, 307
  normalization of, 38–40
text across languages, 305
textual analytical processing, 300–301
textual data
  alternate spellings, 105, 305
  analytics, 35
  data access, 89–90
  direct searches, 306
  in DW 2.0 environment, 34–35
  ETL technology, 308
  evolution of data warehousing, 10
  external glossaries/taxonomies,
    304–305
  homographic resolution, 303–304
  indirect searches, 306–307
  integrating text, 301–307
  NAME data, 308
  normalization, 38–40
  performance, 88–89
  perspective of business users, 310
  relational data base, 309
  semistructured data/value, 307–308
  simple editing, 87, 302
  specific/general, 39–40
  stemming, 305
  stop words, 105, 302

synonym replacement/concatenation, 303
synonyms, 105
terminology, 307
text across languages, 305
themes, 104, 165–166, 304
unstructured processing, 86–90
workload, 88
themes, 104, 165–166, 304
throughput, ETL, 222–223
time capsules, 79
time, performance. *See* performance
time value of information, 279–280
time-variant data
    Archival Sector, 192–193, 199–200
    beginning/ending sequence of records, 197–198
    continuity, 198
    continuous time span data, 63, 194–196
    discrete data, 194, 198
    end-user perspective, 200
    key structure, 192
    nonoverlapping records, 197
    sequence of records, 196
    structure of DW 2.0 data, 191–192
    time relativity in Interactive Sector, 192
    time-collapsed data, 198–199
    transactions in Integrated Sector, 193–194
TIQM (total information quality management) stream, 134–137
top-down modeling, 294–296
total information quality management (TIQM) stream, 134–137
total quality data management (TQdM), 134
TQdM (total quality data management), 134
transaction monitor
    application monitoring, 172
    overview, 169–170
    queue monitoring, 171
    record monitoring, 172
    response time, 171–172
transaction processing. *See also* OLTP
    ad hoc transactions, 340
    in DW 2.0 environment, 339–344

Interactive Sector, 56–57
life cycle of data, 27–30
logic, 339–341
parallelization and performance, 249–250
performance, 253–254
preprogrammed transactions, 340
simple/complex transactions, 339–340
transaction types, 141–142
transformation
    of data. *See* ETL (extract/transform/load) processing
    of data mart data, 325
    of data models, 163–164
    process, 340–341
transparency
    CMSM, 74–75
    data base, 336
triggers for data flow, 206–207

U

unstable/stable data, semantically
    features of stable data, 117
    mixing/separating, 118
unstructured data
    alternate spellings, 105, 305
    data access, 89–90
    data flow, 48–49
    data models, 164–166
    direct searches, 306
    DW 2.0 environment, 299
    ETL technology, 308
    evolution of data warehousing, 10
    external glossaries/taxonomies, 304–305
    homographic resolution, 303–304
    indirect searches, 306–307
    integrating text, 301
    linkages, 87, 309
    metadata, 41, 103, 104–105
    migration to unstructured environment, 267–269
    NAME data, 308
    performance, 88–89
    perspective of business users, 310
    preparing, for DW 2.0 environment, 38–40

processing, 86–90
reading text, 299–300
relational data base, 309
screening for blather, 38
semistructured data/value, 307–308
simple editing, 87, 302
stemming, 305
stop words, 105, 302
vs. structured data, 34–35
synonym replacement/concatenation, 303
terminology, 307
text across languages, 305
textual analytical processing, 300–301
themes, 104, 165–166, 304
volumes of data, 50–51
workload, 88

V

volumes of data
    Archival Sector, 50–51, 80, 85
    business perspective, 26
    for different sectors, 31
    in DW 2.0 environment, 8
    filtering data, 232–234
    Integrated Sector, 50–51, 65
    Interactive Sector, 50–51, 57
    Near Line Sector, 50–51, 76

W

waterfall methodology, 123–126
workload
    Archival Sector, 80
    highway analogy, 64, 66
    Integrated Sector, 64
    Interactive Sector, 56
    Near Line Sector, 73–74
    unstructured data, 88
workload management, 250–251

Z

Zachman framework, 131–133, 289–292